CHINESE WOMEN
THROUGH CHINESE EYES

CHINESE WOMEN
THROUGH CHINESE EYES

Li Yu-ning, editor

An East Gate Book
M.E. Sharpe, Inc.
Armonk, New York
London, England

An East Gate Book

Copyright © 1992 by M. E. Sharpe, Inc.
All rights reserved. No part of this book may be reproduced in any
form without written permission from the publisher, M. E. Sharpe, Inc.,
80 Business Park Drive, Armonk, New York 10504.
Available in the United Kingdom and Europe from M. E. Sharpe,
Publishers, 3 Henrietta Street, London WC2E 8LU.

Library of Congress Cataloging-in-Publication Data

Chinese women through Chinese eyes / edited by Li Yu-ning.
p.   cm.
A collection of essays originally in Chinese
Includes bibliographical references.
ISBN 0-87332-596-6. —ISBN 0-87332-597-4 (pbk.)
1. Women—China—Social conditions. 2. Women—China—Biography.
I. Li, Yu-ning.
HQ1767.C454   1991
305.42′0951—dc20
91-11313
CIP

Printed in the United States of America

The paper used in this publication meets the minimum requirements of
American National Standard for Information Sciences—
Permanence of Paper for Printed Library Materials,
ANSI Z39.48–1984.

BB (c)   10   9   8   7   6   5   4   3   2
BB (p)   10   9   8   7   6   5   4   3   2

To all men and women
East and West
who have helped Chinese women
in their search for a better future

Contents

Preface and Acknowledgments

OF THE many things I have acquired in the United States, one of the most valuable is an appreciation of cultural pluralism. In life and in the study of history I have become increasingly convinced that a variety of cultural perspectives can shed more and better light on any subject, and thereby make any study more stimulating and rewarding. From the historical point of view, human experience and cultural values are perpetually in flux; neither remains permanent, neither is absolute. Born and raised in a Chinese cultural environment and educated in Chinese and American universities, I am acutely aware of the ways each stage of my life influenced my views of my own past as well as my interpretations of historical events.

A major aspect of pluralism is gender equality, in the study of history as well as in life. For some years now I have been working on Chinese women's history, at first collecting and publishing documents and then increasingly thinking about new ways of interpreting the complex history of the many and diverse experiences of Chinese women through China's long history. The rise of feminist scholarship in the United States and Europe has opened up many exciting new approaches and fields. Stimulated by this scholarship, I became interested in Chinese perspectives on Chinese women. In particular, I became increasingly curious about earlier Chinese ideas concerning the history and status of women, and then fascinated by the ways Chinese women in the early twentieth century viewed their own changing world and lives.

This volume is the result of a combination of these interests and my teaching responsibilities. Preparing for my seminars on Chinese women at St. John's University has made me appreciate all the more the excellent works already in print as well as making me aware of the gaps that remain to be filled. *Chinese Women Through Chinese Eyes* is an attempt to fill one of these gaps by presenting earlier Chinese perspectives on women's status in Chinese society and on prospects for the future. It is also an attempt to repay the debt I owe all those who have stimulated my thinking on the subject.

I would like to thank St. John's for giving me the opportunity to develop new courses and for providing me with the research support I needed to begin work on this book. Special thanks go to Dr. Barbara L. Morris, academic vice-president, Dr. Paul T. Medici, dean of the Graduate School of Arts and Science, and Dr. and Sr. Virginia Therese Johnson, former director of Asian studies at St. John's, for their long-standing support and encouragement. Mrs. Sandra M. Esposito was most kind in typing a large part of the manuscript. I have also greatly benefited from discussions with and questions and suggestions from my students over the years.

I have been associated with M. E. Sharpe for over two decades, and, for their help in general as well as their work on this book, I would like to thank in particular Mr. Douglas Merwin, Ms. Anita O'Brien for her skillful editing, and Ms. Helen Albert for her friendship and interest in my work.

Chapters 10, 11, 20, 21, and 22 were translated by Dr. William A. Wycoff and first appeared in *Chinese Studies in History.* I am sure that readers will share my appreciation of Dr. Wycoff's lucid translations.

My husband, Professor J. Mason Gentzler, has been helpful and supportive in innumerable ways since the beginning of this project. His constant encouragement has been important in bringing it to completion. In addition, he translated chapters 8, 9, 13, 14, 15, 16, 17, 18, 19, and 23. Moreover, he helped with the tedious task of reading the galley proofs.

In spite of my great indebtedness to so many people, I remain solely responsible for whatever defects remain.

Most of the essays in part I were originally published earlier in the century, when romanization was far less uniform than now. For the sake of consistency, where possible, romanization has been altered to conform to the Wade-Giles system. Some minor stylistic alterations have also been made, and, in a few cases, footnotes have been rearranged or renumbered. The Chinese characters contained in some of the articles as originally published have been deleted.

Li Yu-ning
Bronxville, New York
May 1991

Introduction

Li Yu-ning

THE STUDY of Chinese women has made great progress in recent years, with the publication of a number of excellent articles, collections of articles, and monographs. The range of subjects has been wide, from palace women in the Sung dynasty to women in contemporary Chinese villages, but the principal focus has been on the post-1949 period, because of the availability of sources and because of widespread interest in the changes in status of Chinese women in the People's Republic of China. Earlier periods have not been neglected, and impressive studies are not lacking, but much remains to be done.

The need for a fuller, more sophisticated understanding of earlier periods has been recognized, both for the intrinsic value of understanding the past and because any evaluation of progress made in recent decades obviously depends on thorough and accurate knowledge of previous conditions. Although the tendency to contrast the present with a stereotyped image of a monolithic past seems happily to have diminished if not disappeared, the need for more detailed knowledge of earlier periods remains urgent. Fortunately, sources are not lacking, though they are more scattered than those for the contemporary period.

The purpose of this volume is to make a step in the direction of a better understanding of the past, especially of the half-century preceding the establishment of the People's Republic in 1949.

The first half of the twentieth century was a period of enormous change, as well as powerful resistance to change. As part of the change, Chinese intellectuals began to reevaluate every aspect of China's history. The history of Chinese women was part of this trend, both as a new field of historical study and as an integral part of the questioning and rejection of many of the values of Confucian society in favor of the new ideals of individual freedom and equality. Many of these pioneer studies remain of value for their solid research, breadth of learning, and stimulating interpretations, including some that have since fallen from fashion and now deserve serious reconsideration.[1] They also provide insights into changes in attitude that were taking place among educated Chinese men and women. The first part of this book contains a number of such essays.

In these decades, Chinese women made limited progress in a number of areas, such as education, employment outside the domestic sphere, and political organization. As part of both the intellectual and social changes, Chinese women began to write about their own lives in unprecedented numbers and with unprecedented frankness. These autobiographies are an invaluable, and largely untapped, historical source. A representative selection comprises the second part of the book.

Thus, part I provides a number of general themes, while part II contains concrete illustrations of these themes and variations on them, and suggests additional themes.

The subjects and perspectives of the seven authors in part I differ in many ways, but the authors have some important things in common. They all take for granted that they are living in a period of transition; they agree that women suffered odious inequities in premodern China and that conditions have improved, and they are optimistic that progress will continue. But, although they are critical of conditions in the past, they also credit Chinese women with significant contributions in traditional society, within the family, in education, in literature, and, to a limited extent, in government. This is a significant qualification, for the opportunity to make a contribution—to the family, to society, or to the nation—was a key aspiration for modern Chinese women, and the authors themselves are in accord that making a contribution is an important criterion for judging women's social status. They see as considerable the influence of mothers and wives, and some believe that literacy among Chinese women, especially those from well-to-do families, was not low by premodern standards.[2] Indeed, it is because talented women could under propitious circumstances distinguish themselves that we have an extensive, virtually unexplored, record of their lives and accomplishments. Unfortunately, the vast majority, whose growth was stunted, are not so well documented, and hence more difficult to study.[3] Enough is known to make some generalizations, and the authors agree about the generally deplorable situation of women in premodern China, and they welcome improvements.

It is important to note that the seven authors in part I were all Western educated and wrote these essays in English. They were aware of contemporary Western views of Chinese women, and in part their essays are responses to contemporary Western perceptions.

In the first selection in part I, Hu Shih questions what he takes to be the common perception of women's place in Chinese history. "There is a general impression," he writes, "that the Chinese woman has always occupied a very low place in Chinese society." He then states his intention to show that "in spite of the traditional oppression, the Chinese woman has been able to establish for herself a position that we must regard as a fairly exalted one." Hu, one of the best-known and most esteemed intellectual leaders of modern China, was by no means unfamiliar with the plight of Chinese women. Raised by a widowed mother and married (through an arranged marriage) to a woman with bound feet, he was a staunch advocate of women's rights. Yet he attempts to evaluate the condition of women in premodern China in the historical context. His main point is that Chinese women did make valuable contributions, in government, in literature, and in education, as well as in the family. It might be objected that his evidence supports only a much more narrowly qualified conclusion—that in spite of great inequalities a very small number of quite exceptional women were not so completely oppressed as to be prevented from having an influence in politics or writing poetry. This would still be an important point. But the shading of Hu's interpretation of the historical record is of interest in itself, as a reminder of the need to look for distinctions among advocates of equality for women. In Hu's case, the implication is that the shackles and fetters of which he writes were perhaps not so powerful, and hence could be overcome through evolutionary change, a position in line with his liberal social and political philosophy.

Hu Shih shows that, although formally there was no role for women in government in premodern China, some did have influence. The best-known tales of women of ancient times were about consorts of rulers who diverted them from their official duties and led to their downfall. It is more than likely that not a few of these famous femmes fatales were more legendary than historical, and that the tales about them were more cautionary fables than accurate accounts or typical behavior. The actual historical record is more complex, as we see in Yang Lien-sheng's study of the conditions that made it possible for women to have political power in the Chinese state and the forces arrayed against them. Professor Yang's solidly documented article also suggests some reasons for rethinking the commonly accepted notion that Chinese women's lives were dominated by the Confucian "Three Obediences": to the father before marriage, to the husband after marriage, and to the sons in widowhood.

The oppression suffered by Chinese women in premodern China was largely by men for the advantage of men (the well-known tyranny of mothers-in-law over daughters-in-law notwithstanding). Yet, as early as the nineteenth century, and increasingly from the late nineteenth century, men played leading roles as advocates of women's equality, especially in promoting women's education and the abolition of footbinding. Lin Yutang, a prominent journalist, writer, and scholar, provides some clues to why some Chinese men were sympathetic toward Chinese women. Like many other critics in China and abroad, then and now, Lin blames Neo-Confucianism, along with hypocrisy, for the double

standard that held women to be morally inferior to men while at
the same time demanding that they live by higher moral standards than were expected of men. Lin is careful to distinguish
between the Neo-Confucianism of the Sung and later dynasties
and original Confucianism, which he sees as more humanistic
and tolerant. He attributes the harmful changes in women's status
under the influence of Neo-Confucianism not to indigenous Chinese ideas but to influences from India, especially Buddhism.
Not surprisingly, the three male writers he identifies as early
"feminists" were men who in general abhorred the narrow restrictions of Neo-Confucianism. Lin indicates, however, that they
were rare exceptions, even eccentrics, and therefore not to be
taken as representatives of any broad indigenous current for reform.

The sympathy for Chinese women shown by these male writers is obviously genuine. Yet it is natural that women should
have expressed greater dissatisfaction toward their past. The personal bitterness of millions can be felt in Ch'en Heng-che's article on the influences of foreign cultures on Chinese women.
Though in later life Ch'en had a highly successful professional
career, as a young girl she had suffered the pain of having her
feet bound, a physical and psychological burden she continued to
bear throughout her life. Not surprisingly, her condemnation of
traditional attitudes toward women is more intense than that of
Hu, Yang, and Lin. Yet, with them she shares a nationalism that
does not condemn the past totally, and, like Lin Yutang, she
places a large share of the blame for the submissiveness of Chinese women in the later imperial period on Indian influences,
brought to China through Buddhism. Ch'en's abhorrence of
women's condition in the past inclines her toward a generally
favorable evaluation of the influence of the West in modern
times. Ch'en belonged to a generation of Chinese intellectuals
who, though not insensitive to negative aspects of Western influence, on the whole saw it as very beneficial. The role of women
in the acceptance of Western cultural influences is a subject in
need of further study; Ch'en's article suggests new insights that

might be derived from looking at this process from the woman's perspective.

Tseng Pao-sun's interpretation of the historical evolution of Chinese women's status is of special interest because of her family background. A great-granddaughter of the eminent nineteenth-century official and Confucian paragon, Tseng Kuo-fan, she was brought up in a lineage famous for its strict Confucian standards. Yet she was allowed to keep her natural feet, to become a Christian, to go abroad to study, and to remain single all her life. Her life thus illustrates how much was changing, and how flexible the gentry elite could be. Credit for this flexibility in her case should be given to her grandmother, an enlightened and wise matriarch, who ruled a large household according to reasonable rules and by setting a personal example for diligence and integrity. Tseng's own experience may have influenced her explanation of Chinese women's lowly status in the past and her optimistic assessment of future improvements. While she agrees with Lin and Ch'en that Indian influences were detrimental to Chinese women, she traces the limitations to women's freedom to the imperial state and the imperial Confucianism of the Han and later dynasties, formulated in the *Li chi* (Book of propriety) and other texts. The disintegration of the imperial system in her own day was thus a cause for optimism about improving women's status. Tseng's explanation for the protracted subordination of women is psychological:

> The stunted growth of Chinese womanhood may be said to owe its origin to the psychological suggestion of society that a virtuous woman should be obedient, quiet, self-effacing, and ignorant, devoting herself only to the service of the family. There is no actual persecution or suppression of feminine activities. A woman under such hypnotic suggestion really does feel that only by striving after such an ideal can she find her true self.

This analysis at first seems similar to the Marxist concept of ideology as "false consciousness." But, unlike the Marxists, Tseng does not see this "psychological suggestion of society" as a means of obscuring the actual situation in which, in a male-dominated social structure, males, as the ruling elite, benefit from women's willing subordination because women are unable to see their true interests. Rather, since she sees these beliefs as imposed by an authoritarian political system that no longer exists, and since she believes Chinese culture does not have the religious and legal obstacles that obstruct women in other cultures, she concludes that "the difficulty lies not in men's opposition but in the women themselves."

> On the whole, Chinese menfolk have taken their changed position sympathetically, and in a reasonable spirit, and thinking men are giving the women's movement much help and encouragement. They realize that it is only by uplifting, educating, and emancipating Chinese women that China can be saved. There is no use in planning all sorts of reform, when about one-half of the nation's population is ignorant of even the most rudimentary facts and principles of life.

Tseng draws the very Confucian conclusion that education is the key to improving the individual and society. Her optimism for the future can thus be seen to be based on a continuity with the past as well as a new feeling of nationalism. The link with the past is also apparent in her vision of the ideal future Chinese woman, who would be both modern and Confucian: "Let her freedom be restrained by self-control, her self-realization be coupled with self-sacrifice, and her individualism circumscribed with family duty." This formulation closely conforms to the standpoint of those conservative reformers from the late nineteenth century to the present who have insisted that freedom and individualism were not absolutes but must always be subordinated to the common interest of society as a whole. Yet, as we shall see, the basic idea has been shared by many women far more radical that Tseng Pao-sun.

The beliefs that the low status of women and the narrow scope of their activities were among the basic causes of national weakness and poverty, and that the emancipation of women was necessarily an integral part of the liberation of the nation, have been expressed by reformers and revolutionaries, women and men, since the end of the nineteenth century. Improvements in the status of women have of course been seen as desirable for their own sake, but equality has more frequently been advocated as a means of providing women broader opportunities to contribute to building a new China, and individual rights and freedoms have been subordinated to the idea of duty to the nation. As China has gone through a series of changes, the Chinese people have repeatedly been exhorted to work for the common good, the collective welfare, the needs of the nation. In the process, the old Confucian ideal of women's self-denial for the sake of the family has been transformed into a new ideal of selfless dedication to the task of creating a new China. The contribution of women to the collective goal is the central theme of "Chinese Women's Fight for Freedom" by Sung Ch'ing-ling, the widow of Sun Yat-sen and a leading figure in Chinese political life for many decades. "From the very start," she writes, "our women fought not under the banner of a barren feminism but as part and parcel of the democratic movement as a whole." Here, Sung is expressing the official policy of the Chinese Communist Party; yet her article reflects perhaps the single most widespread view from the late nineteenth century to present-day admonitions to Chinese women to contribute to the current official goal of modernization. Sung places much more emphasis than the previous writers on the role of government in the success or failure of women in attaining their goals.

During the period of high enthusiasm for Western ideas in the early decades of the twentieth century, many educated Chinese had a tendency to look to the West as a source of ideas for change and to view traditional Chinese ideals and institutions largely, or solely, as obstructions. Movements for women's equality, free marriage, and the abolition of footbinding did owe much to the introduction of Western ideals and the examples of Western societies. Yet, both Chinese and Western traditions were far more complex than such a simple dichotomy allowed, and we can now see that while many aspects of the Confucian tradition, for example, did support the status quo and impede change, other aspects could and did play a more positive role. Continuity with the past has increasingly become a theme in recent interpretations of modern Chinese history. The final article in part I, "Historical Roots of Changes in Women's Status in Modern China," by the editor, is an initial attempt to identify a few possible indigenous origins of the impulse toward improving women's status. It suggests that a feminist consciousness among women was more widespread than a reader might conclude from Lin Yutang's article. It is hoped that a fuller understanding of Chinese women in the past will contribute to a more balanced view of the complex process of change in modern times, in which the influences of both Western and indigenous ideas and ideals can be more precisely assessed.

The focus changes in part II, from general interpretations to the personal experiences of individual women. Autobiography was not a major genre in premodern Chinese literature, but it has thrived in modern China and constitutes a major source for the study of modern Chinese history.[4] The brief autobiographical sketches in part II offer the reader individual perspectives on Chinese women's lives in the first half of the twentieth century—their experiences, emotions, yearnings, and hopes for the future. We hear these women speaking about their roles in a changing society, their attitudes toward the changes going on around them, their personal aspirations and the obstacles frustrating them, and their successes and failures in attempting to overcome these obstacles. As in part I, diversity has been a principal criterion of selection. These women come from different regions of China, from different family backgrounds, and from different socioeconomic groups, and have different levels of education. A few were prominent, while the others were ordinary women about whom little or nothing is known apart from these brief sketches. A few seem fairly content with their lives, but most express a range of dissatisfactions. Yet, most seem determined to struggle, for themselves and for other women.

To begin with one woman's memory of her childhood reaction

to footbinding is appropriate in more than one way. This custom, which had begun by the tenth century and had been widespread (though never ubiquitous) for hundreds of years, was the most blatant, most painful, and most demeaning symbol of the oppression of Chinese women.[5] Yet, it was also an aspect of women's inequality that proved easier to eradicate than many others. Some early opponents of footbinding in the late nineteenth century lived to see the practice disappear. Why some customs were susceptible to reform is as important a question as the reasons for the intractability of others, and much of the task of identifying and classifying the constituent elements of women's subordination remains to be done. In the case of footbinding, intimations of an explanation of why it was eliminated in only a few decades may be detected in the brief memoir of the poet and calligrapher Chang Mo-chün, an early feminist and a participant in the 1911 Revolution. Her moving description of her revulsion at her elder sister's suffering, and the alacrity with which her mother acceded to her refusal to bind her own feet suggest several important themes—the relationship between authentic personal feelings and Western influences, the existence of liberal attitudes toward women among some of the educated elite, and the wide variety of relationships between parents and children. Each of these themes reappears in a number of these autobiographies.

The next two pieces are by two exceptional women, Ho Hsiang-ning and Teng Ying-ch'ao. Both became known through their own activities as well as through their husbands' eminence in Chinese politics. Ho was a rebel from an early age, refusing, like Chang Mo-chün, to bind her feet as a child. Later she went abroad to study and became involved in the revolutionary movement to overthrow the Manchus and establish a republic. Her husband, Liao Chung-k'ai, was for two decades a close associate of the most prominent revolutionary leader, Sun Yat-sen. Ho is a good illustration of how politically conscious women were active within the context of broader reformist and revolutionary movements. It is from this perspective that one can understand what otherwise might appear an anomaly in Ho's account of her life as a revolutionary: by Western standards, entering the kitchen and learning how to cook might seem an unlikely item on a feminist revolutionary agenda. Yet in Ho's eyes, and presumably in the eyes of her readers, this entailed a break with the past and was her way to contribute to the revolution. Women's work with their fellow male revolutionaries earned them a kind of theoretical recognition of equality, but it remains a matter of dispute whether or not by subordinating themselves to male-defined revolutionary goals and male-directed activities, these women may have perpetuated women's subordination to men in new forms.

The demand for equality for women became more widespread after the overthrow of the Ch'ing dynasty and the establishment of the Chinese Republic, as educational opportunities for women expanded. By the time of the May Fourth Movement, there were a sizable number of women students in the large cities, and many of them participated in the antigovernment demonstrations that began in Peking on May 4, 1919, to protest the warlord government's intention to sign the Versailles Peace Treaty, which gave Japan extensive privileges in the province of Shantung. As the demonstrations spread to other cities, once again a rising tide of nationalism became linked to programs for social change, and women's determination to strive for equality was strengthened.

The recollections of Teng Ying-ch'ao, whose many decades of leadership in the Chinese Communist Party's women's activities gave her a prominence in part separate from her husband, Chou En-lai, provide an individual perspective on this important development. She shows how the enthusiastic protests of the patriotic students resulted in the dismissal of pro-Japanese government officials, and how the experience of the effectiveness of organization led to the recognition of shared interests and the potential benefits of further political organization to achieve other goals. Thus Teng links women's liberation to the general patriotic movement, which brought so many political and social issues to public attention, including equality of the sexes, replacing arranged marriage with freedom of marriage, and access to higher education and employment. These were not new issues, but they were first given a prominent place on the public agenda by the May Fourth Movement.

Although initially these ideals were largely articulated by a new generation of educated urban women, they rapidly spread beyond this group. Some of the most moving testimonies of women's experiences and aspirations come from less well known or, more accurately in most cases, unknown women. From them we get a more broadly representative picture of the dissemination of the new ideals and the conflicts between the new ideals and the existing society on the local level.

Most of the next group of selections are taken from women's magazines. Modern Chinese journalism began in the late Ch'ing, and the decade preceding the 1911 Revolution saw the appearance of several women's journals. In the May Fourth period, the number of periodicals proliferated as the thirst for new ideas seemed insatiable—by one informed estimate, over seven hundred new periodicals appeared between 1915 and 1923.[6] Women's magazines were among the more successful. They covered a wide range of topics, from political issues to fiction and advice on homemaking. In 1924, one of the best known, *Fu-nü tsa-chih* (The ladies' journal), solicited brief autobiographies from its readers. From the dozens published, a representative selection is translated here, along with selections from other women's journals from the 1930s and 1940s. Most of the women who submitted autobiographies expressed some degree of dissatisfaction with their lives, but some proudly registered successes, and many encouraged other women to take the initiative in improving their lives.

Although the editors of these magazines gave little or no information about these women, it is clear that they come from a variety of backgrounds. The diversity of background only serves to highlight similarities in experiences and common opinions about the problems facing women and the changes they would like to see. The most common issues are education, marriage, and employment.

Reformers and revolutionaries alike had from an early date stressed the importance of education, so essential for the new scientific skills that would bring economic progress and for the new democratic political and social institutions that were to replace the old authoritarian structures. They agreed that the tasks ahead could not be accomplished if half the population remained uneducated and mired in superstition. Of course, a high value was placed on education in traditional China, and women's desire for educational opportunities long preceded the new situation created by imperialism in the nineteenth century. But with the intensification of the feeling that the imperialist threat required innovative responses, women's education gained a new legitimacy and women's schools proliferated. Before long women graduates were becoming educators themselves, in many local primary and secondary schools, and to a very limited extent in colleges and universities. They in turn disseminated the new ideals to their students, as seen in Fu I-hsing's story, "A Village Schoolteacher."

But educational opportunities did not automatically translate into opportunities for new lives after graduation, and a higher level of education could exacerbate the conflict between the new ideals and existing barriers, a common theme in these autobiographies.

Marriage was a major focal point of conflict between the old and the new, for it pitted an individual woman against those who possessed powerful traditional forms of authority—parents, parents-in-law, and husbands. The new ideal of marriage for love with a freely chosen partner was integrally related to other new ideals—individualism, personal freedom, and self-worth—all of which conflicted with the long-held notion of a woman being confined within subordinate roles. In the changing atmosphere, the responses to involuntary arranged marriage ranged from rebellion, dramatically portrayed in Hsieh Ping-ying's angry confrontation with her parents, to sincere attempts to make the best of an unpleasant situation, as described by Hsiu-ying and Lu Lan, to an extreme case like the unnamed young college graduate who fled from a dismal marriage and sought refuge as a Buddhist nun. Hsieh, who became one of the best-known women writers in modern China, conveys the strength both of her own convictions and of those of her parents, while Lu Lan reveals the sense of helplessness of those who disapproved of the callous ways a young woman's future could be decided but who saw no viable alternative. The new ideals touched many hearts, but they provided no means of implementation in unsympathetic surroundings. The hardships that usually faced those who married for love without parental approval or family support are sadly portrayed in the story of Ah-jung.

The restricted choices felt by women led many to conclude that without economic independence it would be difficult, if not impossible, to attain other goals. Employment would free a daughter from her parents, or enable her to support them, give a wife an alternative to remaining under the domination of a bad husband, or enable her to contribute to family finances, or enable a woman to pursue a career on her own until she found the man she wanted to marry. For women to have such freedom of choice threatened powerful centers of male authority and went against deeply entrenched prejudices. Courage is an unspoken theme in many of these autobiographies, as are support and encouragement. It is interesting to note the sources of support these women had in their struggles, female relatives, brothers, and friends who shared their ideals. Yet none of these could match the security, or the dignity (a theme frequently stressed), of economic independence. As Hsiu-ying so cogently concludes her account of her own experiences:

> If you have a productive job, then you can attain a position of economic independence, and you don't have to depend on a man and submit to the power of a man or the head of a family. You can get away from mistreatment forever, and have a really enjoyable life like a human being. That's not only happiness for women, but also the realization of humanism.

A changing economy did offer women some new opportunities, and many found new forms of employment, in factories, in schools, in government agencies, and even as entrepreneurs. But social attitudes changed slowly, even in the big cities, and prejudices made many jobs unpleasant or difficult. Ms. E. gives a vivid picture of the kinds of petty harassment that commonly occurred. It was not impossible for women entrepreneurs to succeed, like Hung-ying, but the male attitudes that stymied Mrs. A. and disheartened Ms. F. were all too prevalent. And, as career opportunities did slowly open up, the conflict between family and career followed, as seen in different forms in the stories of Ah-jung and Chiang Ch'ing.

Many of these women mention relatives and friends who supported them materially and psychologically in their struggles. Such support was especially important for women struggling precisely against those who under the traditional order should have been their principal sources of support, parents and husbands. Such was the case of Ch'en Heng-che, the author of "Influences of Foreign Cultures on the Chinese Woman" in part I, whose paternal aunt helped her after she had antagonized her father by refusing to marry the man he had chosen for her. Ch'en's brief profile of her aunt is a testimonial to the vital assistance women frequently provided other women.[7] Ch'en's vivid memories of her aunt's kindnesses are tinged with sadness, for her talented aunt never had the kind of opportunities that were available to Ch'en. Perhaps this may help to explain why so many educated women of Ch'en's generation tended to be optimistic about future progress: they knew from their own experience how much had improved in their own lifetimes.

Although many young women came into conflict with their parents over marriage, education, and other problems, it would be misleading to imply that relations between parents and children were uniformly antagonistic. On the contrary, for many the traditional family did provide the support so needed in a time of rapid and unpredictable change. In P'an Ch'i-chün's warm portrayal of one mother-daughter relationship, we see how her mother, for whom old ways continued to provide meaning, played a role in P'an's intellectual and moral growth. While the author no longer shares her mother's beliefs, neither does she look down on them as parochial or outmoded superstitions. She tacitly recognizes that it was through her folk knowledge that her mother conveyed the far more important lesson of love, caring, and respect for learning. Her mother, so rooted in her narrow world, nevertheless provided the guidance that enabled P'an to move into a quite different way of life.

If Ch'en Heng-che and P'an Ch'i-chün illustrate how traditional family relations could provide support for women whose lives were changing, then Chiang Ch'ing's explanation of her difficulties in her relationship with T'ang Na reveals how some traditional male attitudes persisted even among those most associated with rejecting the old and welcoming the new. Chiang Ch'ing, best known as the politically powerful wife of Mao Tsetung and the fiery advocate of revolutionary theater and literature during the Cultural Revolution, was a minor film actress in 1937 when she wrote this self-justification. Her explanation of the problems in her marriage with the actor, director, and left-wing critic T'ang Na shows the continued strength of some traditional attitudes toward women even in the modern cosmopolitan atmosphere of Shanghai. Men who would have ridiculed the idea of binding young girls' feet or forcing a young woman into a marriage against her will still held the double standard in sexual fidelity. Chiang Ch'ing's defensive tone strongly suggests that she believed the propensity to blame the woman for any disharmony in a relationship was still prevalent. Parts of the past were still very much alive in the minds of many in the vanguard of change, and a free marriage was not automatically more successful than one that had been arranged.

"My Life in the Imperial Palace" is of value for Li Yü-ch'in's rare, and in some ways unprecedented, description of the life of an imperial consort. But Li reveals how changed values, as well as changed political conditions, had rendered much of the past anachronistic by the 1940s. Although Li did not object to being chosen as a consort of P'u-yi, the last emperor and the titular head of the Japanese puppet Manchukuo regime, neither did she consider it a special honor. She describes her life not as a glamorous adventure but as a kind of slightly baffling oddity. What she wanted, she explains, was not status but love. Nevertheless, after the war she remained a loyal wife to the now discredited and imprisoned P'u-yi. Like Chiang Ch'ing, Li seems to believe that readers will take it for granted that the women's share of responsibility for the maintenance of the husband-wife relationship is greater than the man's, and she is at pains to make it clear that it was P'u-yi's continued refusal to acknowledge her that finally terminated their marriage. Li's experience, though unique, thus illustrates both the spread of new ideals of marriage and the persistence of old attitudes toward wives.

Li's empty existence in the imperial palace contrasts with the sense of purpose that informs the unnamed nurse's account of her life in the final selection. In the simpleness of her tale she is more typical of the changes that were occurring, as the upsurge of patriotism in response to the Japanese invasion drew large numbers of women into the War of Resistance under the familiar pattern of women contributing in women's ways to the national effort. As the young nurse reveals, her sense of individual autonomy coincides with the shift of primary loyalty from the family to the nation. By now the idea that the needs of the nation take precedence was so familiar that when she informs her parents of her intent not to return home but instead to stay and serve in the military hospital, it is far less an act of rebellion than such an announcement would have been only a short time earlier. Her parents are expected to understand that they must take second place to the nation. But it is clear that second place is also honored, and that the family is still the locus of important obligations and ties of affection.

This is a fitting note on which to conclude. The main themes have been diversity and continuity, within the context of both nationalism and change. New forms of change were soon to appear, and already at the time this young nurse was telling her story, in many areas of China women were organizing for radical change under Communist Party leadership. With the establishment of the People's Republic of China in 1949, a new phase in the history of Chinese women was to begin. It was to be a period in which change intensified and accelerated, but in which both diversity and continuity remained relevant themes. The subject is far too complex to broach here, or to attempt to represent with one or two brief autobiographical sketches.[8] It is hoped that the articles and autobiographies in this book will aid in providing the background for a better understanding of women in contemporary China.

Notes

1. Professor Jonathan Lipman is translating one of the better known of these works, Ch'en Tung-yuan's *Chung-kuo fu-nü sheng-huo shih* (A history of the lives of Chinese women), first published in 1937.

2. For a more recent estimate of female literacy rates, see Evelyn Sakakida Rawski, *Education and Popular Literacy in Ch'ing China* (Ann Arbor: University of Michigan Press, 1979), pp. 6–8, 140.

3. The lives of several seventeenth-century rural village women are skillfully reconstructed in Jonathan D. Spence, *The Death of Woman Wang* (New York: Viking, 1978). For the late nineteenth and early twentieth centuries we are blessed with Ida Pruitt's classic *Daughter of Han: The Autobiography of a Chinese Working Women* (New Haven: Yale University Press, 1945; reprint, Stanford: Stanford University Press, 1967).

4. On premodern Chinese autobiography, see the incisive studies of Pei-yi Wu, "Self-Examination and Confession of Sins in Traditional China," *Harvard Journal of Asiatic Studies* 39, 1 (June 1979): 5–38; and *The Confucian's Progress: Autobiographical Writings in Traditional China* (Princeton: Princeton University Press, 1990).

5. On footbinding, see Howard S. Levy, *Chinese Footbinding: The History of a Curious Erotic Custom* (New York: Bell Publishing, 1967).

6. Chow Tse-tsung, *Research Guide to the May Fourth Movement* (Cambridge: Harvard University Press, 1963), p. 1.

7. On women's support networks, see Margery Wolf, *Women and the Family in Rural Taiwan* (Stanford: Stanford University Press, 1972).

8. The interested reader might start with the biography of Gold Flower in chapter 10 of Jack Belden, *China Shakes the World* (New York: Harper, 1949).

I

Historical
Interpretations

1

Women's Place in Chinese History

Hu Shih

HU SHIH (1891–1962) is familiar to students of modern Chinese history. Scholar, writer, educator, and diplomat, he had broad interests and made a lasting impact in many areas, from the adoption of colloquial Chinese as the standard written language to establishing a Chinese tradition of liberalism. As a liberal, he promoted equal rights for humankind, while as a historian, he praised aspects of China's cultural traditions alongside his advocacy of Westernization.

The following essay reflects Hu's liberal stand on women. His arguments are based on his historical research into the role of Chinese women in politics, literature, and education. This paper was first read in 1931 before the American Association of University Women in Tientsin and was published by the Transpacific News Service of New York City a decade later.

THERE is a general impression that the Chinese woman has always occupied a very low place in Chinese society. The object of this paper, however, is to try to tell a different story, to show that, in spite of the traditional oppression, the Chinese woman has been able to establish for herself a position that we must regard as a fairly exalted one. If there is a moral to this story, it is that it is simply impossible to suppress women—even in China.

I shall begin with these interesting lines from the *Book of*

Odes, which is the richest and most authentic source of materials for our study of the social life of ancient China before the eighth century B.C.:

> When a son is born,
> Let him sleep in the bed,
> Clothe him with fine dress,
> And give him jades to play with.
> How lordly his cry is!
> May he grow up to wear crimson
> And be the lord of the clan and the tribe!
>
> When a daughter is born,
> Let her sleep on the ground,
> Wrap her in common wrappings,
> And give her broken tiles for her playthings.
> May she have no faults, nor merits of her own;
> May she well attend to food and wine,
> And bring no discredit to her parents!

This frank partiality to sons and neglect of daughters does not require any apology or comment. It is simply a sociological and anthropological fact that womankind has always had to face in every part of the world. It is against such a hostile background that woman has had to struggle and slowly win her position in the family and in the larger world.

Even in ancient China, women were playing an important part in political life. Confucius told us that, of the ten builders of the Chou empire, one was a woman. He did not mention who she was, nor what she did. But in those ancient odes, which sang the early history of the Chou people before its eastward migration and conquest, we read high tributes paid to the great women who helped to make their race great. Indeed the poet-historians traced the origin of this race to a virgin woman who, through an immaculate conception, gave birth to Hou Chi, who taught his people the art of agriculture and became the founder of a great race and a great dynasty. Probably women enjoyed a peculiarly high position among this western people. For, in their quasi-historical poems, their great rulers were almost always mentioned together with their wives: the T'ai Wang migrated with his wife; Wang Chi's marriage with T'ai Jen was celebrated in one of the odes; and T'ai Szu, Wen Wang's consort, was praised more than once in these poems. T'ai Szu gave birth to ten remarkable sons of whom one conquered the Yin empire and founded the Chou dynasty, which lasted almost eight hundred years, and another was the duke of Chou, a great general and statesman.

But in the later history of the Chou dynasty, the part played by the women did not seem to be always beneficial. The Western empire fell to the hands of the Barbarians in 721 B.C., and history attributed its downfall to the work of a woman, Pao Szu. Thus the poets sang:

> Glorious was the Chou House,
> It was Pao Szu who ruined it.

Authentic history did not tell us how she did it, but she must have been a truly wonderful woman to be able to ruin a great dynasty. For the poets said in another ode:

> The wise man founded the city,
> But the wise woman destroys it.
> Alas! this wise woman,
> A bird of evil omen is she!
> A woman with a long tongue
> Is surely a stepping stone to ruin.
> Disaster does not descend from Heaven,
> It comes from Woman.

This is a condemnation of women but at the same time a clear indication of the important role played by women in those days. Woman must occupy a very important position before she can ruin a city or a nation.

Throughout Chinese history, there were many great women whose political achievement was not merely due to their status as empresses or empress dowagers. An ordinary person with no marked talents can achieve nothing even though she is placed in the most exalted positions of the empire. But these Chinese women did honor to the positions they occupied in history. Such was the queen-regent of Ch'i who reigned for almost forty years and whose sagacity in internal government and diplomacy kept the Kingdom of Ch'i out of the devastating wars that ruined the nations in the third century B.C. She was once asked to solve the puzzle of unchaining a chain of jade rings. She took a hammer and broke the chain with the exclamation: "I have solved it!"

In the founding of the Han empire, which lasted four hundred years, two women played very important parts. The Empress Lü (died 180 B.C.), wife of the founder of the dynasty, came from the common people and had no education. But she was a woman of great shrewdness and capable of most decisive and brutal action. It was she who murdered Han Hsin and P'eng Yüeh, the two great generals whose power could threaten the safety of the empire. The other woman was the Empress Tou (died 135 B.C.), who also came from the people and was in power for forty-five years. She was a believer in Lao Tzu's political philosophy of noninterference and required all her children and grandchildren and her own clansmen to study the works of Lao Tzu and other Taoist philosophers. Throughout the long reigns of her husband and her son, the imperial policy was one of laissez-faire and strict economy, which allowed the people to recuperate from the effects of long wars and to develop their own resources. At the end of her reign, the empire had attained the height of general prosperity and the government had endeared itself to the people, so that it was possible for her grandson, Wu Ti, to carry out his policy of construction and expansion and to build up an empire of greater China.

In the most glorious days of the T'ang dynasty, a great woman, the Empress Wu Chao, ruled over the empire for forty-five years (660–705), during a part of which period she actually declared herself not merely empress-regent but emperor of her newly founded dynasty of Chou and reigned of her own right for sixteen years. She was a woman of great literary talent and political genius, and her long reign was marked by territorial expansion and cultural advancement.

I shall not go on enumerating the empresses who ruled vast empires, nor the imperial favorites who ruined great dynasties. I think I have said enough to show that the Chinese woman was not excluded from political life and that she has played no mean role in the long history of the country.

In the nonpolitical spheres of life, the Chinese woman, too, has achieved positions of honor and distinction. The greatest honor goes to T'i Ying, of the family of Ch'un-yü, who was responsible for the abolition of corporal tortures under the Han empire. Her father, who was one of the greatest physicians of the age, had been unjustly accused and was to be subjected to bodily tortures. As he had five daughters and no son, the old doctor, on his way to prison, turned to the girls and said: "It has been my misfortune to have only daughters and no son, and I have no one to help me in time of need." T'i Ying, the youngest of his five daughters, resolved to help her father and went to the capital where she petitioned to the emperor offering herself as a slave in the imperial court to redeem her father from the deadly tortures. Her petition touched the heart of the benevolent Emperor Wen Ti, who issued in 167 B.C. his most famous edict ordering the abolition of all the worst forms of corporal punishment.

In the world of scholarship and literature, Chinese women have always made important contributions. In the early decades of the Han dynasty, when the ancient classics were transmitted through verbal teaching, a woman was responsible for the preservation and transmission of the text of one of the classics, the *Book of History*. Three hundred years later, when the great historian Pan Ku died in imprisonment (A.D. 92) and his monumental *History of the Former Han Dynasty* was left unfinished, it was a woman, his sister Pan Chao, who was requested by the imperial government to continue the work and bring it to completion. It was she who taught the great scholar Ma Yung to read the *History of the Former Han Dynasty,* thereby publishing it to the world. Pan Chao was invited to become the teacher of the empress and the other ladies of the court. When the Empress Teng became regent (105–121), she was a kind of political adviser to her. Of her preserved works, the *Lessons for Women* in seven chapters is best known. In these chapters, she taught the virtue of humility, but she also advocated the education of women. "The gentlemen of today," said she, "who educate their sons only and ignore the instruction of their daughters, have failed to understand the proper relationship between the sexes. According to tradition, the boys are taught to read books at the age of eight and will have acquired some knowledge by the age of fifteen. May we not do the same thing for the girls?" These words sound very mild today, but it must have required much moral courage to utter them in the year A.D. 100.

Of all the literary women in Chinese history, the most famous one was Li Ch'ing-chao, a native of Tsinan and wife of the scholar Chao Ming-ch'eng. She was born in 1081 and died about 1140. Both her father and mother being talented writers, she grew up in an atmosphere of culture and refinement. She wrote well both in prose and in verse, but she was particularly noted for her *tz'u* or songs written to popular airs. Hers was an age of songs; but she was very severe in her criticism of the greatest poets of the time. Her own songs, of which only a few score have been preserved, were highly praised by her contemporaries; Hsin Chia-hsien, the greatest master of the *tz'u,* openly admitted that he was sometimes imitating the style of Li Ch'ing-chao.

Li Ch'ing-chao was probably one of the most striking personalities among the Chinese women of historical fame. She was always frank and never hesitated to write of her real life with all its love, joy, and sorrows. As an example of her frankness, I quote these sentences from her preface to her book on a game of chance that was then in vogue:

I love gambling. I am so fond of all forms of gambling that I can easily forego sleep or forget my food. And I always win, be the stake large or small. Why? Because I know the games well. Ever since the war and our migration to the South, frequent traveling under most trying circumstances has scattered all our gambling sets, and I have rarely played. But I have never ceased to think of the games.

With the same candor she wrote her "Second Preface" to the "Catalogue of Bronze and Stone Inscriptions" compiled by her scholarly husband. As this preface gives us a most charming picture of the intimate life of a happily married couple, I quote a few paragraphs to show the place of an educated wife in a scholarly family:

When we were married in 1101, my husband was twenty-one and was still a student at the National University. Both our families being poor, we lived a very frugal life. On the 1st and 15th of every month, my husband had leave of absence from the university to come home. He would very often pawn his belongings to get 500 cash, with which he would walk to the market at Hsiang-kuo Monastery and pick up rubbings of ancient stone inscriptions. These, together with some fresh fruits and nuts, he would carry home and we would enjoy together the edibles and the ancient rubbings, forgetful of all our troubles in this world.

In later years when my father-in-law became prime minister, and a number of influential friends were in a position to loan us rare books to copy, our interest in these antiquarian objects was greatly deepened and we often took great trouble and sometimes suffered privation in order to buy a rare manuscript, a fine painting, or an ancient bronze vessel. I remember once during the Ch'ung-ning era (c. 1105) we were offered a painting by Hsu Hsi for sale at the price of 200,000 cash. Although a son of a prime minister, my husband found it difficult to pay such a high price. We kept the painting for two days and had to return it to the owner. For several days we could not overcome our sense of regret and disappointment.

When my husband became prefect of two prefectures, he spent practically all his income on books and antiques. When a book was bought, he and I would always read it together, mending the text, repairing the manuscript, and writing the captions. And when a painting or a bronze vessel was brought home, we would also together open it, play with it, study its merits, and criticize its defects. Every evening we studied together till one candle was burned up. In this way our collection of books surpassed all other collections in the country because of this loving care which my husband and I were able to give to it.

It was my good fortune to be endowed with a very good memory. Every evening after supper, we would sit together in the Kuei-lai Hall and make our own tea. We would wager against each other that such and such a quotation was to be found on a certain page in a certain chapter of a certain book. We must number the exact line, page, chapter, and volume, and then check them from the bookshelves. The winner was rewarded by drinking the first cup of tea. But when one of us did win, one was so happy that one's hand trembled with laughter and the tea would spill all over the floor. So the first cup was rarely drunk.

We were resolved to grow old and die in such a little world of our own.

Here in this beautiful picture of domestic life in the early years of the twelfth century, we see absolute equality, intellectual companionship and cooperation, and a little world of contented happiness. The picture is too good to be true of most Chinese families; indeed, it is too good to be true of most families anywhere, in the East or in the West. But it is a most interesting human document that tells us that at least some Chinese women once occupied a place that may make some of us modern people feel not a little envious.

The question is often asked, How many women in old China may be said to have received an education? What proportion of the women had access to this literary education?

This question cannot be satisfactorily answered. It varies with the educational opportunities of the different families and with the different localities. A family with a literary tradition usually gave to its women some rudiments of a literary education, while it takes some strikingly exceptional genius to pick up a knowledge of reading and writing in a poor and unlettered family.

Moreover, it is safe to say that women born in the lower Yangtse Delta had a better chance for an education that those born in the other provinces. Again, there seems to have been a gradual spread of the practice of educating women, beginning probably with the invention of the printed book in the ninth century, and becoming more widespread during the last four hundred years when the "literary-talented woman" *(ts' ai nü)* of the popular novels gradually came to be accepted as an ideal for women.

About ten years ago, Mrs. Ch'ien Hsün, wife of a former Chinese minister to Rome, published a "Bibliography of Works by Woman Writers During the Last Three Hundred Years." This lady of seventy years had spent more than ten years in compiling this work, and I was asked to write an introduction to it. I tried to make a statistical analysis of its contents and found the results most interesting and instructive. In the first place, this bibliography tells us that there were 2,310 women in the last three hundred years who had written, and most of them had published, works in the field of literature. This number in itself is a revelation to me. Second, I have classified these lady writers according to their birthplaces and obtained the following results:

Kiangsu	748 (32.3%)
Chekiang	706 (30.5%)
Anhwei	119 (5.1%)
Fukien	97 (4.2%)
Hunan	71 (3.0%)
Kiangsi	57
Chihli	51
Shantung	44
Manchu	42
Kuangtung	38
Hupei	20
Szechuan	19
Honan	18
Kuangsi	15
Shansi	13

Shensi	10
Kweichow	10
Chinese Banners	10
Yunnan	6
Kansu	4
Unclassified	212
Total	2,310

Thus Kiangsu and Chekiang had the highest percentage, each coming very near to one-third of the total. These two provinces plus Anhui make more than two-thirds of the total. Kiangsu, Chekiang, Anhui, Fukien, and Hunan occupy fully three-quarters of the total number. These proportions correspond almost exactly to the ratio of geographical distribution of male authors and of historical personages which has been worked out by other scholars for the same period. All this shows that Mrs. Ch'ien's bibliography was representative of cultural distribution among the female population in the country.

Third, we must note that, out of the three thousand works listed, about 99 percent are poetry. There were a few works on mathematics, one on medicine, half a dozen in the field of history, and about a dozen in classical and philological research. This again is quite significant in showing that the education these women received was purely literary, and that the spirit of critical historical research that characterized the age left no marked influence on the educated ladies. They read and wrote poetry, because it was considered respectable for ladies to be able to do so. Most of these educated ladies learned to paint pictures, and some of them became accomplished artists. That, too, was a part of the literary education.

To confirm Mrs. Ch'ien's investigations, I may point out that the number of women writers of poetry in the last three hundred years is really amazing. As far as I know, there have been three important anthologies of poems written by women during this period. The first anthology was made in 1831 and contained 933 names; the second was a supplement made in 1835 that listed 513 names; and the third was made by Mrs. Ch'ien Hsün in 1918 and contained 309 names. The three anthologies together furnish us with a list of 1,755 women poets. Besides these anthologies of poems in more or less regular meters, which we call *shih*, there are other anthologies of songs of irregular lines, which are written to existing tunes and known by the name of *tz'u*. Most of the women who wrote *shih* also wrote *tz'u*. Mr. Hsu Chi-yu, a well-known collector of books, has recently published a collection of 100 complete works of 100 women songwriters of this period; in addition, he has published an anthology of 2,045 songs by 783 women of the last three hundred years.

It may be asked, what good has all this literary education done to the Chinese women? Has it ever led them to revolt against footbinding? Has it given the women an opportunity to be economically more independent? Has it really elevated their position in the family or in society?

It is true that the literary education for women has not led them to revolt against footbinding, just as seven hundred years of rational philosophy have not opened the eyes of Chinese thinkers to the horrors of such a perverse and cruel form of "beautifying" their women. Nor has this superficial education enabled the women to become economically more independent, although not a few well-known women artists could sell their paintings and calligraphy at a fairly high price. It was considered not highly reputable for good artists to write or paint for pay; and it was only in extreme cases of necessity that educated ladies of good families condescended to sell their pictures or writings.

Nevertheless, this literary education, however superficial and unpractical, has had the good effect of elevating the position of women. In a country where educated men are rare, educated women are even more scarce and are therefore more respected. Moreover, this literary education gave them a key at least to book knowledge, which, while it may not lead to emancipation or revolution, probably made them better wives and better mothers.

It is not always true that "a little knowledge is a dangerous thing." A little knowledge is much better than no knowledge at all.

In particular, this literary education has had tremendous value in enabling the women to become better teachers to their own children. This is invariably true of Chinese girls, who were rarely taught in schools together with the boys, and who would have a better chance for education if their mothers could teach them the rudiments of reading and writing. It is therefore safe to say that the comparatively wide spread of education for Chinese women during the last three hundred years has been largely the work of the educated women themselves.

History is full of evidence of the importance of women's education in the lives of their sons. Many a great man in Chinese history received his early education from his mother. The sage Mencius owed his early training to his mother, whose story has become proverbial. The great statesman and scholar Ou-yang Hsiu (died 1072) lost his father at the age of four and was taught by his widowed mother, who, having no money to buy paper and brush, used reeds to write characters on the ground for her son to read. The great Ku Yen-wu (died 1681), the founder of modern critical scholarship in the last three centuries, told us that his virgin mother, who lost her fiancé on the eve of their wedding and lived a life of widowhood with her adopted son, was responsible for his early training in historical knowledge and in the love for the Chinese nation. When the Manchus had conquered the Ming empire and Manchu troops were approaching her native place, she resolved to die for her country and killed herself by starving fifteen days later. She died the day before her city was taken by the Manchus, and she left her last instruction to her adopted son that he must not accept office or honor under the alien conquerors. Ku Yen-wu lived thirty-six years under the new regime, but he refused to have anything to do with the new government. He was one of the few great spiritual fathers of Chinese nationalism, which ultimately brought about the downfall of the Manchu rule in China.

Thus has China been rewarded by her women for the little education they have received. Against all shackles and fetters, the Chinese woman has exerted herself and achieved for herself a place in the family, in society, and in history. She has managed men and governed empires; she has contributed abundantly to literature and the fine arts; and above all she has taught and molded her sons to be what they have been. If she has not contributed more, it was probably because China, which certainly has treated her ill, has not deserved more of her.

2

Female Rulers in Ancient China

Yang Lien-sheng

YANG LIEN-SHENG (1914–1990), professor at Harvard University and member of Academia Sinica, was an eminent scholar who combined a legendary knowledge of the Chinese historical record with meticulous research and analysis of many aspects of Chinese economic, social, and political history. Among his publications are *Money and Credit in China* (1952) and two collections of articles, *Studies in Chinese Institutional History* (1963) and *Excursions in Sinology* (1969).

The following article appeared first in the *Harvard Journal of Asiatic Studies* in 1960 and is included in *Excursions in Sinology*. It was originally prepared for the Conference on Political Power in Traditional China, sponsored by the Center for East Asian Studies, Harvard University, and held in Laconia, New Hampshire, September 3–9, 1959. In it Yang discusses the ways in which Chinese women acquired and held political power, in both government and the family.[1] "Mothers' rights" and "wives' rights," also mentioned by Yang, are another neglected aspect of Chinese social and family structure in need of further research.

AN INTERPRETER in the British civil service, Thomas Taylor Meadows, stationed in China before and during the Taiping Rebellion, had the following comment to make on the position of woman in China:

16

Woman is still more of a slave of man among the Chinese than among Anglo-Saxons. The quality of her slavery is, however, much tempered by the great veneration which Confucian principles require sons to pay both parents. The Imperial Government dare not refuse leave of absence to a mandarin if he, as an only son, requires it in order to tend his widowed mother during her declining years; even though the government may know that the real cause of his asking for leave is to escape from some impending official difficulty. On the other hand, a mandarin dare not (as we may do) ask for leave in order to tend a suffering wife, or to visit one from whom official duties have long separated him. Nothing surprises and amuses mandarins more than the frequent reference which foreign functionaries *will* make to their conjugal relations as affecting, in one way or the other, their official avocations and duties. A Chinese will rarely introduce his most intimate male acquaintance to his wife. It is hardly considered a compliment. Introductions to mothers are, on the other hand, not infrequent. The friend introduced then performs the kow tow to the lady, i.e., he kneels before her and touches the ground repeatedly with his forehead. The son does not prevent him, but he returns the salute by kneeling and kow towing to his friend. Thus two men, and often, of course, grey bearded men of high stations, will in China be found knocking their heads against the floor in honour of a women of their own class in society. Add to this that if a mother accuses her son before the magistrate, the latter will punish him as a black slave is punished in an American flogging-house, i.e., without inquiry into the specific offence. The reader will conclude that this great social and legal authority of mothers in China must operate to raise the position of females generally; and this it does in fact: though in the contraction of their own marriages each is but a passive instrument.

These interesting observations on what may be termed a mother's rights are found in Meadows's *The Chinese and Their Rebellions* (pp. 634–35), published in 1856. Had the book been written only five or six years later, the author would probably have made the natural connection between the rights of mothers and the regency of empress dowagers or the institution of female rulers in China.

It is common knowledge that, in the whole history of imperial

China from 221 B.C. to A.D. 1912, Chinese society was predominantly patriarchal and patrilineal. Attention is rarely called, however, to the fact that in many periods of its long history the country was governed by female rulers. Empress dowagers served as regents for both Chinese and alien dynasties, and they were particularly powerful under the Han, the Northern Wei (Hsien-pi), the Liao (Ch'i-tan), the Sung, the Yüan (Mongol), and the Ch'ing (Manchu). The T'ang dynasty witnessed the unique female emperor, Wu Chao, who founded her own dynasty (r. 690–705, d. 705, age 80). Altogether, these female rulers exerted considerable influence in Chinese history.

In spite of their importance, studies of these female rulers are scanty and not always critical. In Western languages, one finds only a few biographies translated from the Chinese standard histories: biographies of Empress Lü (r. 188–180 B.C., d. 180 B.C.) of the Former Han,[2] of Empress Teng (r. A.D. 105–121, d. A.D. 121, age 41) of the Later Han,[3] and of Empress Feng (r. 465–471, 476–490, d. 490, age 49) of the Northern Wei,[4] as well as several full-length biographies of Wu Chao[5] and of the Empress Dowager Tz'u-hsi (r. 1861–1872, 1874–1889, 1898–1908, d. 1908, age 74).[6] The high position enjoyed by empresses in Liao society has been discussed in detail by Wittfogel and Feng,[7] but no similar studies are available for the other dynasties. The Liao cases, however, were not typical because regular intermarriage between the emperor's clan (Yeh-lü) and the empress's clan (Hsiao) was not the rule under other dynasties. The importance of the Hsiao empresses as rulers and campaign leaders in the Ch'i-tan state is still reflected in Chinese opera today.

Although traditional Chinese scholars have paid some attention to regencies of empress dowagers,[8] their discussions are often sketchy and tend to be overloaded with conventional ethical judgments. One modern study is fortunately rather concise and objective and may serve as a starting point for our investigation. It is the section on "Empress Dowagers and Regents," (pp. 111–14) in a book entitled *Chung-kuo fu-nü tsai fa-lü-*

shang chih ti-wei (The woman's position in Chinese law) by Chao Feng-chiai. The study was made by Professor Chao in 1926 as postgraduate work on a China Foundation Scholarship at Peking University and was published in 1928. Although more than thirty years old, the book as a whole and this section in particular are still useful. I would like to present a translation of Professor Chao's text and notes and add a supplementary discussion of some of the political and social problems involved in the hope that other scholars may be stimulated to undertake a more thorough and critical study of the reigns and personalities of these female rulers.[9]

Translation of Chao Feng-chiai's Text

Although China did not have a written Salic law, nevertheless there was a prohibition, silently observed through dynasties, that a woman was not to become emperor.[a] In history, from the time when the Great Yü of Hsia transmitted the throne to his son, Ch'i, the rulers of the following dynasties all passed the throne to a son and never in a single instance to a daughter. Hence the principle is obvious.

There are warnings against the regency of an empress dowager in the Classics,[b] and no written law sanctioning it exists in history. Moreover, there have been orders prohibiting empress dowagers from interfering in government, notably during the Ming

---

[a]In China there were two cases in which women became emperors. One was Nü Kua in ancient China, traditionally known as the sister of Fu-hsi (Endō Ryūkichi, *Shina shisō hatatsu shi*, part 1, section 5), but she lived in such remote antiquity that her story seems unreliable. The other was in medieval China. The Empress Tse-t'ien of the T'ang dynasty changed the dynastic name from T'ang to Chou and assumed for herself the title of Shen-sheng huang-ti (Holy Emperor). She was on the throne for fifteen years (annals of Wu Tse-t'ien in the *Old History of the T'ang Dynasty*), but both contemporaries and later people considered her a usurper.

[b]*The Classic of Documents,* "The Speech at Muh": "The hen does not announce the morning. The crowing of a hen in the morning indicates the subversion of the family" (Legge, *The Shoo King,* pp. 302–3).

dynasty.[c] Actual cases, however, have existed, beginning with Empress Lü of the Western Han and ending with Empress Dowager Tz'u Hsi toward the end of the Ch'ing dynasty. This type of regency has a history of over two thousand years, and certainly it should not be regarded as something accidental.

It may be observed that from the Han dynasty on, whenever there was a regency of an empress dowager, precedents from earlier times were invariably cited as an established model.[d] This indicates that the regency of empress dowagers first created in the Han period had in later times at least the effect of customary law. Coming down to the Ch'ing dynasty, one finds that the *Ta Ch'ing hui-tien* (chapter 291) even includes a section on empress dowagers' "Attending to the business of government behind a lowered screen" (*ch'ui-lien t'ing cheng*),[10] which constituted a major statute of the dynasty. There seems no doubt that it had become a dynastic institution.

Although the regency of an empress dowager was a dynastic institution, it does not necessarily follow that all empress dowagers could serve as regents. In general, this was possible only

---

[c]Prohibition of interference in government by empress dowagers did not begin in the Ming period. In the third year of Huang-ch'u (A.D. 222), an edict ordered that the officials should not memorialize the empress dowager and that the members of the empress's clan should not take part in the government[11] (annals of Wen-ti in the "Wei chih" [of the *San-kuo chih*]). But in the time of Shao-ti, Empress Dowager Ming-yüan again dominated the government (annals of Shao-ti in the "Wei chih"). Only during the Ming dynasty, in the first year of Hung-wu (1368), T'ai-tsu decreed, "Although the empresses and imperial concubines should serve as models of mothers in the empire, they are not to be permitted to take part in government affairs." This was observed throughout the Ming dynasty, which had no cases of regencies of empress dowagers (biographies of the empresses and imperial concubines in the *History of the Ming Dynasty*).

[d]According to the biography of Empress Yü in the *History of the Chin Dynasty*, "When Ch'eng-ti came to the throne, she was honored as Empress dowager. . . . The officials memorialized that, the Emperor being young, the precedent of Empress Teng of Han should be followed. She declined several times but was finally obliged to appear in court and serve as regent." (Empress Teng served as regent for Shang-ti from the first year of Yüan-hsing [A.D. 105].)

when certain conditions were fulfilled. These conditions were not set forth in any written law. History shows that altogether there were three of them, as follows:

1. When the emperor was very young. For instance, when Empress Dowager Tou served as regent, Ho-ti was ten years of age (annals of Ho-ti in the *History of the Later Han Dynasty*); when Empress Dowager Teng served as regent, Shang-ti was only just over the hundred days after his birth (annals of Shang-ti in the *History of the Later Han Dynasty*); when Empress Dowager Liang served as regent, Ch'ung-ti was only two years of age (annals of Ch'ung-ti in the *History of the Later Han Dynasty*). But when Empress Lü of the Western Han assumed the rule, Hui-ti was already seventeen (annals of Hui-ti in the *History of the Former Han Dynasty*). This occurred because Empress Lü was greedy for power.

2. When the emperor was ill and unable to attend to affairs. For instance, when Sung Ying-tsung was ill, Empress Dowager Ts'ao was asked to make decisions temporarily with him on military and civil [literally state] affairs *(ch'üan t'ung ch'u-fen chün-kuo shih)* (biography of Empress Ts'ao in the *History of the Sung Dynasty*). Again, when Shen-tsung was ill in bed, Chancellor Wang Kuei memorialized to ask the empress dowager to attend temporarily to governmental business together [with the emperor] *(ch'üan t'ung t'ing-cheng)* (annals of Che-tsung in the *History of the Sung Dynasty*).

3. When the emperor died suddenly or left a posthumous edict. For instance, upon the death of Han An-ti, Empress Dowager Teng first served as regent and then decided to put Shao-ti [the young emperor] on the throne (annals of An-ti in the *History of the Later Han Dynasty*). This is an example of the former situation. Upon the death of T'ang Kao-tsung, a posthumous edict ordered that all major military and civil affairs were to be decided by the Heavenly Empress [i.e., Empress Wu] (annals of Empress Wu in the *History of the T'ang Dynasty*); again, upon the death of Sung Chen-tsung, a posthumous edict ordered that the heir apparent should assume the throne and temporarily make deci-

sions on major military and civil affairs together with the empress dowager (annals of Jen-tsung in the *History of the Sung Dynasty*). These are examples of the latter situation.

According to the "Treatise on Rites" in the *History of the Sung Dynasty,* when Hui-tsung came to the throne [1100], the empress dowager was to join him temporarily in attending to governmental affairs, and the Three Secretariats and the Privy Council jointly discussed the precedents. Tseng Pu said, "The present emperor is an adult; how can the empress dowager attend to governmental business behind a screen? I propose that the precedent of the Chia-yu [1063] era be followed." Ts'ai Pien said, "In the cases of T'ien-sheng [1023] and Yüan-feng [1085] and the present time, the decision was made entirely by a posthumous decree. The situation is different from that at the end of Chia-yu, when Ying-tsung requested the empress dowager to attend to governmental affairs." Tseng Pu said, "Although the order of regency is found in the posthumous decree, in actuality, it was issued in accordance with the wish of the empress dowager."

Discussion

The section translated above leads us to an obvious conclusion involving three points; namely, regencies of empress dowagers existed in Chinese history (1) as an established institution, which, though (2) occasionally prohibited and criticized, was often resorted to (3) as a measure of emergency and expediency. Each of these points requires further elaboration and clarification, but before discussing them, I would like to say a few words on the political position of the empress dowager as a regent.

Regent Empress Dowagers as Chiefs of State

Students of government may ask: Was the regent empress dowager the chief of state or only the head of government, if a distinction can be made between the two in Chinese history? My tentative reply is that such a distinction existed only in a rather vague fashion, but it is clear that at least several of these empress dowagers wanted to be recognized as the sovereign or supreme ruler, even though their wishes were not always carried out. The subtlety of the situation can be illustrated by the various official expressions used to define the regency.

In the annals of Empress Lü in the *Records of the Grand Historian (Shih chi),* one first encounters the phrase *lin-ch'ao ch'eng-chih,* a phrase also found in the annals of Empress Lü in the *History of the Former Han Dynasty* and translated by Professor Dubs as "appeared in court and pronounced [that she issued] the [imperial] decrees." Here a footnote of Professor Dubs reads: "Ever since, when an empress had assumed the emperor's power, her act has been called by this phrase, so that it has become an idiom. . . . An empress could issue edicts [*chao*], but the issuing of decrees [*chih*] was the sole prerogative of the emperor" (vol. 1, p. 192). When Empress Lü put the second Shao-ti on the throne in 183 B.C., she did not allow him to proclaim the next year as the first year of his reign (*yüan nien*), thus emphasizing the fact that it was she who "issued the imperial decrees" (*ch'eng chih*). She seems to have been successful in her claim in Former Han times, as she was referred to as the *nü-chu* or "female ruler," and her reign was recorded in the section called "Annals" in the *Shih chi.* Only in the early years of the Later Han did Emperor Kuang-wu order her tablet to be removed from the Temple of Emperor Kao-tsu as a sign of disapproval.

Forces trying to check empress dowagers became stronger from the third century on. These comprised at least the emperor, his clansmen, and many aristocratic families during the period of the Six Dynasties and included literati-officials in T'ang, Sung, and later times. The Sung literati-official scored a point by putting in the word *t'ung,* "together with, jointly," in proclamations of the regency of empress dowagers to emphasize the principle that the emperor, even in minority or illness, remained sovereign of the state. This principle is comparable to the interesting concept in English common law:

> In judgment of the law the king, as king, cannot be said to be a
> minor, for when the royal body politic of the king doth meet with the
> natural capacity in one person the whole body shall have the quality
> of the royal politic, which is the greater and more worthy and
> wherein is no minority. For *omne majus continet in se minus*.[12]

Another interesting term in this connection is *hsün-cheng*, "tutoring (the emperor) in government," introduced in 1886 to justify the continuation of the regency of Tz'u-hsi when the emperor
was coming of age and was supposed to attend to government
business in person *(ch'in-cheng)*.[13] The term later became applied to one of the three stages (military, tutorial, and constitutional) of gradual realization of constitutional government for the
Republic of China according to the teaching of Dr. Sun Yat-sen.

Regent Empress Dowagers as an Established Institution

Regencies of empress dowagers became institutionalized in Later
Han times. The rituals required for such regencies are recorded in
the *Tu tuan* of the second-century scholar, Ts'ai Yung: "When
the empress dowager serves as regent, she will appear in the front
throne hall to receive the officials; she [will be seated] facing
east and the young emperor facing west. When the officials send
in memorials, two copies should be made, one for the empress
dowager and one for the young emperor."[14] Nothing is prescribed
about a lowered screen or curtain, which seems to have been a
later innovation made by Empress Wu.[15]

During the Sung, another Chinese dynasty with several regent
empress dowagers, the rules became more elaborate, and subtle
distinctions were drawn between two types of precedents. One
was that of Dowager Empress Liu (r. 1022–1033, d. 1033, age
64), who came to the Ch'eng-ming Tien (a major throne hall),
with the young Emperor Jen-tsung and made decisions there behind a screen. Her example was followed by Grand Empress
Dowager Kao (r. 1085–1093, d. 1093, age 62), who came to the
Ying-yang Men with Emperor Che-tsung on an odd-numbered

day *(chih-jih)* in every five days and was seated with the emperor behind a screen. The other precedent was established by Empress Dowager Ts'ao (r. 1063–1064, d. 1079, age 62), who attended to business only in a small throne hall with a screen in front of her. She did not set up a special name for her birthday, nor did she send any envoys in her own name to the Ch'i-tan. These imperial prerogatives, however, were assumed by Empress Dowager Liu and Grand Empress Dowager Kao. The discussion in 1100 was to decide which of the precedents was to be followed by Empress Dowager Hsiang (r. 1100–1101, d. 1101). The decision was in favor of the example of Empress Dowager Ts'ao.[16]

Empress Dowager Liu was undoubtedly the most ambitious and aggressive of the Northern Sung empresses. In the year 1032, she performed the imperial ceremonial plowing and made offering herself with the emperor in the Temple of the Imperial Ancestors. Both rites were prerogatives of the emperor. In her posthumous order *(i-kao)* in 1033, she wished to pass on her regency to Imperial Concubine Yang, who was to become empress dowager. This part of her order, however, was disregarded and omitted when the posthumous order was announced to the empire.[17]

The Manchu rules concerning the regency of an empress dowager reached a climax of detail. These rules, of course, are found only in the Kuang-hsü edition of the *Ta-Ch'ing hui-tien* and not in the earlier editions, because such a regency had not been sanctioned in the earlier part of the dynasty when the Ming policy of prohibition was still followed. According to these rules, the screen was to be lowered in front of the empress dowager but not in front of the emperor. Certain major sacrificial offerings were to be made by designated imperial princes in place of the emperor *(ch'ien wang kung tai),* and certain ceremonies, including the ceremonial plowing, were to be temporarily suspended.[18]

Criticism and Prohibition of Regent Empress Dowagers

Criticism of female regents began as early as the Later Han period, when in 107 Tu Ken, a court gentleman, and one or more of his colleagues criticized Empress Dowager Teng and petitioned that she return governmental power to the emperor. Infuriated by this request, she ordered these gentlemen to be placed in heavy silk bags and beaten to death in the imperial court. Tu Ken narrowly escaped because he revived after his body had been placed outside the city; after pretending to be dead for three days, he fled to an obscure place where he served incognito as a waiter in a wine shop. Fifteen years later, in 121, when the empress dowager died and the Teng clan lost its influence, he identified and presented himself when the emperor wished to honor his family for his loyalty.[19] Tu Ken remained an inspiring example for literati-officials as late as the end of the Manchu dynasty, as may be illustrated by a reference to him in a four-line poem by T'an Ssu-t'ung, one of the six martyrs in the reform movement of 1898, written shortly before their execution.[20]

Fan Yeh, in the annals of Empress Teng in his *History of the Later Han Dynasty,* also criticized the empress dowager for her lifetime regency *(ch'eng-chih chung-shen),* although he praised her ability and the achievements of her reign. In his preface to the annals of the empresses, Fan also spoke strongly against such a regency, particularly because it tended toward dominance by imperial in-laws in the government. In this sense, we may agree in part with the remark of Professor Fitzgerald: "The empresses of the Han dynasty had played the role of the Trojan horse, introducing a crowd of ambitious relatives to the citadel of power, but themselves only providing the lure, and remaining the tool of their king."[21] After all, the road from concubine to empress was neither smooth nor easy. Imperial favor was difficult to secure or maintain. The numerous delicate situations in the palace required much charm, ability, and luck (such as the bearing of a son, a very important factor) on the part of the Trojan horse. Court intrigues and even murder were not infrequently resorted to whenever they were considered necessary. These conditions were true through all of Chinese history. Another side of the coin is that there were also wise empresses and empress dowagers who realized the virtue of self-discipline. These declined excessive honors, wealth, and power for members of their own families, and exercised control over their ambition or unlawful activities.

As Professor Chao Feng-chiai points out, prohibition against regencies and against interference in government by consort families began with the imperial decree of Wei Wen-ti in A.D. 222. This prohibition was echoed by Wu-ti, founder of the Liu Sung dynasty in South China, in his posthumous decree of 422: "In later generations, if there are rulers who are minors, governmental affairs should be entirely entrusted to the chancellors, and the empress dowagers need not bother to appear in court."[22] Obviously, the lesson of the Later Han was still fresh. Similarly, the prohibition of regent empress dowagers by Ming T'ai-tsu ordered the Board of Works to manufacture *hung-p'ai*, "red tablets," bearing his warning against their interference in governmental affairs and had the tablets placed in their living quarters. These were to be made of iron, presumably painted red, with the incised characters decorated with gold.[23]

Emergency and Expediency

The conditions that required the regency of an empress dowager have been thoroughly discussed by Professor Chao. Such situations as the disability or minority of the emperor have also been conducive to regencies in other cultures. The Chinese definition of minority, however changed from time to time. This was true not only of the emperor but of commoners as well, for whom age-groups were defined, at least from Ch'in and Han times on, to determine their taxes, labor, and military services. The subject is so complicated that it must be left for a later paper. For the present purpose, it may be sufficient to remember that for the most part in Chinese history, an emperor of seventeen *sui* (actually sixteen years of age) was considered to be not young, or at least not very young.

Empress dowagers were sometimes asked to exercise power or authority temporarily as an emergency measure, particularly when it was found necessary to dethrone an emperor, to enthrone a prince, or to announce surrender to an enemy. The first and most famous case of dethronement by an empress dowager was that in 74 B.C. when the influential General Huo Kuang asked the empress dowager to dethrone Prince Ch'ang-i.[24] Another famous case was under the Chin when the powerful General Huan Wen dethroned the emperor and made him Duke of Hai-hsi by order of the empress dowager.[25] These cases have been known in history as the precedents of Han Ch'ang-i and Chin Hai-hsi. They have been copied by later generations, most frequently under the Southern Dynasties, a fact that seems to reflect the dominance of powerful clans and the quick shifts in their balance of power during that era.

An unusual case of emergency occurred in 1127. The two Sung emperors and most of the imperial consorts had been captured and sent to North China by the Jurchen. The puppet ruler, Chang Pang-ch'ang, not wishing to assume the imperial authority, invited an imperial consort to become empress dowager and issued in her name a proclamation enthroning an imperial prince (later Kao-tsung) as emperor and founding the Southern Sung dynasty. The proclamation, beautifully composed by Wang Tsao in the double-harnessed style (*p'ien-t'i*) has long been considered a true masterpiece. It includes, for instance, the following lines: "When the Han House suffered misfortune in its tenth generation, it was fitting for Kuang-wu to restore the dynasty. Of the nine sons of Duke Hsien of the state of Chin, there was only Ch'ung-erh who was still available for succession. Such indeed is the will of heaven, which requires hardly any planning by man."[26] Readers of the translation can appreciate the appropriateness of the historical allusions; the beauty of the balanced words and phrases in Chinese, however, is practically untranslatable.

If the enthronement of an imperial prince was a happy occasion, the offering of surrender to an enemy was the contrary. This case often occurred at the end of a dynasty, when the empress dowager and the young emperor faced oncoming conquerors. The sad duty of sending a memorial of surrender (*hsiang-piao*), very much like selling the last real estate of a family, had to be performed in the name of both mother and son. An unusual example of this case was the so-called abdication by the empress dowager and Henry P'u-i in favor of the Republic in 1912. The decree on this occasion, like the memorials of surrender of earlier times, was well composed. Actually, its style was more dignified because, after all, the surrender was made to the people, and the decree included expressions of friendly hope for the Republic.

Mother's Right and Wife's Right

Modern writers differ considerably in their estimation of the extent of a mother's authority in traditional China. For instance, Lin Yutang in *My Country and My People* (New York, 1935, p. 137) says: "The Chinese woman is, on the whole, a constitutionally sounder animal than her male companion, and we still have plenty of matriarchs even in the Confucian households." On the other hand, Olga Lang in *Chinese Family and Society* (New Haven, 1946, p. 52) remarks: "The widespread idea of a Chinese dowager with enormous power does not hold up under careful analysis of the position of women as represented, for example, in Chinese fiction." On this subject I am inclined to agree with Dr. Lin. To the best of my knowledge, up to the early years of the Republic, there were still many "matriarchs" or "dowagers" in large families of the higher classes. The extent of their power, although varying from case to case, was on the whole considerable.

Similar to the mother's rights were the wife's rights, which were to be respected even if the wife did not bear a son. This fact explains why, of the coregents toward the end of the Manchu dynasty, Empress Dowager Tz'u-an took precedence over Empress Dowager Tz'u-hsi, because, although Tz'u-hsi was the mother of T'ung-chih, Tz'u-an was the first wife of Hsien-feng. In this connection, attention may be called to a study by Dr. Niida Noboru on the position of the mistress of the household in China and her *Schlüsselgewalt*. This study of the authority and duties of the woman in charge of the household covers the practice of both higher and lower classes, including that of farmers.[27]

To conclude our discussion, some conjectural hypotheses may be advanced about the position of women in Chinese and some neighboring societies and the possibility of mutual influence. The position of women was relatively higher in the royal house of the Shang, which had its basis in the eastern part of North China. The high frequency of fraternal succession of Shang kings is possibly a remnant of an earlier matrilineal society. As late as early Han times there existed in Shantung the institution of *wu-erh*, "priestess" or "witch-child," an eldest daughter who was not married but was asked to play the leading role in making sacrificial offerings in the family.[28] This, together with other evidence,[29] indicates that the ancient Chinese culture, or at least its eastern branch, may have been matrilineal or even matriarchal. Whether this characteristic had anything to do with neighboring peoples in Manchuria or Korea remains to be investigated.

In Han and later times, the position of women in neighboring societies to the north of the Chinese world seems to have been on the whole higher than that of their sisters in China. For instance, females under the Northern Dynasties were said to have been active in society and in politics; a woman could seek official posts for her son or protest wrongs done to her husband. In contrast, women under the Southern Dynasties rarely had any activities outside their households.[30] Empresses of the Northern Dynasties were notoriously jealous, and it was at least partly because of their influence that few princes or officials dared to have more than one wife.[31] This higher position of women in North China may have helped to inspire Wu Chao to declare herself emperor. In turn, the Sung empress dowagers may have been influenced by Wu Chao and by the powerful empress dowagers of Ch'i-tan.[32] That the Jurchen Chin did not produce regent empress dowagers may perhaps be explained by several factors: (1) The Jurchen at first practiced polygamy without making a distinction between the chief wife and other consorts. (2) The rise of the Chin was sudden, and their rulers quickly adopted Chinese thought and institutions. (3) The Chin had several long-lived emperors, and (4) the Chin dynasty did not last very long. The case of the Manchu dynasty was similar to that of the Chin, but it lasted long enough to witness the reign of Tz'u-hsi for nearly half a century.

Notes

1. Professor Yang's findings have been confirmed in a detailed study of empresses and other imperial consorts during the Sung dynasty: Priscilla Ching Chung, *Palace Women in the Northern Sung* (Leiden: E. J. Brill, 1981).
2. Edouard Chavannes, *Les memoires historiques de Se-ma Ts'ien* (Paris, 1895–1905) 2:406–42; H. H. Dubs, *The History of the Former Han Dynasty* by Pan Ku (Baltimore, 1938–49) 1:191–210.
3. Nancy Lee Swann, "Biography of the Empress Teng: A Translation from the Annals of the Later Han Dynasty *(Hou Han Shu, Chüan 10a),*" JAOS 51 (1931): 138–59.
4. A. G. Wenly, *The Grand Empress Dowager Wen Ming and the Northern Wei Necropolis at Fang Shan* (Washington, DC, 1947).
5. C. P. Fitzgerald, *The Empress Wu* (Melbourne, 1955); Lin Yutang, *Lady Wu, A True Story* (London, 1957); Nghiem Toan and Louis Richard, *Wou Tsö-t'ien* (trans. of Empress Wu's biography in the *New History of the T'ang Dynasty)* (Saigon, 1959).
6. J. O. P. Bland and Edmund Backhouse, *China under the Empress Dowager, Being the History of the Life and Times of Tz'u Hsi* (London, 1910); Philip W. Sergeant, *The Great Empress Dowager of China* (New York, 1911); Princess Der Ling, *Old Buddha* (New York, 1928); Charles Pettit, *The Woman Who Commanded 500,000,000 Men* (New York, 1929) (trans. from the French by Una, Lady Troubridge); Daniele Vare, *The Last of the Empresses and the Passing from the Old China to the New* (London, 1936); Harry Hussey, *Venerable Ancestor, The Life and Times of Tz'u Hsi, 1835–1903, Empress of China* (New York, 1949).
7. Karl A. Wittfogel and Feng Chia-sheng, *History of Chinese Society, Liao (907–1125)* (New York, 1949), pp. 199–202.
8. E.g., the opinions of Hu Yin and Ma T'ing-luan, quoted in *Wen hsien t'ung-k'ao* (Shih-t'ung ed.) 251.1908a–c; Chao I, *Nien-erh-shih cha-chi* 3, on imperial in-laws in Han times, and 4, on empress dowagers of Eastern Han.
9. A translation of Chao Feng-chiai's notes, indicated by letters, appears as footnotes to the translated text.
10. The screen was lowered to observe the segregation of men and women as required by the rules of propriety for the higher classes in traditional China.
11. (*Yü-cheng*) "to take part in government," but the "Wei chih" text has (*fu-cheng*) "to assist in government," which, as a technical term used especially by imperial in-laws or princes, meant to serve as chancellors or in similar key government posts.

12. *Encyclopaedia Britannica* (11th ed.) under "Regent" quotes Coke upon Littleton 43a and adds, "But for reasons of necessity a regency, however anomalous it may be in strict law, has frequently been constituted both in England and Scotland." The position of male regents, who were rare in Chinese history, tended to approach that of the chief of state; for instance, the Duke of Chou, Wang Mang, and Dorgon. Also compare the position of regents (called *sesshō* and *kampaku*) in Fujiwara Japan.

13. *Ta-Ch'ing hui-tien* (Kuang-shü ed.), 293.13b–22a. This section contains no provisions about *ch'ui-lien* but requires only a temporarily erected gauze screen. Compare with Daniele Vare: "During the audiences given by Yehonala and Sakota in the name of the child emperor whom Hsien-feng had chosen to be his successor, a curtain of yellow silk was suspended in front of each empress, so as to render her invisible to the person kneeling in front of the platform on which the throne was raised. In the Chinese phrase, 'the empress dropped the curtain' or 'the empress governed from behind the suspended curtain.' This formality was observed during the first regency, which lasted from 1861 to 1873. But during the subsequent two regencies (1875–1889 and 1898–1908), Yehonala acted for an emperor of her own choosing, therefore with greater authority, and the yellow curtain was done away with. The sovereign will was no longer made manifest through a veil" *(The Last of the Empresses,* p. 65).

14. *Tu tuan* (SPTK ed.), B.3a–b.

15. See the annals of Kao-tsung in the *Old History of the T'ang Dynasty.* Under the Eastern Chin in A.D. 344 when the empress dowager held the two-year-old emperor to hold court in the major throne hall, a white gauze curtain was placed in front of them.

16. "Treatise on Rites" in the *History of the Sung Dynasty,* ch. 117; *Sung Hui-yao kao,* vol. 6, "Empresses and Imperial Concubines," 1.10ab, 13b, 17a–18b, 20ab.

17. *Sung hui-yao kao,* vol. 6, 1.11ab.

18. *Ta-Ch'ing hui-tien shih-li,* 291.1a–17b.

19. Biography of Tu Ken in the *History of the Later Han Dynasty* 87 (*lieh-chuan* 47). Tu Ken is also referred to in the comments by Fan Yeh at the end of the annals of Empress Teng, a reference that is omitted in Dr. Swann's translation.

20. The poem reads: [The Chinese original is omitted here.]

21. Fitzgerald, *The Empress Wu,* p. 113.

22. *History of the (Liu) Sung Dynasty (sung shu),* annals of Wu-ti.

23. *Ch'un-ming meng-yu lu,* 6.50b–51a.

24. Arvid Jongchell, *Huo Kuang och hans tid* (Göteborg, 1930) (trans. of the biography of Huo Kuang in the *History of the Former Han Dynasty* 68 [*lieh-chuan* 38]).

25. Biography of Huan Wen in the *History of the Chin Dynasty* 98 (*lieh-chuan* 68).

26. *Sung Hui-yao kao,* vol. 6, 1.25ab.

27. Niida Noboru, *Chūgoku no nōson kazoku* (Tokyo, 1952), pp. 243–310.

28. "Treatise on Geography," in the *History of the Former Han Dynasty,* ch. 28B.

29. E.g., Lin Yutang, *My Country and My People,* pp. 136–37; Lü-Ssu-mien; *Ch'in Han shih* (Shanghai, 1947), p. 487.

30. *Yen-shih chia-hsün,* ch. 1.

31. *Nien-erh shih cha-chi* 15, on empresses of Northern Ch'i and Sui.

32. Taking a lesson from earlier empress dowagers and following the model of Sung emperors, the female rulers of the Sung period were on the whole kind to the literati-officials. There were no cases of dethronement.

3

Feminist Thought in Ancient China

Lin Yü-t'ang

LIN YÜ-T'ANG (1895–1976), better known in the West as Lin Yutang, whose versatility and prolific output had few parallels in modern Chinese letters, enjoyed a long and distinguished career as a writer, scholar, journalist, publisher, educator, and inventor of the first Chinese typewriter. A gifted stylist in both Chinese and English, he wrote and translated several dozen books. Among the best known are *My Country and My People* (1935) and *The Importance of Living* (1937), which established him as a leading interpreter of Chinese culture in the West. Toward the end of his life, Lin thought that his most enduring work would most likely be *Lin Yutang's Chinese-English Dictionary of Modern Usage*, published in Hong Kong in 1972.

The following article appeared in the first issue (September 1935) of *T'ien Hsia Monthly*, an English-language magazine published in Shanghai. In a characteristically witty and pungent vein, Lin criticizes what he calls the neo-Confucian "semipathological state of mind that reveled in darkening women's souls and torturing women's bodies." His sympathy is with three unorthodox eighteenth-century literati, Yü Cheng-hsieh, Yüan Mei, and Li Ju-chen. The article reveals not only the author's forte—erudition combined with wit and humor—but also the humanist strain of Chinese thought, which informed much of the writing about Chinese women and the attempts to improve their status.

IT IS a truism that Chinese ethics is essentially a masculine ethics. What particular form and development this masculine ethics took, however, is not quite fully known to the West. For instance, Chinese history itself has always been written with a masculine bias. Thus, whenever the men rulers made a mess of the business of government and lost a dynasty, the men scholars were always able to point out a woman as the cause of their downfall. "Cherchez la femme," they seem to say. Queen Ta-chi was made, by common consent, responsible for the downfall of the Shang dynasty during the reign of the tyrant King Chou. Another queen, Pao-szu, was by the common verdict of the men historians, responsible for the fall of the East Chou dynasty under another tyrant, King Yu. It seems very curious that these scholars never noticed the point that it was the virtue of Queen Pao-szu, and not her immorality, that provoked the catastrophe; Pao-szu's only fault was her extreme decorum and disinclination to giggle, which provoked the king to play the shepherd-boy's trick by sending rockets as alarm signals to his vassals, when there was no danger at all. The vassals came with their troops, saw that they had been made fools of by the king, and the queen finally smiled. That smile, our historians say, cost King Yu his empire. And the king who made fun of official war signals and of his vassals was exonerated. And so on ad infinitum, from the ancient beauty Hsi-shih who was made responsible for the loss of the ancient Wu Kingdom to the twentieth-century Miss Butterfly, who was hounded out of Nanking in 1934 with threatening letters condemning her as responsible for the loss of Manchuria. It took a Hou Ch'ao-tsung, the lover of Li Hsiang-chün (to whose case we shall come presently), to reverse the old dictum that "Hsi-shih was responsible for the loss of the Wu Kingdom" by pointing out that, with the sort of misrule and licentiousness going on at the court, the Wu Kingdom would have been lost anyway without a Hsi-shih. According to the undisputed Chinese orthodox point of view, therefore, Marie Antoinette, or at least Madame Pompadour—and not Louis XVI—was responsible for the collapse of the first French Empire.

Chinese feminists, therefore, have a slightly different task from that of Western feminists, owing to the fact that such feminist thinkers as there were had to fight against a different background or a different social system from that of the West. While the general trend may be the same, such as, for instance, the fight for a single sex standard and the privileges of education for women, there are different evils of injustice to women, such as concubinage, footbinding, encouragement of a woman's suicide in defense of her chastity, and the forbidding of widows to marry, which form the special objectives that any independent Chinese thinker with a feminist leaning had to fight against in the first place. Part of the barbarity, to which Chinese Confucian scholars had allowed themselves to descend, will be reflected in the following discussion of the views of Yüan Mei, the rebel thinker of the eighteenth century. It is only necessary here to point out some salient points of the puritanico-sadistic background created by the Confucian scholars from the tenth century onward.

These scholars, calling themselves *li-hsüeh* or "scholars of reason" (which term in time became synonymous with goody-goody hypocrites), had drifted a long way away from the sane and healthy humanism of Confucius and turned it into a killjoy doctrine. Influenced by Buddhism, they began to cultivate the mind, regarding it as something apart from and set above the human passions and the life of the senses, in that way drifting into a pseudointellectualism which has good enough parallels in the West. These Confucian village schoolmasters, with their large mouthfuls of morality and righteousness, were always anxious to maintain the sanctity of society's morals, but being men themselves, naturally threw the great burden of upholding social morality upon the shoulders of women. The forbidding of widows to marry was erected into a doctrine,[1] compelling lifelong celibacy on the part of widows and even of girls whose fiancés had died before the wedding, and often encouraging suicide by erecting stone *p'ailou* in honor of those who did so. These were labeled "heroic women," so that the quality of heroism began to be very much admired in the *female* sex, since men had no occasion to defend their own chastity, even if they were of a heroic turn of mind. Women's feet were to be bound. Baby girls were often killed or drowned or sent into a monastery, without eliciting a protest from these austere souls who had the morality of the nation so much at heart. Toward the end of the Ming dynasty, the curious doctrine was discovered or invented that "In a woman stupidity is virtue." This callousness and lack of fine feeling went so far that at times women have been compelled to commit suicide by hanging themselves in order that their male relatives may wallow in the glory of having a "chaste woman" in the family, with the privilege of exemption from conscript labor for themselves. Yü Cheng-hsieh mentioned in his "Essay against Chastity" a poem that runs as follows:

> It is the custom in Fukien that half of the baby girls born are not brought up, and those that do grow up are expected to be heroic women.
>
> When a husband dies, the woman dies also without any reason; poisoned wine is in the cup and the rope hangs ready from the beam.
>
> The woman loves life, but what can she do under oppression? Her sorrows and her anger are concealed in her breast.
>
> Her clan relatives laugh and are happy that the woman dies; they petition for decorations to glorify their clan.
>
> A thirty-foot-high p'ailou [honorific arch] stands gloriously before their housedoor—but at night, they hear the new ghost wailing and begging to come back to life.

Is it not possible that a few independent minds should have risen and raised a voice of protest against this barbarism? There were, but one would have to look for them among the less orthodox and more frivolous and undegenerate writers, for it would be hopeless to look for originality among the high priests of the Orthodox Confucian Church. Curiously and yet naturally enough, too, not a single woman's voice was to be heard in this group, which is but a reflection of the tyrannical power of the Confucian system of ideas. Chinese women put up with this sexual injustice as naturally as Chinese people put up with political injustice. It was rather from among the more heterodox and independent thinkers that the voice of protest was to come. A number of orthodox scholars have occasionally given expression against various points of this social order, but such expressions are comparatively few. The reason is that the Chinese classic view, holding the male and female principles as necessarily com- plementing one another, is so essentially correct and true that it apparently gives a broad enough basis to excuse, in their minds, the existence of its unpleasant individual aspects. With all his fine feeling, all Su Tung-p'o could say was: "Don't be born a girl!"

I have found only three writers whose views on the woman problem entitle them to be called Chinese feminists. These are Yü Cheng-hsieh, the scholar (1775–1804); Yüan Mei, the poet and great rebel thinker (1716–1799), who made it his special job to take women poets as his pupils and publish their writings; and Li Ju-chen (c. 1763–c. 1830), the author of *Ching-hua yüan*. This is a feminist novel written in 1825, with a hundred talented girls as its heroines, all passing official examinations and becoming officials under the regime of the nymphomaniac Empress Wu of the T'ang dynasty. Yü approached his problem with the calm and dignity of a scholar, setting his important and revolutionary conclusions in one or two bare and apparently harmless lines. Yüan, on the other hand, threw down the gauntlet against the entire pack of Confucian Tartuffes, and with his great vogue as the first poet of his times definitely wielded an important influence for the emancipation of women. Li, the novelist, made the novel a channel for propagating his ideas, and the adoption of this channel gave him a free scope for satires on men, and on the system of footbinding in particular.

It is interesting to note, however, that all three writers had to establish their plea, not by an appeal to logical arguments alone, but by profuse quotations from Chinese history to show that such existing evils were by no means traceable to Confucius, but were the inventions of later days, in that way tearing away from them the cloak of time-honored sanctity.

I

The ideas of Yü Cheng-hsieh are contained in four essays arranged together in Book 13 of his *Note-Books*, the *K'weissu Leikao*: (1) "Essay on Chaste Widows," (2) "Essay on Chaste Maidens" (who refused to marry after their unwedded fiancés died), (3) "That Jealousy Is Not a Vice in Women," and (4) "A Postscript to the *Book on Costumes* of the Old T'ang History" (a long historical study of four thousand words on the rise of footbinding, one of the longest essays, in fact, of his entire *Note-Books,* ending up with just two lines of conclusions against foodbinding). Owing to the style and academic tone of his *Note-Books*, Yü never attained the influence that Yüan exercised over the public, although his *Note-Books* were popular enough among the scholars. In contrast to Yüan, Yü put forth his views in a few succinct words after a cool, dispassionate review of historical facts. It lacks, therefore, the force and vigor of the prose writings of Yüan the poet. Nevertheless, his conclusions seem to have a wider philosophic import and are theoretically just as devastating.

Yü Cheng-hsieh called the system of encouraging chaste widows a "shameless" masculine point of view to enslave women.

> It is true that women should not remarry, but neither should the men. The sage did not lay down this point because he had taken it for granted. . . . Ever since people lost sight of the true meaning of "propriety," they have interpreted it with a bias, making unreasonable demands upon women. According to the ancient rites, the husband and wife are united in wedlock on an equal basis, but some scholars have lowered the position of the wife. The ancient people said that "one's body is bound in marriage for life," without making a distinction between a male body and a female body. When men began to sanction divorcing their wives on "seven grounds," they broke the bond seven times. And when they began to remarry after their wives died, they broke the marriage bond for the eighth time. With their masculine logic and their sophistry, they have woven a web to enslave women. This is a shameless theory.

His conclusion was: "We should not blame women if they remarry; it is enough that we respect those who refrain from doing so."

It is with the nicety and skill of a dissecting surgeon or the flair for distinctions of an expert lawyer that Yü handles the problem of jealousy in women. Jealousy has a definite special origin in China, because it was concomitant with the concubinage system, as anybody might easily perceive. Jealous women, for instance, became most conspicuous in the Wei and Chin dynasties when the concubinage system flourished most and the aristocrats of those times had women entertainers by the scores, and sometimes by the hundreds, in their homes. The direct result of this was that at this period high ministers of state and officials often appeared at the imperial audience with their faces bruised and scratched. It was obvious, therefore, according to these men, that the good old times were gone and women were degenerating into devils. The evil became so rampant that in the Wei dynasty, a scholar by the name of Yüan Hsiao-yu (Filial Friend) petitioned to the king to have a definite system of concubinage established and to dismiss from their office those officials who did not keep concubines of the required number or who allowed their jealous wives to maltreat their concubines. An official who had no progeny with his wife and failed to take concubines, this "Filial Friend" suggested, should be punished for the crime of filial impiety, and his wife should be divorced. Looking at it from a cold, legalistic point of view, Yü pointed out that jealousy should be distinguished from acts of cruelty. He suggested that jealousy was entirely normal and human in women, but if the wife should go to the extent of murdering the concubine or otherwise giving bodily injuries, there was ample provision in the law for punishment of murder or acts of cruelty as such. According to him, therefore, the establishing of jealousy as a crime in law is entirely superfluous. With a sort of dry, Kantian humor he remarked, "The doctrine of marriage provides for mutual devotion. If a man takes concubines and his wife is not jealous, the implication is that the wife cares for him no more, and when the wife does that, the basis of the family is already ruined."

What strikes me most is the principal reason Yü gave against footbinding, which seems rather rare in the literature of the period. Yü actually protested against the system of footbinding on the ground of its effect on physical health. After a critical review of the origin of footbinding, he said, "In ancient days we have compulsory labor for both men and women, but with their feet bound, women are no longer fit for government labor. *And when the female sex is weakened, then the harmony which comes from the complementing of the male and female principles will be imperfect.* Moreover, the bow-shoes used in footbinding originated with ballet girls, and *when you lower the position of women, by implication you lower the position of men also.* The reason why women are not willing to give up this custom is because they are not aware that in ancient times there were big, beautiful shoes for unbound feet worn by the aristocrats. As they cannot be convinced by reasoning alone, I have therefore gone to the trouble of making this point clear to them."

All in all, Yü's ideas contain the seeds of true sexual equality and a system of monogamy in marriage. While Yüan, the poet and epicure, fights for a more liberal standard of morality for both sexes, it is characteristic of Yü that his ideas tend toward a tightening of marriage standards for both men and women.

II

Bare and terse as the utterances of Yü Cheng-hsieh were, they at least helped to save the face of Chinese scholarship.[2] He made it possible for one to believe that the scholarly mind is not necessarily a crass mind, impervious to all sense of right and wrong. It took, however, a more vigorous voice than Yü's to put over a message to the public and stir up a little turmoil in the snug nests that the Confucian males had built for themselves. This was the voice of Yüan Mei, with the literary name Tzu-ts'ai, considered by some the first poet of his time.

Perhaps it may sound strange that Yüan, who specialized in securing concubines for others and had several himself, should be called a feminist, and this seems on the surface allowable only in an Oriental sense. But the matter is not so simple as that. In the first place, Yüan's liberal views of sex, while they seem a little selfish and masculine, are nevertheless applied to the female sex as well. In his opinions on sex matters, he took a liberal point of view that is decidedly Oriental and pagan, but it is hard to prophesy at this moment whether Yüan's views are out-of-date or really too much in advance of the twentieth century.

In the second place (and this is the really important point), Chinese feminism could fight its way out to the open, not by a more austere view of sexual morality, but only by pointing a mocking finger at the really obscene puritanism of the then prevailing type of Confucianism. And so, paradoxically enough, Yüan took concubines in the cause of emancipation of women in China. Yüan was a philosopher in rebellion against the orthodox school of his time. Is it strange that of all writers in old China, he should express the most devastating views about sexual ethics, seeing that here was a man who dared to defy orthodoxy on its own ground? Here was a poet and a prose writer of great power and brilliance, a skeptic in all things and an apostle of skepticism;[3] anti-*li-hsüeh,* anti-Buddhist;[4] anti-vegetarian and anti-geomancist[5] and hater of all forms of superstition,[6] cant, and hypocrisy,[7] constantly turning his ire against the Confucian respectability; fond of female company and proud and unashamed of it;[8] a critic who decried all conventional rules of rhetoric in prose[9] and inveighed against the carcass of neoclassical poetry made up of quotations and quotations from quotations from books instead of real sentiments from life;[10] a critic, too, who challenged the infallibility of the Six Confucian Classics,[11] who openly denied that the word "orthodoxy" should have any meaning[12] and who even dared to doubt the authorship of the *Spring and Autumn Annals* by Confucius,[13] to doubt the reliability of the *Analects* itself as correct reports of Confucius's sayings,[14] and even to suggest that Confucius had his nodding moments.[15] In a word, Yüan was a naturalist in morals,[16] basing his naturalism on the broad basis of Confucius himself, and it took a man of his independent mind to doubt the correctness and justness of the social order of his day. On the whole, the position of Yüan Mei vis-à-vis Confucianism is very similar to that of Martin Luther vis-à-vis Christianity, representing the same rebellious tendencies, based on the same naturalism in morals, and entailing the same type of personal attacks from the orthodox camp.

As has been pointed out above, the special nature of Chinese feminist thought is determined by, and best understood through, the puritanico-sadistic background that Yüan Mei had to fight against. According to these Confucianists, not only was the act of sexual intercourse highly immoral, but even the love poems that Confucius had incorporated in the *Book of Poetry* were obscene in their eyes. The poem that describes the love and longing of King Wen for his queen and with which the *Book of Poetry* begins was good enough for Confucius, but too obscene for these latter-day prophets. There was a scholar by the name of Shen Lang who memorialized to Emperor Li-tsung of the Sung dynasty that this poem should be struck out from the *Book of Poetry* and two poems on the virtue of the emperors Yao and Shun should be inserted in its place.[17] It is against this type of stupidity that Yüan Mei constantly turned the full force of his satire and humor. On the whole, Yüan took the view that private morality was chiefly a private affair, and he never failed to remind his correspondents that Confucius appreciated love lyrics and that there was recorded in the *Book of Poetry* a mother with seven sons who still remarried, but who was regarded by Mencius himself as committing only "a slight misbehavior." To the founder of the Confucian orthodox school, Chu Hsi, he threw a challenge. It was reported that when Chu Hsi was staying at Lingan, he heard one day the sound of temple bells and remarked to himself with fear and trepidation, "Hearing this sound almost causes me to lose hold of my rational mind," which according to Buddhist-Confucian philosophy was something that should be carefully guarded as the light of the soul by quiet and meditation, in order to subjugate the desires of the flesh surging from underneath. About this story Yüan Mei sarcastically remarked: "What kind of a rational mind was it that he was trying to guard, and what kind of a mind was it that he was so afraid to lose hold of?"[18] Against this pseudointellectualism or pseudorationalism, Yüan championed the life of the senses and the passions, for just as the essence of the bell is shown in its resonance, so the mind pure and simple has no existence except in its manifestations of different passions or sentiments of pleasure, anger, sorrow, and the like.[19] He seemed to have derived a satanic pleasure in twice referring to the case of the Sung scholar Lü Hsi-che, who believed in quietism and cultivated his mental quiet to the extent that when his sedan-chair bearers fell into the river while crossing a bridge, there was not even a flutter in Lü's heart.[20] A similar instance was the case of Chang Wei-kung, who during his defeat saw the massacre of 300,000 soldiers and whose son Nan-hsien was able to boast that his father's mind was so cultivated that he went on snoring like thunder in his sleep after seeing the massacre.[21] It was against this form of Buddhist quietism under a Confucian cloak that Yüan Mei raised a banner of revolt and preached a wholehearted and clean enjoyment of life, going back, as he always reminded his readers, to the broad humanism of Confucius himself, as against that of the moral smugs.

Perhaps an instance or two may be given of this straitjacket type of morality that Yüan had to fight against and so constantly made fun of in his "Letters." One incident is that of Yang Li-hu, an old scholar in his seventies, who took exception to a little anecdote about him that Yüan Mei had incorporated in his book *Tzu pu yü*. This refers to the story Yang had personally told Yüan in his young days that, when Yang was official examiner, the ghost of a famous courtesan, Li Hsiang-chün, appeared to him one night in his dream and begged him to pass a certain candidate by the name of Hou who was a clan descendant of the courtesan's lover, Hou Ch'ao-tsung. This so scandalized the Confucian Pecksniff (Yang) that he wrote to Yüan Mei, denying the truth of the entire episode, offering certain corrections in its wording, and even suggesting to him to burn up the wooden blocks for his book. Such a puritanical protest coming from an old scholar approaching his eightieth year amused Yüan Mei so much that he wrote three successive replies, which are fine examples of his pungent, satirical style. For this reason, I am translating part of the first letter here.[22]

> Alas! What a musty soul thou art! . . . It seems to me that when you were young and clean-minded, you were frank and straightforward, but now in your degenerate old age, your only worry is how people are going to write your epitaph and your funeral eulogy, and you are therefore forced to deny the story. What harm is there in seeing the ghost of Hsiang-chün? Could it ruin a man's moral character? . . . Hsiang-chün must be over two hundred years old now, and if she were living, she must look like a white-haired old crone. She could no longer be young, nor do I think she was particularly beautiful, since she had the nickname of "a little pendant." What harm can it do to a highly moral and upright person like yourself to see her and be pleased, I wonder? For she can do no harm even to a low-down frivolous person like myself. Do you suppose that Hsiang-chün is to be despised just because she was a sing-song girl? She remained faithful to her hounded and persecuted lover and repudiated all advances of influential officials at a time when her lover's enemies were at the height of their power. I am afraid this sort of moral courage is rare even among the great gentry. . . . I should have thought that you should feel proud and regard it as a sign of your love of the ancients that you were able to see the ghost of Hsiang-chün, and I am amused that you regard the whole affair as immoral. How comes it that you have such an indecent mind and hold such a low opinion of yourself?
>
> Especially amusing to me is your correction of the words "she lifted the curtain and whispered [to you]" and substituting for them other words "she knelt beside [your] bed and begged you." After all, Hsiang-chün had come only to beg for your favor on behalf of a candidate. What crime had she committed that she should kneel down to you like a criminal before a magistrate? By the way, you have retired from the magistrate's office for a long time already, and isn't it rather a shame for you to put on the air of a district magistrate before a dead female ghost of two hundred years ago? Once and again in your letter you refer to Hsiang-chün's "chaste soul." How are you to know whether Hsiang-chün is chaste or not? Even if she were not Hsiang-chün, but another plain-dressed woman of forty, her

chastity or lack of chastity is something which does not quite properly lie within the bounds of your knowledge. If your mind is pure, what harm could come from her lifting the curtain and whispering something in your ear? And if your mind is impure, and she should be merely begging on her knees beside your bed, couldn't you pick her up and put her on your lap?

I noticed that in your corrections you managed to put in a phrase about "her dress being plain and her demeanor dignified and proper," and am amazed at the minuteness of your observation; I am afraid, therefore, you have already transgressed the Confucian rule of not looking upon improper objects, and your chances of being worshiped at a Confucian temple with Confucius and Mencius and having a share of the cold pork offering are rather slim.

You mustn't forget that it is most easy for the names of monks and talented women to go down in history. At present, of course, you, Mr. Yang Li-hu, are high up and Hsiang-chün is nothing but a courtesan. But I am afraid that in thirty or fifty years the world will know and remember Hsiang-chün and be entirely unaware that a certain Yang Li-hu ever lived. A gentleman scholar ought to conduct himself like one in a sedan chair: he must be carried high by others, but must not try to carry himself high.

Again your letter says that you are quite "romantic," but only object to being "romantic with a prostitute." This is very strange. Now I ask you, if you are not going to be romantic with a prostitute, with whom are you ever going to be romantic? It is not so bad to be romantic with a sing-song girl, but it would be extremely awful to seduce young girls. The matter of sex is like wine. Some cannot touch a drop of it and some can drink gallons. We are born so differently, in our nature as in our face. There is no use trying to cover up one's romance or lack of romance. And a man's character after all doesn't depend on his being romantic or not. King Wen loved women and Confucius approved; King Ling of Wei also loved women and Confucius disapproved. Lu Chi had not a single concubine and yet he was a cad; Hsieh An went about with sing-song girls and yet he was a gentleman. I know very well that you are a highly respectable person and don't understand what romanticism means, and I give you my respect for it, too. Why on earth, then, must you try to pretend to the honor of being a dandy or a lover of women? There were ancient people who wanted to be counted among the sages, but now there are people who covet to be counted among the dandies. What a

funny world we are living in now! I hear that on your seventieth
birthday, you celebrated the wedding ceremony again, asking your
sons and daughters-in-law to escort you into the bridal chamber, and
there you sat squarely with your dear wife on the bed and pulled
down the bed-curtain. That did give you a chance of priding yourself
on being a dandy! . . .

Remember there was a man who dreamt that he took a concubine
and told his wife about it and his wife severely reprimanded him,
forbidding him to have such dreams thereafter. Is it owing to the
unholy fear and respect for your wife which have been so thoroughly
instilled into your breast that you must try to avoid scandals even in
your dreams? . . . Let me tell you what I think. Perhaps you are still
capable of going to sleep with your wife, but if you are trying to pose
as a dandy and a lover of women, you are a long way from it yet. A
gentleman looks after the important points in his conduct and character, while a common man attends to the trivialities. Huang Shu-tu
was like a great sea, whose water won't become purer for a little
dredging, nor muddier for a little stirring. Now my dear sir, you have
walked in the path of righteousness for so many years, and yet your
point of view is so narrow and the water seems to get muddy at the
slightest shake-up. Am I not, therefore, right to think that after all
you are just like a gutter? Its water will dry up very soon, however
clear it may be! I hope you will have a little humility and accept my
kind advice. Fetch a hundred gallons of spring water from the Huei-
shan Mountain and make a general cleansing with it of all the dirt
and mud that is clogging your soul. This, I tell you, will be more
efficacious than taking a strong laxative or reciting the Diamond
Sutra.[23]

The above helps to show the mud and dirt that have clogged
the orthodox Confucian soul and that stand in the way of anyone
fighting for a more healthy view of sex and of women. It enables
us to see how such barbaric customs as the encouragement of
suicide among women and the system of footbinding could be
tolerated by the Confucianist minds—minds putrid, minds stale,
and minds, it seems to me, that had very little sunlight in them.
Such minds were decidedly psycho-pathological with a sadistic
taint in them. Without such a type of culture, footbinding could
not have persisted. A thousand times better this shameless

libertinism of Yüan Mei's, if you prefer to call it that, than the semipathological state of mind that reveled in darkening women's souls and torturing women's bodies. I need only point out that the system of footbinding, which repelled Yüan Mei,[24] had given birth to the custom of the taking off of a sing-song girl's shoes as a form of wine game. In one shoe was contained the wine cup, while the other shoe was used as a target at which these scholars were to throw peanuts or hazelnuts, with the wine in the other shoe as forfeit. Another ridiculous game was similar to the "clap seven" game. A small shoe would be taken off a sing-song girl's foot and passed around the table by the guests in succession, while counting from one to thirty by turns, corresponding to the thirty days of the month. For each number, the shoe was to be held in a special designated position, whether by the tip or by the heel, turned upside down or sideways, raised above the table or hidden beneath it. Anyone who made a mistake was to be fined by drinking wine. Here is the merry song giving the directions:

> On even days shout loud, on odd days low,
> On the third day take the shoe like a bow.
> Turn the sole up on the eighth day,
> Like the crescent moon that goes its way.
> On the fifteenth, lift the cup up high,
> Turn the shoe outwards and pass it by.
> On the twenty-second, lift shoe and cup
> Down on table when the thirtieth is up.
> Those who miss a number must repeat.
> Fine those who are wrong or obstinate.

Illustrative of Yüan's point of view regarding the so-called sexual morality of women, which was so far apart from that of the Confucianists, are, for instance, his views on rape, on virginity, and on the remarriage of widows. Yüan evidently thought nothing of the virginity of maidenhood, upon which all the Confucian scholars had set such a high store. I am not sure but

Yüan's view on this point is anything except out-of-date. What seems to me actually pathological is the craze men had about virgins, which was largely brought about by Taoistic superstition, while the purity of young men was something that nobody ever discussed. I quote from Yüan's letter to his sister's husband, which allowed him to speak out his mind freely:

> Your letter says that you will not marry a virgin, and this seems to fit in so well with Lao Tzu's advice, "Never be the first in the world." Do people really believe that a woman is impure simply because she is not a virgin? When Yü Jang met Chih-po, he became a hero, and when Wen-chün married Hsiang-ju, she remained faithful to him for life. Those who look for virtue in others should first look at themselves. If they think that women who are not virgins are ipso facto impure in character, why is it that we allow our cook to have a first taste of the food at our table, and allow the carpenter to stay first in the house we build? What's the harm in marrying a widow?[25]

In strong contrast to the austere morality of the orthodox school, which considered that a woman had lost her character once she had been raped, and actually encouraged her suicide, Yüan took the view that adultery by rape did not constitute a blemish on a woman's character. He was inclined to a less severe and more human view toward women in such a situation. "Life and death is a serious matter. No one except those Confucius called 'the courageous' will gladly seek death. If a woman is truly pure and faithful to her husband, her submission to adultery by force is but like a passing cloud overshadowing the sun and cannot be considered wrong. Some of them have [something] besides old parents to look after and young children to bring up, and their life is worth something to them. The Sage never really taught these women to end their lives."[26]

An actual instance of sadism is the case of Ch'üan-ku, a girl who committed adultery with her lover and was caught and punished. Hearing that Ch'üan-ku still went to stay with her lover after the case was dismissed, the magistrate had her brought to court, stripped naked, and flogged, which he personally looked on with pleasure. If this is not sadism, I do not know what is. When a friend of Yüan's told him the story, this infuriated him so much that he wrote a letter to the magistrate, scolding him in biting sarcastic terms, accusing him of sham and hypocrisy, of playing into the hands of crooks and gangsters and purposely making an example of Ch'üan-ku in order that he, the magistrate, might enjoy the name of moral uprightness. Yüan actually compared him to tigers, wolves, and other wild beasts in his treatment of women, and he took the standpoint that Ch'üan-ku's conduct in remaining faithful to her lover was to be encouraged instead of being punished.[27]

Yüan also took exception to the current view that widows should not remarry. He pointed out, like Yü Cheng-hsieh, scores of historical facts to prove that this doctrine was a wicked invention of later days.[28] In this connection, however, it is curious to note that both Yüan's sister, who was divorced from her gambler husband, and his own daughter, who became a widow at nineteen, were never induced by Yüan himself to marry a second time. In the case of his sister Su-wen, who was a poet, it was evident that she chose of her own accord to remain a widow. But in the case of his own daughter, there was comparatively little excuse for the father not to find a second husband for his young widow daughter. Yüan was perfectly aware that any number of righteous Confucian scholars in the T'ang and Sung dynasties had daughters who married for the second or third time, but apparently he never had the courage to put his own doctrine into practice himself.

What made Yüan so popular or so notorious in his time was the fact that he had scores of lady poets for his "pupils" whose writings in verse he undertook personally to publish. Actually the entire *Sui-yüan shih-hua,* a book devoted to the discussion of anecdotes in connection with certain poems, was only half-concerned with the verification of lady poets of ancient and modern days. This set such a fashion for ladies not only to write but also to publish their poems that it became a general vogue. A protest from Chang Hsüeh-ch'eng (1738–1801), a younger contemporary of Yüan's and a noted scholar, will serve to show both the great influence of Yüan Mei and the point of view of the scholars whom Yüan opposed.

> Recently there is a shameless fellow who prides himself on being romantic and has led astray a number of men and women, mainly by offering as their models the talented men and women on the stage enacted by actors and actresses. Most of the ladies in rich families south of the Yangtze have been led astray by him. They publish their manuscripts of poems and get a lot of publicity for themselves, in total disregard of the separation between men and women and almost forgetting that they are females. These ladies do not cultivate the proper culture of women; how can they ever have any really poetic talent? For now they have been corrupted by immoral people and this has become a general custom. Indeed, I am sorrowful for the degeneration of mankind.[29]

Such an expression coming from Chang Hsüeh-ch'eng is important, for Chang was representative of the better and more sincere and critical-minded type of scholars. What this scholar actually said was, it was all right for sing-song girls to write poetry, but not for family girls; furthermore, that it was all right for family girls to write poetry, but not to publish it. "A good girl," Chang said, "should be a quiet girl, for in quietness lies a woman's culture. Alas! how is it that these modern so-called talented girls must make such a fuss about themselves!"[30]

III

We come now to *Ching-hua yüan*, which is a novel of ideas put in the framework of a story of overseas travel through different countries, with strange customs affording convenient points of comparison with the "Celestial Empire." There are, for instance, countries like the "Gentlemen's Kingdom" (in which everybody is such a gentleman that, in a shop bargain, the merchant would try to push down the price and the buyer would try to raise it as high as possible, in a heated exchange of politeness), the "Women's Kingdom" (where the relations between the two sexes are completely reversed and where the women rule and the men powder and rouge and bind their feet, awaiting the women's pleasure), and other countries like the "Double-Faced Kingdom," "The Black-Teeth Kingdom," "The Bifurcated-Tongue Kingdom," and so forth.

Running through this thread of adventure, however, is another story that chiefly takes place in China itself, and it is this story that has a decidedly feminist purpose. The main point of the story is that when the great empress of the T'ang dynasty, Wu Tset'ien, was ruling over China, this strong woman who was suffering from a type of acute megalomania,[31] one day, with the courage inspired by alcohol, gave an imperial order for all the flowers to bloom in the imperial garden the next morning. This was in winter when only the narcissus and the plum flowers were in bloom, and the fairies in charge of the different flowers did not know what to do. It happened that the Queen of Flowers was playing chess somewhere with Maku, and these flower fairies, failing to locate her, took the matter into their own hands and ordered their respective flowers to bloom, for fear of offending the powerful empress. Everything then happened as the empress wished, with the exception of the peony, whose fairy was away somewhere and unaware of the imperial edict. Fairy Peony came back six hours too late, and although her flowers finally bloomed along with the rest, these flowers were henceforth removed from the imperial garden and "exiled" to Loyang as a form of punishment by this megalomaniac empress. However that may be, what happened in Heaven was this: the Queen of Flowers was punished for negligence of duty, and she and all the other ninety-nine flower fairies were to be sent down to earth to live over their human life once more. These were, of course, all reincarnated as talented girls, and as the story proceeds, the empress issued an edict for civil examinations to be held for women, besides those for men. In the end, these hundred reincarnated fairies passed the examinations and were made officials of different ranks. The latter part of the story is mainly occupied with the leisurely conversations and wine games and literary pastimes of these talented ladies—to the extent that they seem to be the main concern of the author.

In this novel we find the frankest discussion and an amusing satire on footbinding. Quite early in the novel (chapter 12) there occurs a conversation with the two ministers of the ''Gentlemen's Kingdom.'' They were discussing with the principal character of the story the ridiculous customs and superstitions of the Celestial Empire and condemning them—such as geomancy, expensive weddings and funerals, the keeping of coffins for a long period in one's home before burial, the belief in fortune-telling, the offering of blood sacrifices ("trying to please the gods by killing or destroying lives"), the sending of poor and helpless girls into a nunnery, and finally, footbinding. With regard to the last evil, Minister Wu Chih-ho said:

> I hear that in your esteemed country, the women's feet are bound. When young girl's feet are being bound, the pain is something terrible. Their skin is inflamed and the flesh decomposes, smeared all over with blood. At this time they moan and cry, and can neither eat in daytime not sleep at night for the pain, and develop all kinds of sickness. I thought that these must be bad girls being punished by their mothers for filial impiety, and therefore submitted to this kind of torture which is only better than death. Who would suppose that this was done for their benefit to make them look beautiful, as if girls could not be beautiful without small feet! Now it seems to me when you cut off a superfluous part of a big nose or slice off a part of a high forehead, you would consider that man disfigured; and yet you regard girls who have disfigured feet and walk with a kind of tortured gait as beautiful! Just think of the famous beauties of old, Hsi-shih and Wang Ch'iang, who were beauties although they did not have one-half of their feet cut off. When one comes to think of it carefully, I don't see what's the difference between footbinding and a regular form of torture for criminals. I am sure this would never be approved by the sages and the truly wise. Only by all the gentlemen of this world agreeing to stamp out this custom can an end be put to it.

This idea is developed in chapters 32 through 38 in the form of an amusing satire, when Lin Chih-yang, one of the principal men characters in the story, visiting the "Women's Kingdom," is arrested and presented to court as one of the queen's concubines. In this kingdom, the men were powdered and rouged and attended to domestic duties. Some men had their beards picked so that they might look young and please the women, and some old men painted their white beards black in the hope that they might still look young. Lin first underwent the torture of having a hole drilled through his ears for the purpose of wearing earrings, and then

> a few black-bearded palace maids [who are by the way males] appeared, holding a long white silk band in their hands and knelt before Lin, the man, saying, "We beg to report to Madam that we have received the royal order to bind your feet." Then came two other palace maids who knelt down to the ground to hold Lin's feet and took off his silk socks. The other black-haired maid brought a stool and seating herself on it, began to split the white silk band in two. She first took up Lin's right foot and placed it on her knee, first sprinkling some alum between his toes. Then, holding his toes tightly together, she began to bend Lin's foot upward into the form of a bow and tie it up with the white band. As soon as she had tied two rounds, another maid came forward with thread and needle to sew it up. And so it continued, one tying the feet as tightly as possible and the other sewing the stitches as close as possible. Lin just lay there on the floor completely helpless, with these two maids binding his feet and another two holding his legs still. When the whole thing was finished, he felt a spell of burning pain creeping up from his feet. Unable to stand the pain, Lin thought of his sad plight and broke down weeping aloud, "You are killing me!"

And so the farce continued until that night when Lin, unable to sleep owing to the excruciating pain, got up and stealthily tore off the silk band, after which he felt an immense relief in his toes and fell asleep, exhausted. This was discovered the next morning, and Lin was flogged until he had to submit to the process again. This was continued for some days until Lin was considered presentable at court, and there he came powdered and rouged and, assisted by palace maids on both sides, looking as shy as a girl. The queen looked carefully at his feet and then at his hands and began to smell him all over, from his perfumed hair downward to his body and upward again to his face, until Lin was ready to die with shame. After this smelling and pawing continued for some time, the queen was delighted, for the more she looked at him, the more he found favor in her eyes. She ordered that Lin was to be formally brought into the palace the next morning, meanwhile allowing him to pass the time outside the prison. . . . "That night Lin cried himself to sleep."

Afterward when Lin escaped with the help of his friends, he spoke thus to his wife: "I was beaten and hung upside down in the tower and had my ears drilled through. All these tortures, however, were comparatively easy to stand. What I absolutely could not stand was to have my two big feet bound until the bones were cracked and the tendons torn, leaving nothing except a bony skeleton covered by a thin skin. And when I moved about in the day or at night, my toes smarted until I was ready to die with pain. Just think that I have escaped from such a humiliation, which I am afraid even among the ancient people very few persons could stand!"

While Li Ju-chen is to be credited with writing the first Chinese feminist novel, indirectly working for the advancement of female education, he did not go so far as Yü or Yüan in the attack on the inhuman sex-standard for women. In the imperial edict issued by Empress Wu in chapter 40, there are twelve articles or statutes designed especially for the welfare of the female sex, such as the provision for special decorations for women, for the marrying off of maid-servants at their proper age, the establishing of pension houses for women and special orphanages for girls, pensions for widows, free medicine and free medical advice for women, and free burial at the state's expense for women who died without relatives or friends to bury them, and so forth. It is interesting to note that chastity in widows and in betrothed but unmarried maidens is expressly encouraged in these statutes, which provide for special decorations for them.

However, it is not fair to say that the problem of a double sex-standard has entirely escaped the author, for in chapter 61, we find the one and only protest against concubinage, which neither Yü nor Yüan had the courage to express. Three educated girls in the company of Lin had fallen into the hands of a robber in the Double-Faced Country. The robber chief was going to take them as his concubines, but it happened that he held his wife in unholy terror. After the robber chief was beaten in his wife's presence until, as she said, "all pride and stubbornness were beaten out of him," he began to plead for mercy: "Have mercy upon me, Madam! I can stand this no longer!" The robber's wife replied:

> Yeah? You know it now! You should have known it before, and then you would not have thought of taking concubines. Suppose I take a few male concubines and gradually leave you in the cold, would you like it? You men are all like that. When poor, you remain good husbands and have some respect for your wives, but once you are high up and rich and powerful, then off you go like a different person. You begin to think a lot of yourself and look down upon your friends and relatives and even begin to forget about your wife. As you are, you are all thieves and scoundrels and if I have your body slashed into ten thousand bits, you certainly deserve it! What do you know about the doctrine of "reciprocity"? I'll have you flogged for thinking only of yourself and not of others, and I am going to flog this idea of "reciprocity" into your head before I quit. After that, I'm through with you and won't bother you any more. What I say amounts to this: You either take or don't take concubines; but if you do, you must first get some male concubines for me before I'll give my consent.

My feeling about the whole affair is that it always requires some measure of feminine ferocity to put through a feminist program. This robber's wife could have smashed shop windows in Piccadilly, true to Western feminist style. Women who are sweet-natured always marry off and shut up, and that is the secret of the defeat or lull in the feminist movement today.

Notes

1. This applies chiefly to widows of scholars and officials. These were not forbidden by law to remarry, and they were free to do so, if they dared defy the social convention. But the power of social convention was more tyrannical than the law.

2. In this section, the references to Yüan Mei's *Sui-yuan ch'üan-chi* (Collected works) are as follows: A—*Hsiao-ts'ang shan-fang wen-chi*; B—*Hsiao-ts'ang shan-fang ch'ih-tu*; C—*Sui-yüan shih-hua*; D—*Sui-yüan sui-pi*; E—*Tu-wai yü-yen*.

3. A. Book 18, Second Letter in Reply to Hui Ting-yü ("I Doubt This Is Not What the Sages Prohibited").

4. A. Book 37, Letter in Reply to Wang Ta-shen; B. Book 4, Letter in Reply to a Certain Secretary; E. 4, 5, 21, 41.

5. B. Book 2, Letter to Subprefect Chang; for antivegetarianism, see A. Book 22, and his entire "Cook Book."

6. B. Book 1, Letter to Yüeh Shu-hsien.

7. B. Book 4, Letter in Reply to Lieutenant Governor T'ao Hui-hsien; B. Book 3, Letter in Reply to Provincial Graduate Chia Hui-hsiang.

8. B. Book 9, Letter to Chu Shih-chün; B. Book 7, Second Letter in Reply to Yang Li-hu; B. Book 8, Letter in Reply to P'eng Pen-yuan.

9. B. Book 10, Second Reply to Li Shao-ho; E. 16; A. Book 30, On Mr. Mao's *Anthology of Writings by Eight Masters* ("One Needs No Rules in Writing").

10. A. Book 30, Letter in Reply to Chi-yuan on Poetry and History; A. Book 18, Preface to *Ou-pai chi* by Chao Yun-sung; B. Book 8, Letter in Reply to Li Shao-ho; A. Book 18, Letter in Reply to Shih Lan-t'o on Poetry and History.

11. See note 1. "The Six Confucian Classics are the progenitors of writings, just like the great grand ancestors of the people. The descendants naturally should listen to the words of their great grand ancestors, even though their ancestors' words are not all necessarily right, . . . nor all necessarily pure."

12. A. Book 17. Letter in Reply to Libationer Lei Ts'ui-t'ing on Behalf of Secretary P'an; particularly against Chu Hsi; B. Book 6, Letter in Reply to Shih Chung-ming; A. Book 24, 4.

13. B. Book 8, Letter in Reply to the Supervisor of Imperial Instruction Yeh Shu-shan.

14. B. Book 7, Second Reply to Yeh Shu-shan.

15. E. 24.

16. See the most important essay "Ch'ing-shuo," A. Book 22.

17. C. Book 7, 2.

18. B. Book 4, Letter in Reply to a Certain Secretary.

19. See note 16.

20. See note 18.

21. Ibid.

22. B. Book 7, Letter in Reply to Yang Li-hu.

23. An interested reader may read A. Book 23, where Yuan makes fun of a scholar who has not seen his wife for seven months during his mourning, and discusses it in a manner perhaps too indelicate for the average respectable reader of this journal.

24. D. Book 20, 26, "Footbinding Did Not Start with Li Hou-chu"; E. Book 1, 28.

25. B. Book 3, Letter to Huang Ch'ao.

26. A. Book 15, Letter in Reply to Mr. Chin Chen-fang on Legal Regulations.

27. B. Book 4, Letter to Chin Kuei-ling.

28. D. Book 13, "On Remarriage."

29. Chang Hsueh-ch'eng, *Ting-ssu cha-chi*.

30. Chang Hsu-ch'eng, Wen-shih t'ung-i, chapter on "Fu hsueh" (Studies for women) (inner chapter 5).

31. This is a historical fact, her love of bigness manifesting itself in many strange forms.

4

Influences of Foreign
Cultures on
the Chinese Woman

Ch'en Heng-che

WRITER and historian Ch'en Heng-che (1890–1976) was a notable
woman of the Republican period. As early as 1917, while a student
at Vassar College, she published in the United States a short story,
"One Day" (*I-jih*), written in colloquial Chinese, which was later
regarded as the first new-style work of fiction in modern Chinese
literature. She also wrote poetry and prose in the colloquial
language.

In 1920, Ch'en became the first woman professor at Peking
University, teaching Western history and English literature. She
was an outspoken social critic and an early advocate of women's
rights. She and her husband, Jen Hung-chun (1886–1961), who was
a leading promoter of science education in China, shared liberal
views on government and education, and both were founding
members of and regular contributors to *Tu-li p'ing-lun*
(Independent critic), a journal published in the 1930s by liberal
intellectuals headed by Hu Shih (see chapter 1).

The following essay was included in a volume entitled *The
Chinese Woman and Four Other Essays*, published in China in
1934 under the author's English name, Sophia H. Chen. In it, Ch'en
discusses two main foreign influences on Chinese women, the
Indian and the Western. Like some other Chinese intellectuals of
the time, she believed that Buddhism, which had been absorbed by
Neo-Confucianism, had been inhibitive, especially the custom of

forbidding widows to remarry, and that Western influence was "wholesome" and was helping Chinese women to regain the status they had enjoyed in ancient times before the impact of Indian ideas.

———————

IT IS idle to say whether a foreign culture is desirable or undesirable by itself, for its influences cannot be felt until it has gained entrance into the heart of the native culture. If the good qualities of the alien culture fall in harmoniously with those of the native one, or if they succeed in stimulating the growth of the native culture in the direction of improvement, then we say that the foreign influence has been good. If, on the other hand, an alien culture succeeds only in giving an impetus to the growth of the ugly qualities in a native culture, then we say that its influence has been bad. But as a rule, these influences are rarely of unmixed good or evil, for very often both of these factors are at work at the same time; so that the nature of the outcome will have to depend a great deal on the amount of conscious and guiding effort that the human mind is capable of giving.

China has met, in the long course of her history, many a foreign culture, but only two have been sufficiently great as to disturb the stabilized system of her own culture ever since the time when she was politically united under the Ch'in dynasty, almost twenty-two centuries ago. The first of these two great cultures that invaded China came from India, and the second came from Europe and Europeanized America. Both of these two cultures have shaken the original culture in China at its foundation, and both have compelled China to feel their influences.

I am not undertaking the ambitious task of telling you the whole history of the impact of these two cultures on China with their consequences. What I shall attempt to do will be confined to the most significant changes brought about by these cultures to the life of the Chinese woman, especially the changes that were caused by the impact of the European culture.

In spite of the fact that Buddhism from India had enriched the

Chinese culture in general and Chinese philosophy in particular and had produced, by its union with Confucianism, the Neo-Confucianism of the Sung dynasty, its influence upon the life of the Chinese woman was decidedly that of an unmixed evil. Two of the most deadly weapons for the oppression of a woman in China were either elaborated or had their origin in the Sung dynasty, and they have remained in power until recent times. I mean the custom of footbinding and the moral philosophy that condemns the marriage of widows, with its many corollaries that also help in the suppression of a woman's freedom. While the custom of footbinding was not imported from India, no enlightened society could ever have tolerated a custom such as this, and without the preparation of that mental background and social environment which regarded a woman as a necessary evil, whose presence was both degrading and dangerous to men, a custom like this would have been cut dead in its bud. In fact, evidences in Chinese history have shown that long before the Sung dynasty, leisurely ladies in the palace had often resorted to this special practice as a means to beautify their bodies; but it never became a universal custom until the Sung dynasty and was practiced only in tolerable measures, perhaps not any worse than the tight shoes and high heels that our modern ladies wear, East or West. It is therefore that particular mental background under the influence of the Indian attitude toward women that made it possible for this torture of womankind to develop and flourish for almost a thousand years.

The custom of forbidding widows to marry doubtless had its origin in Indian philosophy, as no disgrace had ever attached to a Chinese woman who married a second time, either through divorce or through the death of her husband, before the Sung dynasty. And if proofs are needed to show that this attitude toward women in general and widows in particular had its origin in the Indian culture, let me quote a few paragraphs from *The Ordinances of Menu,* or Manu, which took its present form as early as the first century A.D. The following quotations are from chapter 5, "On Diet, Purification, and Women."

148. In childhood must a female be dependent on her father; in youth, on her husband; her lord being dead, on her sons; if she has no sons, on the near kinsmen of her husband; if he left no kinsmen, on those of her father; if she has no paternal kinsmen, on the sovereign: a woman must never seek independence.

154. Though inobservant of approved usages, or enamored of another woman, or devoid of good qualities, yet a husband must constantly be revered as a god by a virtuous wife.

157. Let her emaciate her body, by living voluntarily on pure flowers, roots, and fruit; but let her not, when her lord is deceased, even pronounce the name of another man.

161. But a widow, who, from a wish to bear children, slights her deceased husband by marrying again, brings disgrace on herself here below, and shall be excluded from the seat of her lord.

163. She, who neglects her former (purval) lord, though of a lower class, and takes another (para) of a higher, becomes despicable in this world, and is called parapurva, or one who had a different husband before.

166. Yes; by this course of life it is, that a woman, whose mind, speech, and body are kept in subjection, acquires high renown in this world, and, in the next, the same abode with her husband.

Notice the striking similarity in sentiment, expression, and even the use of terms, that one discovers between the above sentences and the customs and usages regarding the status of women in China, both married and unmarried. Notice, for example the term parapurva, which must denote the same kind of stigma as the term "twice-married woman" has denoted in China in the recent thousand years. It is a stigma worse than death, at least to those of the Chinese women who regarded themselves as daughters of culture; but no such stigma had ever attached to a "twice-married woman," nor did a woman ever need to feel ashamed of her status if she married a second time, before the influence of Buddhistic India had penetrated the Chinese nation. It was during the Sung dynasty, when Buddhism had been assimilated into the national philosophy of China, that its accompanying culture made its conquest, until that notorious saying "to die by starvation is a small matter, to lose one's chastity is a great one" became a sacred commandment for the Chinese woman, a commandment first admonished by a person no less illustrious than the great Neo-Confucian scholar, Ch'eng Yi. It is true that this custom was never forced by law, but like many customs in China, it was made effective by the social opinion and moral force which are often much more deadly than the hands of the law. And through the admonishment of scholars who have always been leaders in Chinese social opinion, this attitude toward a woman's chastity was elaborated and exaggerated to such a ridiculous degree that on one hand, social life between men and women became entirely forbidden, so that the only men a woman was allowed to see besides members of her family were her cousins and brothers-in-law. On the other hand, the idea of preserving one's chastity was so exaggerated that a little girl of five or six, or even younger, would sometimes be asked, if her boy fiancé should have died, "Would you remain faithful to your 'man' or marry again?" "Of course," her parents would continue to say, "we would not force you not to marry again, but what a great honor you would bring to our family as well as to his if you should keep your celibacy and go to live with his parents!" The little girl, knowing nothing about life and the world, would naturally choose the path which her parents had chosen for her, thus dooming her entire life to a miserable and inhuman existence.

However, I shall not let myself be tempted to dwell on this point too long. Suffice for it to prove that the first of the two great cultures that ever disturbed Chinese life and custom had been most detrimental to our womankind. Now how about the second one, the one that was brought to China by missionaries and merchants from America and Europe? The answer is, that though the impact of this culture is not an unmixed good, it nevertheless points to a direction quite different from that of its Indian predecessor, at least so far as its influences upon the life of a Chinese woman are concerned.

For the sake of clarity, I shall classify the influences that this new alien culture have been exerting on the Chinese woman into three kinds; namely, those that restore what there had already been in the native culture of China before the Indian culture took them away; those that enlarge and elevate or exaggerate and degrade what the Chinese woman has always possessed; and those that give the Chinese woman what she never had before, be it for better or for worse. We shall now call these influences, respectively, the restorative, the evolutionary, and the revolutionary. It must be borne in mind, however, before we proceed further, that these influences sometimes work together, though often alone; or they may work in opposite directions, thus leaving the Chinese woman in greater perplexity and her problems the more difficult to solve. I shall make this point clear presently.

First, let us see what this Western culture has restored in the Chinese culture that directly affects its women members. In my opinion, for all the wrongs that the Western culture might have done to China, one thing alone would have redeemed them, and that is, the conviction that their early missionaries aroused in the Chinese minds that the practice of footbinding was absurd and wrong. Prior to this, scholars did sometimes criticize this absurd custom, but the criticism was always casual, and no serious thought was ever given, nor effort ever made, for the abolishment of this custom until toward the end of the last century, when not only missionaries began to preach against the evil of this practice, but also the Chinese minds were prepared to be convinced through their observation of the natural feet custom of the Western women and of the Manchu ladies. Even till now, more efforts have still to be made toward that direction, especially in the country districts, and this task is now generally undertaken by Chinese social reformers themselves. Nevertheless, the first rolling of the stone, so to speak, was started by our sisters from the West.

The strong conviction that a remarried woman deserved only contempt in respectful circles in China received its first shock, not through the preaching of missionaries, who, being strictly moralistic in those days, perhaps wished to remain on good terms with a custom that upheld chastity, even at the expense of humanity, but through comparison with the Western custom, which could respect a woman who had married a second husband. This was a real revolution as well as a revelation to a Chinese woman of the educated class, who had so long been accustomed to the ignominious stigma attached to the title "twice-married woman" that death had seemed an easier sting to bear than to incur the disgrace and dishonor of such a label. Though it would be unwise now to try to push to extreme this practice, restored to China by the Western culture, nevertheless, it is only fair that young widows and divorced women should be encouraged to marry again if they choose to do so. And though "twice-married women" are still the exception and not the rule in China at present, the attitude toward them has already been changed. And attitude after all, is all that really matters in a situation like this, for it is the main factor that decides future deeds by individuals as well as by social groups.

While there are many other illustrations of the restorative influence of the Western culture on the life of a Chinese woman, none of them can speak more eloquently for the unmixed good that it has bestowed on her than the above-mentioned cases, which therefore will suffice for our purpose at present. And on the whole, this particular phase of the influence from the Western culture has been wholesome, for it has helped the Chinese woman to regain what had been lost to her for almost a thousand years, so that she is now able to stretch her limbs again, literally as well as figuratively, and to live the life of a free individual as her female ancestors had lived a long time ago.

The second point for our consideration is the evolutionary influence from the Western culture. But in order to do this, we must first find out what is the cultural background of a Chinese woman and what are its deficiencies. Briefly speaking, the education that a Chinese woman of the literati class received could be summarized by what is termed the "Culture of Four Arts," namely, music, chess, calligraphy, and painting. The accomplishment of these four arts, combined with the basic education in literature and poetry, and sometimes even scholarship, would enable a woman to receive the honorable title of "*ts'ai-nü*," that is, a talented or accomplished lady. Unfortunately, the range of subjects for her education stopped here, nor was a thought ever given to the women of the great mass. It is true that dreamers like the author of the novel *Flowers in a Mirror* did suggest through the portrayal of his Utopia for women that all women should receive education equal to that of their brothers, that they should be eligible for public offices, even as reigning sovereigns, just as men had been. But this remained only a dream until a generation ago, when an alien force began to penetrate the Chinese mentality until it became useless to refuse its entrance.

As this alien force from the West was itself a recent product of the Industrial Revolution, its evolutionary influence on the Chinese woman has not been fundamentally different from the same influence that it had exerted on the women in Europe and America of the Victorian age. We find, therefore, that as this influence had enlarged the field of a woman's education in the West, as it had made education a thing of democracy, extending to the dark region of that great mass of womankind, and as it had prepared a woman to lead the life of an independent individual, so has it done the same to the Chinese woman. Doubtless there are differences in the results, but these differences are only like different flowers from different trees. A peach tree will bear peach blossoms, and no other, a cherry blossom cannot be found anywhere but on a cherry tree, this is difference; but spring has caused all buds to open and become beautiful flowers, and this is similarity, which is more significant than the difference. Does not this realization make us feel closer together, we from China and we from the West, as well as making us more sympathetic and understanding in our efforts to solve our somewhat similar problems, which after all are caused by the same fundamental force?

Thus we find that after half a century of knocking and calling, the torchbearers from Europe and America have succeeded in bringing out the latent powers of a Chinese woman until they begin to blossom. The independent spirit that was the pride of the Chinese woman in society and at home in the old days has now become the chief weapon with which she is transforming herself into an independent individual, a specimen so rare in other Oriental countries; and a *"ts'ai-nü"* of the Four Arts that was only a decoration of culture is now being transformed into an international scholar, a medical doctor, a great musician, an educator, a social reformer, and whatnot. But unfortunately while some of the half-developed talents of the Chinese woman have been thus brought to full power, other undesirable traits have also been given unnecessary encouragement. For example, the petty politician in the old-fashioned woman that had enabled her to gain power and prestige, favor and fortune, in the clanlike family of her days is now being developed into a full-fledged and much more annoying politician in the person of her daughter, whose sphere of ambition is no longer limited to the little home, but must be extended to the whole state. This is an example of what an ugly result the impact of the Western culture could produce if it stimulated the Chinese culture in the wrong way, and no guiding hand was given to its direction.

Under the category of revolutionary influence of the Western culture on the life of a Chinese woman, none could be more fundamental and significant than the changes that this influence has brought to the family and to the society in which a woman in China has always figured prominently.

To understand the radical nature of the changes that have taken place in the institution of the family with its corollaries of marriage and love, we must first acquaint ourselves with the structure of the Chinese family itself, which is fundamentally different from the same institution in Europe and America. In the first place, a Chinese family is not merely a love-nest for a man and a woman but is a state in miniature, and its functions are carried out by a government with the mother or the father as the supreme sovereign. And in the second place, the spiritual tie that binds a family together is a complicated system of mutual duties of the members in the family toward each other; the love between a man and his wife is not denied, but it is considerably subordinated to his duty as a son, as a brother, as an uncle, and whatnot. The result of these two peculiar phenomena in the fam-

ily structure is that motherhood and wifehood become only sub-
serviently important to a woman's duty as daughter-in-law,
"daughter-in-lawhood," as it is called in China. And the supreme task of a Chinese mother in the old days was to prepare
her daughter to be a good daughter-in-law, before she taught her
how to be a good wife. For the same reason, marriages were
always arranged by the parents, and if by chance love came in, it
only peeped in shamefacedly through the cracks of the wall,
never in broad windows or through wide-open gates. While many
records of beautiful deeds have come down to us from noble
women either as mothers, wives, or daughters-in-law, much inward suffering had darkened this external beauty, and great and
intense became the suppressed desire in the hearts of young men
and women to live a life of their own. But though freedom to live
and freedom to love were denied them, especially since the Sung
dynasty when a strict conventionality was developed that tabooed
anything that savored the enjoyment of life or the beauty of love
between the youth and the maiden, they had not forgotten this
freedom, and sometimes they even sought for it. But they lacked
self-confidence, these youthful seekers of the Elysian Garden,
and they were not sure that their natural desire was right, so
puritanical had been the moral atmosphere under which they
were brought up.

Then comes the Western culture, which teaches the Chinese
young men and women that young people are doing nothing
disgraceful if they choose their own mates, and that family is
neither a clan nor a miniature state, but is the expression of love
between a man and his wife. And when this Western influence
has succeeded in convincing the Chinese young people in this—
be it remembered that this task is no more difficult than to per-
suade a starving man to take a dish of palatable food—there
comes at once the revolutionary institution of "small families,"
that is, families composed of only the man, his wife, and their
children. Needless to say that this is the place where people can
go very far and get lost, and that they may exchange some cheap
commodity, so to speak, with a beautiful jade that had been the

cherished inheritance from their culture. Thus, for example, instead of merely getting rid of the parasite members and lateral
relatives in the clanlike family, some Chinese young couples may
go as far as the American man in the story, which says that when
an American man was asked to declare who were with him on his
trip to the Orient, he replied, "My family and my mother"! But
come as they may, these black horses in a big herd, the tide of
revolution must go on. Perhaps one might say that after thousands of years of a dry and dull life, of a moral bondage that
mortified anything alive in a young heart, it is only natural and
fair that these youthful adventurers should be regarded with some
indulgence, even if they go a little too far. The important point
here is not whether their reckless adventures should be checked
or not, it is rather whether there is a guiding hand, an understanding mind, and a sympathetic heart, in the persons of their leaders,
especially their mothers and fathers, who will thus consciously
and tactfully keep the black horses away from the imported herd.

Of the effects that this revolutionary influence has caused in
the Chinese society with relation to its woman members, only a
few important changes could be mentioned. First, the question of
double standard of morality. Hithertofore, none except one or
two utopian writers had ever expressed any doubt as to the right
of a man to live beyond that moral standard which controlled a
woman's life, namely, loyalty and faithfulness to one's mate.
Thus, the label of "jealous wife" is only next in disgrace to the
label of "twice-married woman," but a jealous husband is the
most injured and most righteous being on the surface of earth,
and even murder would be justified if he could prove definitely
his wife's faithlessness. Under circumstances such as this, the
custom of taking concubines seems trifling indeed.

While there is no lack of hypocrites among the Western men,
and while their standard of morality is far from being single, one
thing in their life at least has aroused the curiosity of men and the
envy of women in China, namely, the institution of monogamy,
and the entire absence of concubinage. With the aid of traveling
and studying the Chinese students who thus come into close contact

with the life of European and American women, who are already emancipated, though still in an incomplete form, the eyes of a Chinese woman begin to open more and more widely, until she decides that concubinage and double morality are to go forever. This conviction is made effective through the newly introduced custom of choosing one's own mate; the man being anxious to gain favor in the eyes of his lady, it is not difficult for him to share her point of view not only in words but also in the depth of his heart. The consequence is that while it was an exception for a man to refuse to take a concubine in times past, it has become an exception for a man to take one now.

Another revolution in a woman's life in society is the right to inherit property and money, a right even the European and American women did not acquire until the latter part of the last century. This right, however, seems to me to be only a mixed blessing, as it will also encourage the possessive instinct in a human being and may lead to very ugly consequences.

The same may be said of the right to hold public offices and government positions, recently conceded to women in China as well as in other countries. While the right itself is a blessing, great discretion is needed in the exercise of it, and a high sense of duty as well as a noble esteem of one's mission are necessary conditions if this right is to transform a Chinese woman into a great statesman instead of turning her into an ugly politician of dubious character, as many politicians are all the world over, and as some woman politicians in China have already proved to be capable of becoming.

Another phase in the revolution of a woman's social life is the new conception of the social relations between a man and a woman; but we will not be able to grasp the radical nature and its revolutionary significance in this seemingly trifling change if we do not understand its background. For thousands of years, the golden rule for social life in China had been this: "Between a man and a woman there shall be no handling of things." So there was no social life whatsoever, and as a thing became rare, it also became very attractive. And there developed, as a compensation for this dry and dull life, a highly romantic tendency in the Chinese youths and maidens, who fell in love with each other so easily and so precipitately that it became the more dangerous for them to see each other. Thus the vicious circle went on, making it more and more difficult for anyone to break it. But at last a break came through the influence of the Western culture, which tolerated a restricted mingling of the young even in conventional circles, while in Greenwich Village communities one may even abandon oneself utterly in order to taste the cup of life to the full. Knowing the background of Chinese youths and the prudish conventionality under which they have been brought up, do we still wonder why the young men and women in China prefer social life of the Greenwich Village type to the one supported by Western conventionalities with which the youths in China naturally have no sympathy, because these conventionalities are entirely foreign to their understanding? We are therefore forced to the conclusion that no moral standard in the West may be imparted without discrimination; but experience and wisdom, a youthful heart and a mature mind, must all unite in the common effort of creating a new and noble standard that would not only suit the changing society of China, but will also elevate and beautify the social life that young women in China are to share with their young men.

This last point is both a wish and a symbol of what the Western culture ought to bring to the Chinese woman; for if this culture could succeed in giving the right kind of impetus to the native one so that it will grow and develop toward the direction of a bigger, richer, and more beautiful culture, the ugly qualities in the foreign culture will have little chance to succeed. But how can this happen without the conscious mind and the sympathetic heart that constitute the necessary guidance referred to a minute ago?

—December 1932

5

The Chinese Woman Past and Present

Tseng Pao-sun

TSENG PAO-SUN (1893–1978), known in the West as P. S. Tseng, was an outstanding example of gentility imbued with a spirit of dedication to Confucian and Christian ideals. A great-granddaughter of the eminent statesman Tseng Kuo-fan (1811–1872), she was brought up in the Confucian tradition and became a Christian as a result of her education in mission schools. In 1916, she received the bachelor of science degree from the University of London, becoming the first Chinese woman to receive an academic degree in England.

Tseng never married, for she wanted to devote herself to women's education, which she believed to be fundamental to the task of building a modern China. The I-fang Women's School, which she founded and administered for two decades in Changsha, Hunan, was one of the best middle schools in central China during the Republican period. Her educational principles were: "Enjoy studying without becoming dull and pedantic," "Appreciate Chinese culture while possessing a scientific spirit," and "Believe in Christ without forgetting the Way of Confucius and Mencius."

The following essay was included in *Symposium on Chinese Culture*, edited by Sophia H. Chen (see chapter 4), published in Shanghai in 1931. In it, Tseng shows her evenmindedness, derived from her Confucian-Christian beliefs. She neither condemns the past nor demands radical emancipation, attempting, like many Chinese reformers, to balance freedom with self-discipline, and individualism with dedication to the family and the nation.

THERE IS little doubt that civilization depends much on women, for not only do they make up about one-half of the world's population, but also the entire future generation is in their hands for early nurture and training. It is not too much to say that no nation is higher than its womanhood. A brief study of the Chinese woman will throw much light on ancient Cathay.

There is evidence that in the earliest times China owed much to the fair sex. Not only was the Chinese woman, in common with her sisters elsewhere in the ancient world, the founder of the family, but she was also the inventor of many household things. We were told in Ssu-ma Ch'ien's history that the queen of Huang-ti discovered the art of rearing silkworms, presumably for silk weaving; in the *Book of Odes* we read of women making garments, shoes, and even practicing the art of dyeing colors.

The influence of a woman in her home, and especially on her son, is repeatedly noted. Thus we read much of the wisdom of the mother of Confucius and the mother of Mencius. In the *Book of Odes,* one entire section is given to eulogizing the queen T'ai Szu, whose good influence on her husband, and indirectly on the state, was considered one of the prime factors in the founding of the Chou dynasty. Even Confucius, who did not approve of women's meddling with state affairs, admitted the importance of their contribution. As a matter of fact, women were not entirely barred from political activities at that time; we read of Ch'i Chiang, who cooperated with state ministers in sending off her husband, the Prince of Ch'in, to claim his kingdom; of Ch'in Mu Fei, who made her husband, the Prince of Ch'in, release her brother, Prince Hui of Ch'in, a prisoner of war; and of Chao Wei Hou, who was petitioned by her ministers to send her son on an important diplomatic mission. Chinese ancient history is full of examples of this kind. Judging from the foresight and wisdom of these women, we gather that they were as well educated as men.

In the early Han dynasty there were many highly educated women. In the reign of Wen Ti (179–157 B.C.), Fu Nü, the daughter of a great scholar, was the only authority on ancient classics, and she lectured to the doctors of the Imperial Academy, by order of the emperor. About the same time, a young girl by the name of T'i Ying sent a petition to beg Imperial pardon on behalf of her father. The petition was written by herself and attained a high standard of literary merit, besides being an exquisite expression of filial sentiment. In the reign of Emperor Ho (A.D. 89–105), Pan Chao, a sister of the great historian Pan Ku, completed the *History of the Former Han Dynasty,* which her brother began but which was interrupted by his death. She was also a teacher to the empress and the ladies of the court; for them she wrote seven chapters on women's conduct. Thus we see that at least a woman of high rank was educated, and there was no prejudice against her taking part in public affairs.

It seems to be a universal rule that when men have established themselves as rulers, they proceed at once to make laws and evolve doctrines to limit the freedom and power of women. China is no exception to this rule. Stable central government only began with the Han dynasty. Before that, for about two thousand years, a feudalistic system prevailed, and the various states were in constant competition or active warfare, which gave no chance for any theory or practice to consolidate or develop on a nationwide scale. Everything was in its changing youth. The Han dynasty (206 B.C–A.D. 220) marked the close of ancient China and opened a new era. With the state becoming more stable, men's predominance over women began to be evident. The *Book of Propriety,* which imposes strict discipline on women, was therefore adopted as the authority on feminine conduct. The movement was so subtle that even such an educated woman as Pan Chao deprecated women's independence. As a result, the latter part of the dynasty was devoid of women of genius or outstanding character, though not lacking in women of conventional virtue.

This state of affairs continued to the period known as the Southern and Northern dynasties (A.D. 420–580), when China was divided and much harassed by foreign invasions from beyond the Great Wall. The emperors, instead of attempting to improve their respective empires, or working for the unification of China, expended their energy and money on luxury and indulgence. The courts were filled with ladies of exceptional beauty, accomplished in poetry, painting, music, and dancing. Describing a court of the Southern dynasties the well-known poet Li Shang-yin said:

> The palaces were filled with ladies chosen for their beauty as well as scholarship.
> They thus surpassed Chiang An in that he was only chosen for his learning.

The ladies were always devising new plans to capture their emperor's favor. Various means of improving physical attraction were invented; among them may be mentioned the beginning of footbinding, which became a fetter to the Chinese woman for more than fifteen hundred years and is still practiced in backward districts of China. With her feet deformed, she was more easily confined in the house, and her interests and pastimes became progressively more circumscribed, as did her character and intelligence. Her status was no better than that of a toy or serf of her husband. The Sui dynasty (A.D. 581–617) marked the highest point of imperial luxury and despotism in China, and it was no coincidence that women's position sank lower than ever before.

During the T'ang dynasty (A.D. 618–906) favorite wives of emperors constantly got the country into trouble. The dynasty was known as the dynasty of "Female Perils." The empress of Kao Tsung, Wu Tse-t'ien, actually ruled the empire for fifty years (660–705), changed the name of the dynasty into Chou, and established herself as the emperor of China, using the masculine term. Other notable examples were Empress Wei and Yang Kuei-fei. The fear of women thirsting for power called forth men's theories that further restricted what was meant by maternal duty and feminine virtue. Roughly, they amounted to absolute obedience of women to men, contentedness in an ignorant and limited life, and utter self-abandonment in the service of the husband's family. This tendency reached it highest in the Sung dynasty (960–1276), when the influence of Hindu civilization had been incorporated with Chinese culture, an influence that was rather detrimental to women's development. The greatest moral authority for the last eight hundred years, Chu Hsi (1130–1200), interpreted the Confucian classics in such a way that an entirely new meaning was put into the Confucian ideals of womanhood. Chastity and absolute loyalty to one man was made the cardinal virtue of a woman. Everything else must be subordinated to it. According to him it was a small matter to die of starvation but a serious matter to lose one's virtue by marrying a second time. Previous to his time, widows or divorced women marrying a second time were quite common and were recorded without any criticism. But the Sung scholars never let such a case pass without due censure. Great poetesses of the time such as Li Ch'ing-chao and Chu Shu-chen were condemned simply because they held different moral views. Orthodox Neo-Confucianists would not even read their works. In general, the woman of the Southern and Northern dynasties was frivolous though accomplished; the woman of Sung was serious and narrow. However, the ideas of womanly virtue in the Sung dynasty did rescue her from her former position of a mere pleasure-mate to man.

With such a historical background, we may consider the typical Chinese woman from three aspects: education, marriage, and social status.

When a girl is unfortunately born in a poor family, apart from learning household duties, she has no chance of obtaining a decent education. If, however, she is fortunate enough to be a daughter of a well-to-do man, she is taught to read and to write under a governess or even a master. She has to learn Confucian classics, poetry, embroidery, painting, and music, as well as household duties. We read in a poem called ''The Peacock'':

> At thirteen I could weave silk,
> At fourteen I learnt to cut out a garment,
> At fifteen I played Kung Hou [a musical instrument],
> At sixteen I finished the Book of Odes and other classics.
> At seventeen I married thee.

This is a fair example of an educated girl. The final destiny of the Chinese woman is always marriage. Unmarried women are almost unknown, unless the betrothed men should die before the marriage and the girls choose to become virgin widows; or when the girls renounce the world and take to the veil. The marriage is always arranged by the parents. In exceptional cases, the girl may be given a choice between two eligible young men. It is not a marriage of mutual love between the young people themselves, but one of mutual esteem and friendship between the families. The girl is not only married to the man, but she is also pledged to his family, to serve its aged, to tend its young, and to care for its various relatives. The man's family, that is, his parents and relatives, expect a great deal from the bride; so much so that the customary dowry has become a burden to the richer parents who have a marriageable daughter. Yet they will cheerfully bear it, for they realize the importance of marriage to their daughter. For the man, marriage means the taking of a lifelong mate, the perpetuation of his family name, and the continuation of his ancestral worship. Important as it is, it is not to be compared with the case of the woman. To her, it is her one and only destiny, her completion of life, and her meaning of existence. Without marriage she has no status of her own in home or society. On account of its importance, every marriage is carefully safeguarded and widely published by means of the so-called six ceremonies and festivals, with as much pomp and show as the families can afford.

After marriage the wife acquires the social position of her husband. If in due course she should have a son, then her status is further raised. If she fails to do so her lot is not to be envied. The very object of marriage itself is, in theory at least, to keep up the family line. Formerly a wife could be divorced on account of sterility; now, however, this is rarely done. On the other hand, the husband can take secondary wives as an alternative. If she is still more unfortunate as to lose her husband without an issue, then she is indeed to be pitied. She is more often than not subject to maltreatment by her husband's clan. They may insist on her adopting a son of the same name. If her husband should have died rich, then many will be the quarrels, and bitter will be the feelings among the different branches of the family; some would wish to give him an heir, and some would object to others giving him an heir. The crux of the matter is that she has no rights of her own, but only those of a wife or mother. The doctrine that a woman before marriage must identify her fate with that of her father, after marriage with that of her husband, and after the death of her husband with that of her son, is still largely true in conservative families. Yet the married woman is not without power or prestige in her home. She has control over her children and her daughters-in-law. She is the helpmate and companion of her husband, though often she is not educated enough to use this right. There is no such strong prejudice against a woman having a share in her husband's public work as exists in Japan. As compared with her Indian sister, the Chinese woman is certainly immeasurably better off, especially in the case of a widow. A Chinese widow has at least the rights of a mother, since she would be given an adopted son even if she has none of her own.

The stunted growth of Chinese womanhood may be said to owe its origin to the psychological suggestion of society that a virtuous woman should be obedient, quiet, self-effacing, and ignorant, devoting herself only to the service of the family. There is no actual persecution or suppression of feminine activities. A woman under such hypnotic suggestion really does feel that only by striving after such an ideal can she find her true self. The result is that the woman who brings herself forward to the public eye is generally bold or even dangerous in seeking self-gratification. Empress Wu Tse-t'ien, mentioned before, and the famous empress dowager of the Manchu dynasty are good examples. It is therefore small wonder that antifeminists fling these cases up as arguments against women's taking part in public affairs. They forget that the best womanhood has been penned up within homes by their theories of womanly virtue.

Within the last thirty years a vast change has come over the mentality and the status of women in China. The nature of the change will be dealt with later on. Four factors made such a rapid change possible. In the first place, the older ideal of womanhood, being based on psychological suggestion, has no religious or legal foundation. It is therefore easier to break down. In the second place, the Chinese mind is tolerant and conciliatory. Nothing will be pushed to the extreme. Any woman who wishes to make herself a public figure is only looked upon with social disapproval. Society will rarely endanger her life or ostracize her as an outcast to the community. In the third place, the Chinese pride themselves as rational beings, and will always yield to reason. They are also intensely practical. The justice and advantage of emancipation of women cannot but win general approval. And lastly, many of the higher-class Chinese women were educated. So the change was more in the nature of evolution than revolution.

The instruments that brought about the change are modern schools, modern literature, and the political revolution.

Early girls' schools were founded by Christian missionaries, on whom so much blame has been heaped in recent years that we are apt to forget this great service they have rendered to the women of China. Mission schools are certainly open to criticism in many important respects, but their attitude toward women has been consistently liberating. Government and other private schools were opened later on where girls were taught regular high school and teachers' training courses. Through education, many of the Western thoughts and ideas on freedom were introduced. At the same time, literature of all kinds, propagating the rights of women and their need of emancipation, spread all over the country. The woman therefore became conscious of her personality and demanded to be treated on the same footing as man, to have access to the knowledge and facts of life, and to enjoy equal rights with man. These were the fuel that fed the smoldering fire before the Revolution of 1911; when that came, the fire broke into conflagration. Some women took active part in that political upheaval. The fetters on women were broken once and for all.

A foreign student of China is simply amazed at the rapidity of the changes, and perhaps above all at the change in Chinese

women. He notices the natural feet and the bobbed heads of the
girls, the free mixing of the sexes, and the freedom and ease with
which women appear in public. These facts, remarkable as they
are, only indicate some outward signs of the inward changes in
the mentality of the women themselves, and of society at large.
Briefly, these changes are as follows:

The first and most important one is the change in moral conception. The old moral codes have undergone a thorough meta-
morphosis. Though filial piety is still considered the highest
virtue, blind obedience to parents is no longer upheld. Chastity
has received a new meaning, in that an element of love is taken
into account. Women demand to be judged by the same moral
standard as men. Monogamy is recognized as the right form of
marriage. Sexual taboo is becoming a thing of the past, and problems of sex and love are frankly studied. A woman does not lose
her individuality after marriage; she retains her profession, political views, and property. Very often she keeps her maiden name,
simply because she demands to be somebody in her own right,
independent of her father, husband, or son. Marriage is looked
upon as an institution founded on mutual love and help, rather
than a one-sided surrender of the woman to the man; it is only
natural that divorce should be allowed when the basis of love and
mutual help is gone. In fact, a marriage can be dissolved by
mutual consent on account of incompatibility of temperaments,
without even going through the law courts. How different from
the old idea of a woman's loyalty to one man!

The second is the change in the outlook on life. The modern
Chinese woman is not content to live a life in the home only. She
has a mission to fulfill and a contribution to make to China. The
desire for higher education, the seeking of a profession, and the
demand for suffrage are some results of this outlook. In short, she
has discovered the vast potentiality of life and will not be satisfied until she has lived her life to the fullest extent. Though she
realizes the importance of the home, she will not allow it to fill
the whole of her horizon. She endeavors to be a worthy citizen,
as well as a loving wife and good mother.

The third is the change in social status. As subjectively the woman has changed her moral standard and outlook on life, so objectively society has begun to treat her differently. On the whole, Chinese menfolk have taken the changed position of women sympathetically, and in a reasonable spirit, and thinking men are giving the women's movement much help and encouragement. They realize that it is only by uplifting, educating, and emancipating Chinese women that China can be saved. There is no use in planning all sorts of reform when about one-half of the nation's population is ignorant of even the most rudimentary facts and principles of life. Hence in political, educational, and business circles, men and women have worked side by side without prejudice or friction. Compared with the women of the West, who had to fight hard for their rights of education, profession, and suffrage, the women of China gained theirs at very little cost. The difficulty lies not in men's opposition but in the women themselves.

From the above changes we glean some idea of a modern Chinese woman, free in mind and behavior, eager to learn and to serve, seeking to work out the destiny of her people, and striving to set right the social and economic wrongs of her nation. But she is not without grave problems confronting her, in spite of the help and encouragement of her countrymen.

It is difficult to define freedom, to know exactly where individual freedom ceases and social restriction begins, or to draw the line where liberty becomes license. It requires the highest idealism and the best judgment to maintain this delicate balance in the use of liberty. Some of the farsighted reformers are already perceiving a tendency to misuse this undefined liberty by some of the modern Chinese girls. The problem, then, is how to get the freedom for developing oneself and at the same time to keep in view the good of all.

Though there are many girls' schools in China today, a thorough study of girls' requirements in life is lacking. Therefore the proper kind of curricula and school life for girls have not been designed. The girls' schools are simply replicas of boys' schools, with a few subjects such as needlework, cookery, theoretical domestic science, and so forth thrown in haphazardly. These subjects are usually given an insignificant position and allowed the minimum of time, often neglected by teachers, and despised by students. Thus the girls leave school without any idea of homemaking. Moreover, they are apt to develop a wrong notion of the equality of the sexes. Instead of realizing that true equality lies in each developing along its own line, they try to approximate the male standard of thought and life, thus turning themselves into pseudomales. This is a serious problem indeed, and it can only be solved by women themselves.

Another problem is how to make education for modern girls a practical and living thing. They should consider education primarily as something that enlarges their personalities and enriches their lives. Unfortunately, this is often not the case. Many a girl desires a diploma as she does a diamond. It gives her better prestige, better chances in marriage, and something to boast of among her friends. She does not make any practical use of her knowledge, or live up to what she knows to be right. The idea that education is but a stepping-stone to official rank has had such a degrading effect on Chinese men that we do not want it to contaminate our newly freed women. Let them be educated for education's sake, and let their education permeate their daily lives.

The problem of sex life is a complicated one. Now that a woman is free to choose her mate, the question is how to exercise this freedom wisely. It is true that marriages arranged by parents are very often miserable, but it is equally true that a large number also turn out to be successful. Before making a betrothal, the girl's parents usually carefully consider the social position, the family, and the suitability of the young man. When a girl makes her own choice, owing to lack of experience with the world and with men, she is liable to be dazzled by superficialities, taking no account of the man's upbringing and social standing. As a result, the couple cannot get on after marriage; they begin to quarrel and often end in separation or divorce.

When marriage and divorce are both easy, we have the grave danger of destroying the family, and consequently ruining the future generation. For the family to absorb all the time and energy of the mother is certainly robbing her of her due; but has the mother the right to deprive her children of their claims? Is it not the same kind of injustice that she cried out a while ago against her husband, viz., sacrificing one person's rights for the pleasure of another? The old-fashioned mother may be ignorant and superstitious, but her very sacrificing life has inspired many a son to achieve noble deeds and form an exceptionally fine character. To her we owe forever an obligation for raising such pillars of Chinese civilization. It is well for the modern Chinese women not to give up the right of motherhood, but to learn something of the tremendous value of maternal love, which, after all, is the foundation of social morality.

Loyalty in marriage should be given a fair consideration, not only for the sake of the children, but for the women's movement as a whole. A marriage is a serious affair, and a decision should not be lightly reached when so weighty a matter as the merging of two lives is being contemplated.

A Chinese schoolgirl is inclined to feel that she is so burdened with national and social welfare that she should devote herself entirely to these and live a single life. She often shuns such subjects as domestic science, child welfare, or nursing, but chooses others as far deviated from home and marriage as possible. In her profession she tries to do man's work. For instance, she will decline to be a school matron or a hospital nurse if she can help it. But a time comes when sex as a natural instinct will assert itself. A few exceptional women may be able to sublimate it into some other creative work. The majority will be forced to marry. Such marriages naturally cannot be very successful. There are still a few others, who, having lost their chances of marriage, partly through their own obstinacy, and partly through their parents not daring to interfere, develop into miserable and sour-tempered old maids. Consequently, the problem is how to make our modern women treat love and marriage rationally, and to give scientific sexual studies due emphasis.

A profession for women is certainly one of the most important factors in their emancipation. Without economic independence, a woman is not truly free. Although all professions are open to women now, they are not able to avail themselves of most of them. This is due to the insufficiency of their education in general and lack of vocational training in particular. Where there is real equality of sexes there is also real competition. Since men are usually better qualified, they easily oust women. A well-known publishing house in Shanghai may be cited as a concrete example. The company opened all its departments to women between 1920 and 1923, and many women were admitted, but gradually most of the women were replaced by men. They were dismissed chiefly through want of intelligence, inefficiency in work, and a general lack of earnestness in profession. The company declared that they did not dismiss them because they were women, but simply because they were poor workers. This is a serious charge. Until women are really needed on the ground of their invaluable work, the position they enjoy in a profession on courtesy is false and not enduring. Women, if they take up any profession at all, must do so in earnest, and with thorough preparation.

Perhaps it is not out of place to say a word here about women's choice of professions. It is necessary for them to survey the field and find out what kind of workers are needed before making a decision. As it is, women will go in for fashionable training without reference to the requirements of society, or to their own temperaments. This is not only a waste of money and time but a waste of the nation's potential energy, for many of them will not be employed at all. For example, it is fashionable for girls to get into government service, and not to be primary school teachers in the country districts. As a matter of fact, government appointments are most insecure, and also sought after by too many competitors, while in the country districts there is a dire need for trained women teachers. Unless women are willing to do the nation's spade work, and not consider any profession *infra dig.* so long as it is useful to the country, their professional career is doomed to failure.

The question has often been raised whether a woman can have a real profession and run a good home at the same time. In theory, professional activities can always be pursued by a capable woman with family duties. But in practice the mother nearly always finds the work, the care, the fatigue, and the mental strain that the home and children involve so unending and tedious that she is forced to give up her professional zeal. The modern Chinese woman must try to discover a means of harmonizing her threefold duty to herself, to her home, and to society. This is certainly a difficult problem to many, but a solution should not be impossible to some.

The above are some of the difficulties that confront the modern Chinese woman. The writer does not attempt to offer any solution, but simply to enumerate them. All these problems are real and concern masses of people, and therefore they cannot be expected to conform to abstract theories. Every step in the women's movement will have to be guided and checked by actual facts. It is hoped that what has been said is sufficient for the reader to see that this is a critical time for the Chinese woman. China is an old country, tied down by various conventions and traditions, torn asunder within, defeated and humiliated without; yet she is trying to regenerate herself, to take her rightful place in the family of nations, and to find her own soul. It is out of this melting pot that the Chinese woman is trying to emerge as a new being. She is at the cross roads; it is difficult to say which road she will take. Will she revert to the old as the pendulum swings back? Or will she throw over all her heritage and become a totally new person, unknown to her land, and alien to her civilization? Or will she retain what is best in China and supplement it with the best from the West? The third possibility is naturally what we want. To achieve this it is necessary for the modern Chinese woman not to be denationalized, but to have such a thorough knowledge of the culture and civilization of her own country that she will personify what is best in them. For then, and not until then, will she be able to reevaluate and make the best use of those desirable old Chinese ideals, such as maternal love and wifely devotion. With a foundation like this she can build a superstructure of Western training in arts, science, and philosophy, or anything else she chooses. Therefore, for the modern Chinese woman, let her freedom be restrained by self-control, her self-realization be coupled with self-sacrifice, and her individualism be circumscribed with family duty. Such is our new ideal of womanhood, and to realize this is our supreme problem.

6

Chinese Women's Fight for Freedom

Sung Ch'ing-ling

SUNG CH'ING-LING (1883–1981), also known as Soong Ching
Ling, was a controversial celebrity throughout most of her long life.
As widow of Sun Yat-sen (1866–1925), who was esteemed as the
leader of the 1911 Revolution and the founder of the Chinese
Republic by both the Nationalist and Communist parties, she
enjoyed an eminence that gave her a high degree of security in
times of rapid and unpredictable political change. But, like her two
sisters, Ai-ling and Mei-ling, she attained public prominence without ever holding real political power.

In 1927, when Sung Ch'ing-ling's brother-in-law Chiang
Kai-shek (1887–1975) rose to national leadership and suppressed
the Communist Party, she openly declared that he had violated Sun
Yat-sen's political principles and his policy of cooperation with the
Communists. This was the beginning of the public differences
between the Sung sisters, which reflected conflicting convictions
and ambitions and which were to continue throughout their lives. In
the 1930s, she lent her support to the China League for Civil Rights
and the National Salvation Association, both of which opposed
Chiang's Nationalist government. During the period of the united
front against the Japanese in the second Sino-Japanese War, she
joined the Chiang government in Chungking. But after the war and
during the civil war between the Nationalists and the Communists
that followed, as the honorary chairperson of the Revolutionary
Committee of the Kuomintang she engaged in a wide range of
activities in support of the Communist Party.

When the People's Republic of China was established by the Communists in 1949, Sung was appointed a deputy chairperson of the new government, and her name appeared prominently in a number of Chinese and international Communist organizations. In 1951, she was awarded the Stalin Peace Prize. In 1952, she helped found the magazine *China Reconstructs*, which enjoyed an international circulation. As chairperson of the China Welfare League, she promoted various projects for the welfare of women and children. In 1959, she was elected a deputy chairperson of the government, a largely ceremonial position, as was the position of honorary chairperson of the All-China Women's Federation, to which she was elected in 1978. Two weeks before her death from leukemia in Beijing in 1981, she was made a member of the Chinese Communist Party and an honorary chairperson of the People's Republic. Sung was given a state funeral and eulogized by the government as "a great patriotic, democratic, international and Communist fighter and outstanding state leader of China."

The following article, which appeared in the July 1942 issue of the magazine *Asia*, was later included in a collection of Sung's articles, entitled *The Struggle for New China*, published in Beijing in 1953. It demonstrates the relationship between her analysis of Chinese women and her political position.

———————

CHINA'S women, no less than her men, are fighting the battles of their country. In the present struggle, in which its entire future is at stake, they have shown themselves worthy daughters of the heroines of our past.

From ancient times, individual women have participated actively in the defense of the nation and the molding of its destiny. Hua Mu-lan, a Chinese Joan of Arc, is reputed to have led the armies against foreign invasion from the north. Her exploits are remembered to this day in the songs and the theater of the people. Liang Hung-yü, the wife of a famous Sung general, also fought against the invaders. In the field of our culture, Pan Chao helped to compile and edit the *History of the Former Han Dynasty*;

Ts'ai Wen-chi was one of the most famous of the ancient com-
posers; Li Ch'ing-chao, Chu Shu-chen, and Yü Hsuan-chi wrote
poems that are still read. Despite the fact that in the old Chinese
society their position was unvaryingly that of obedient servants
of the men of the family, the education, breadth of vision, administrative capacity, and even military prowess of exceptional
women left their mark on the history of the land.

Contact with the West, and the rise of the national revolutionary movement, opened new and greater vistas for Chinese
women. Many entered the factories and became independent
wage earners. Though it was still a long way from potentiality to
fact, the basis had been laid for the participation of women in
national life not merely as the wives and mistresses of the great,
but in their own right as citizens.

The process began with the upper and middle classes. Women
began to appear as doctors, public health workers, and teachers.
On the political scene, many of them were self-sacrificing members of the revolutionary parties.

An outstanding part was played by the latter in the struggles
for the overthrow of the Manchu dynasty. Ch'iu Chin, one of the
noblest martyrs of the revolution, was second in command of an
underground republican organization with its own armed forces
in Chekiang. She lost her life when she failed in an attempt to
assassinate En Ming, the Manchu governor. Ho Hsiang-ning
(Mme. Liao Chung-k'ai), who at sixty-four is still among our
foremost progressives, was an original member of Sun Yat-sen's
first united revolutionary party, the T'ung Meng Hui. Many
women of this period helped both in the direction of the movement and in the execution of its most difficult and dangerous
enterprises.

The proclamation of the Republic was not the end but only the
beginning of the fight for a new China. The form of government
had changed, but the power was still substantially in the same
hands, and life remained what it had been. This was apparent in
the field of women's rights as everywhere else. When two
woman leaders of the Kuomintang, T'ang Ch'ün-ying and Chang

Chao-han, presented a bill for legal equality of the sexes to the first republican parliament, the reactionary majority easily voted it down.

During the First World War our own industrialists were able to build many new factories. A natural accompaniment to this was the rise of a labor movement. The conscious political fight for democracy in China widened to include not only the middle class but also the working people and the peasants. China began to witness not only the outstanding deeds of individual women, but also examples of heroic activity by women in the mass striving to create a better Republic.

Tens of thousands of worker, peasant, and student women participated in the great military campaign for the eradication of the northern warlords in 1925–27. They performed auxiliary services, spread the slogans of the national movement far and wide, and on many occasions fought shoulder to shoulder with the troops. In the course of the struggle, large numbers of girls from field and factory grew from the status of semislaves and the stupor of endless toil to full human stature and leadership. It was not for nothing that the feudal leaders of reaction paid the homage of bitter hatred to the "bobbed-haired girls" of the time and made the gutters of our cities run red with their blood.

Women were represented also in the directing body of the great campaign. The Central Committee of the Kuomintang elected at the First National Congress in Canton in 1924 included, among others, Ho Hsiang-ning, Teng Ying-ch'ao (Mrs. Chou En-lai), and Ts'ai Ch'ang; the latter two were leading workers in the Communist Party, which contributed so much to the progress of the movement. Ho Hsiang-ning organized the Kuomintang Woman's Department.

From its inception, our national revolutionary movement has made the liberation of women one of its basic demands. The advance of our women to equality in legal status, educational opportunities, and social position has been and is an essential part of China's march toward full independence and democracy. No nation can claim to be free when half its citizens are dominated by the other half. From the very start, our women fought not under the banner of a barren feminism but as part and parcel of the democratic movement as a whole.

When the forces of domestic and foreign reaction proved too strong for the first heroic assault of the people and China's initial effort to achieve democratic unity broke on the rocks of renewed civil war, it was natural that the trend toward women's emancipation should also suffer a check. Careers in medical, educational, and welfare work remained open, but politics and administration were again barred, as if one out of every two human beings in China had no conceivable right to participate in the ordering of the society in which all lived.

The Kuomintang, captured by and held securely in the grip of its right wing, abolished the woman's department that had done so much to bring it victory. The women members who continued nominally to belong to its Central Committee remained there not in recognition of their own work, but on the strength of the previous leadership of their dead husbands. They did not acquiesce in the new trend and, from exile, declared their opposition to the flight back to the past. But, unfortunately, there were other women who made their peace with things as they were and counseled their less privileged sisters to abandon their seeking for a wider life. This was the dark period during which civil war raged for ten years and a policy of external appeasement allowed the Japanese to get a grip on large parts of our territory and much of our political life.

The new democratic movement that broke this discouraging pattern arose, some two years before the war, in circumstances of great danger to the country from Japanese encroachment. Ever since the seizure of Manchuria in 1931, the students in our universities had been active in pressing the government to fight Japan. Thousands of young people marched in protest demonstrations, moved on foot to the capital itself, starved in hunger strikes, and braved the beatings of the police, imprisonment, and execution to make their voices heard. At the end of 1935, the students of Peiping came out into the streets, ready to stop with their bodies the attempt of the Japanese to establish a puppet government in the capital of China's culture. The time was ripe, and their action not only accomplished its purpose but launched the new, organized wave of popular sentiment that we know as the National Salvation Movement. As many girls as boys took part in this heroic initiative, and the causalities among them were as great. Chinese women will always remember that it was a girl marcher who, when the gates of the city were locked against the procession, squeezed her slim body through the space under them and, ignoring the swinging broadswords of the guards, explained the purpose of the demonstration and appealed to them to let the students through.

Within a few weeks, hundreds of National Salvation Associations had been organized in all parts of the country and among all groups of the population. Not the least of these was the Women's National Salvation Association established in Shanghai on December 22, 1935, only two weeks after the Peiping demonstration. On the day of its founding, a thousand members paraded through the city with slogans identical to those of the general democratic upsurge: "Stop civil war!" "Chinese must not fight Chinese!" "Form a united front against Japan to save the nation!" "Women can emancipate themselves only through participation in resistance!"

The new body soon organized many separate occupational sections—for professional women, teachers, students, workers, housewives. It established close relations with others working in the field, such as the YWCA. Woman writers formed discussion groups and planned the production of literature. Three women's magazines, *Woman's Life,* a monthly, *Woman's Masses,* published every ten days, and *Little Sisters,* a fortnightly, began to appear.

After the student marches, the next great action of the people against Japan was carried out by the textile workers of Shanghai and Tsingtao, who walked out in tens of thousands from enemy-owned cotton mills. Among them there were far more women than men. Their courage was even greater than that of the students, because they faced not violence alone but immediate starvation. These miserably underpaid factory girls, with patched clothing and wisps of cotton in their hair, working sixteen to eighteen hours a day from early childhood, many of them already coughing from the tubercular seeds of death in their chests, will always remain heroic figures in the annals of our awakening.

When the strike broke out, the various National Salvation Associations in Shanghai formed a committee of leading intellectuals to support the workers. Under Japanese pressure, seven members of this committee were arrested by the government, charged with "endangering the safety of the Republic," for which the maximum penalty was death. Among these seven, who submitted voluntarily to trial, was Miss Shih Liang (now minister of justice), one of our few women lawyers. They remained in jail until after the outbreak of war.

The countrywide movement against the imprisonment of the patriots served further to strengthen the anti-Japanese mobilization of the people. In the Sian Incident, the next great landmark on the way to unity and active struggle against the invaders, the release of the seven was one of the important demands made on the Generalissimo. These events, and ever-increasing Japanese pressure, led rapidly toward the achievement of the immediate goals for which every progressive, patriotic, antifascist Chinese had been working—the cessation of civil war, and armed resistance to external aggression.

For the patriotic women of China, as for every other group of the population, the war was the great test. They rose to meet that test well. In the very first days after the clash on the Marco Polo Bridge, they organized nursing, bandage making, and political propaganda units to work in conjunction with the local garrison—the 29th Army. But within three weeks the bulk of this courageous but ill-led and ill-equipped force had been smashed, and the whole region fell into the hands of the enemy. Peiping and Tientsin witnessed considerable fighting, but they did not suffer as other cities did later from the occupation. There was nothing except their patriotism to stop the more active young women who lived there from going back to their very comfortable homes for the most part, and reconciling themselves to fate. But this is precisely what they did not do. Thousands left the two cities for points behind the Chinese lines. Many went by boat to Tsingtao and overland to Nanking. Some slipped through the Japanese cordon, joining the regular Chinese forces along the Peiping-Hankow Railway and the Grand Canal. Still others entered the guerrilla detachments that were springing up in the hills around Peiping or struck west to meet the advancing Eighth Route Army, in whose schools they received training. They traveled in groups, and everywhere, in boats, on trains, in wayside villages, they spoke to the people of resistance.

Those who remained behind did not stay idle. They published underground papers, assisted in organizing secret contacts between the occupied cities and the ever-growing strength of the guerrillas, carried on propaganda among the Japanese troops, garnered intelligence, and in general constituted a fighting column operating in the rear of the enemy.

While these developments were taking shape in the north, the tremendous battle for Shanghai broke out and raged fiercely for a full three months. Volunteers helped to bring the wounded back from the front, rolled bandages and sewed hospital clothes for their needs, nursed them, wrote letters, organized entertainment. Hastily set up classes trained two thousand emergency nurses in two months. Many women worked right in the zone of fire—mill girls, society matrons, students, and girl scouts side by side. Thousands gave money, strength, or both.

The barbarous sack of Nanking proved conclusively to every Chinese that life under the invaders would be impossible. In particular, the Japanese army showed there that it was warring not only against men, but against women also, taking special and brutal advantage of the defenselessness of the sex. Chinese women replied with the formation of the Kwangsi Woman's Battalion and training in armed self-defense in many places. But the deeper and more important reply was their greater activity everywhere in the task of helping the war.

The first nine months of 1938, during which the government

had its headquarters at Hankow, marked the high tide of democratic unity for national resistance in China. It marked the high tide also of the women's movement. All women's organizations—the National Salvation societies, old neutral bodies like the YWCA, new wartime products like the National Women's Relief Association with over one hundred branches throughout the country, the National Association for the Care of War Orphans, and others—were united at the Kuling Conference of July 1938 into an all-embracing women's organization. This was the Women's Advisory Committee, and its plan of work embraced not only aid to the orphans and the wounded, but also club activities for the troops at the front, education of village women, publication of magazines, encouragement of local production through the revival and improvement of handicraft methods, and the training of skilled leaders and organizers along all these lines.

The committee grew rapidly because it began as a truly united front organ. Kuomintang, Communist, and nonparty women participated equally in its deliberations. Delegates to the Kuling Conference included many extremely able women whom the civil war had driven underground with a price on their heads, such as Teng Ying-ch'ao, whom I have already mentioned as an active leader in the 1925–27 period. Moreover, it could lean on organizations that had been created by the needs of the war and acquired much experience applicable on a broader scale. These organizations were widely different one from another, but all had something to contribute. The Hunan War Service Corps, for instance, accompanied one military detachment through a battle-studded march from Shanghai to Hankow. The Yunnan Women's Battlefield Service Unit, starting from that remote southwestern province, proceeded by foot almost two thousand miles to the central China front. The aforementioned Kwangsi Women's Battalion covered fifteen hundred miles from Kweilin to the Fifth War Zone north of the Yangtze and worked among the soldiers there. Ting Ling's Northwest Women's Battlefield Service Group, the most versatile of all, carried on every conceivable type of educational and agitational work. It drew posters, composed and acted its own plays, initiated production and recruiting campaigns, organized the people for specific tasks, and was in almost every way an example of what such a unit should be.

The women's work in the northwest and in the new guerrilla bases behind the Japanese lines needs stressing because, although the Advisory Committee rendered extremely important auxiliary service, it was only in the Shensi-Ningsia-Kansu, Shansi-Hopeh-Chahar, and other border areas that a true women's movement was created, carrying on the great tradition of 1925–27. Here the women organized into associations numbered not in the thousands but in the hundreds of thousands, and their functions not only dealt with relief but involved full participation in the war and in political and economic self-rule. The organizers of the Eighth Route Army came to some of the most backward regions of China, devitalized by long misrule and shaken further by periods of Japanese occupation. In large sections of Shansi and Shensi provinces, women still had their feet bound. Illiteracy was 95 percent or higher. Oppressed and embittered husbands made up for the hopelessness of existence by exercising boundless tyranny over their wives. Girl babies were sold or killed almost as a matter of course. The very sight of the uniformed organizers, these strange and terrible free-striding "girl soldiers," frightened the local women indoors. They had to be approached carefully, first only with offers to help with their washing and their baby-minding, and with suggestions for better methods of doing these things. They had to be encouraged to talk about their lives, to be told of their rights in relation to their men, to be given a sense of their worth and their own importance, then to be helped into fighting with their families for the few hours needed to attend meetings and receive education, then to be entrusted with responsibilities. And the results of this patient and painstaking labor? Today, women in the border areas have become real people and real fighters, not only matching but often outdistancing the men. The system of democratic self-rule has placed women in administrative positions put there by the votes of their fellow villagers of both sexes, and it is not uncommon to find women district magistrates, mayors of townships, and heads of villages. In North Shensi alone, women hold two thousand elective positions in local administration. Women's organizations are responsible for livestock raising, for the weaving of uniforms, for the care of wounded and children, aid to soldiers' families, control of travelers, and, when the men are away fighting, the farm work of their villages as well. In many cases they have brought traitors to book, done intelligence work among the enemy, guarded wells and crossroads, and performed other functions of military value.

No one who comes back from these areas fails to tell of the part played by women in every phase of life, of how, in the midst of the war, they have moved from the darkness of the feudal past to a position which, for their sisters in the rest of China, lies only in the future.

On a more limited scale, the Chinese Industrial Cooperatives have also made a great difference to the position of women wherever they have been established. One such body began with the opening of two textile cooperatives for some factory girls evacuated from Hankow. Today, after three years, it has organized some twenty-five thousand soldiers' wives, refugee and peasant women for home spinning of wool, runs schools for over seven hundred children and adults, and sponsors a production program for crippled veterans and Japanese war prisoners. Its efforts have been responsible for giving the country 1,240 tons of wool for army blankets and have saved great numbers of women from beggary. Literacy groups, clubs in which the women learn collective self-management, training classes to give them the skills that lead to independence, and clinics for them and their children have been built up from the profits of the common productive effort. In CIC centers throughout the country, many women hold positions as district organizers, and they head some of the best and most efficient units, famous far and wide throughout the movement. In the recent enforced evacuation of cooperatives from the Shansi bank of the Yellow River, where a large-scale Japanese offensive achieved success, the workers put themselves voluntarily under semimilitary discipline. "Desertion in the face of the enemy" became one of the statutory justifications for the displacement of officers and expulsion of members. Not one woman was so disgraced. On the other hand, it was the woman chairman of a textile unit who ordered her colleagues to go ahead and stayed behind herself to bury immovable machinery and carry away some lighter equipment on her own person when the Japanese had surrounded the cooperative on three sides at a distance of less than a mile. In the ranks of the cooperatives there are also women who a short time ago were mill-slaves under the galling conditions to which Chinese labor is subject. They were unskilled peasants, uprooted from their land and seemingly condemned to slow starvation as refugees, or local girls and housewives whose existence had been dislocated by the war. Now they have become people worthy in themselves and valuable to the country's present and future, no longer "just women," but full and respected citizens.

In 1938 a very real effort was made to unify all women's activities under the Advisory Committee, to which Teng Ying-ch'ao reported in detail on the work in the guerrilla areas which was then in its exciting early experimental stages. Under the committee, the groundwork was laid for the friendly cooperation of Chinese women of all classes and parties.

During the past two years, however, and especially in recent months, conditions on our united front have deteriorated greatly. Defeatists and fifth columnists have had altogether too much success in straining relations between the two major parties, between the guerrilla areas and the rear. Reactionaries who have lain low since the beginning of the war have been enabled to raise their heads and set to work busily to annul the democratic gains won by the people in four years of war. Once again, this process has shown how intimately the position of women is connected with the relative ascendancy of the forces of progress or backwardness. In the summer of 1940, women who, in Chungking and elsewhere, had worked faithfully in government departments since the outbreak of the war, carrying on through repeated evacuations, bombings, and wartime economic earthquakes, began to feel once more the weight of the old prewar type of discrimination. The post office, for instance, suddenly declared that it would no longer employ married women. Education projects of the YWCA in the countryside were closed. A meeting of all women's organizations in the capital, held under the auspices of the Advisory Committee, was called to devise measures of self-protection, and the committee itself immediately attracted the attention of the secret police and pressure-group political manipulators. When reaction reached its zenith in the attack on the New Fourth Army, the wave of arrests throughout the country took in many workers in women's organizations, including one member of the highest coordinating body. Under these circumstances, some of the most active organizers were compelled to leave the country.

Finally, the official convening message of a conference of women's work leaders called by the Central Organization Department of the Kuomintang in the spring of 1941 showed that, despite such outward signs as the presence of a number of woman members in the appointed People's Political Council, the reaction had by no means been defeated. The message advised women to strengthen their organization, to increase their individual skills, to join the party, and to have more children. On the participation of women in politics it had this to say: "It is harmful for every woman to strive to take part in politics. . . . Work in the women's movement should be concerned with general education, vocational training, women's service, and welfare and daily problems. The women's movement will have succeeded when women reach the level of men in character, knowledge, physical condition, and technical abilities." In other words, women are urged to equality of attainment but are denied equality of rights. It is hardly necessary to say that such a conception is opposed both to the ideas of Sun Yat-sen, who held strongly that it is the duty of everyone to take an active part in the workings of government and its improvement, and to the whole trend of painfully won progress in China.

Nevertheless, forward-looking Chinese women are far from discouraged. They know that so long as the war against aggression continues, the objective preconditions for the growth of democracy, and the demand of life itself for such growth, will increase and not diminish, whatever the resistance of those who can only look back. Also, they know that the awakening of our womanhood is only beginning. Every traveler in China can tell how much the vast majority of women, even in their still backward state and whom the wave of emancipation has not touched, are doing for the common effort. The Burma Road and the great Northwest Highway to the Soviet Union, those two heroic breakthroughs of fighting China to the outside world after the Japanese had blockaded her by sea, were largely built by the labor of women. The Kwangtung trade route, which, dodging the blockade for more than a year, secretly moved far more goods each week than the Burma Road could manage in a month, was composed of endless lines of sturdy Hakka woman-porters, carrying hundred-pound loads in thirty-mile stages.

Women have not only worked but fought. I know personally of an instance in which the female population of a village in Hainan Island fought off a small Japanese landing made when their menfolk were away. They had only farm implements to fight with, and many were killed, but the enemy force was compelled to reembark. Similar happenings must have occurred in a great many places throughout the country, unheralded and unknown. As for individual cases, there is a story in almost every district of some girl who, emulating Mu Lan of old, changed into men's clothing and fought in the army.

The fighting record of our women does not permit us to believe that they will ever again allow themselves to be enslaved either by a national enemy or by social reaction at home. Only an extension of democracy, including the rights of women, can bring real victory in this war. Such a victory, won by the united efforts of the people, will leave no room for any scheme of things other than democracy.

When the victory over aggression is achieved, Chinese women

will stand with the women of all countries, as those who have suffered so much more than even the men in the mad revel of fascism and war that has spread throughout the world, ready and willing to see that in the future all movement shall be forward, that the earth's present frightful testing-time shall be the last of its kind.

7

Historical Roots of Changes in Women's Status in Modern China

Li Yu-ning

BORN in China, Li Yu-ning received her B.A. degree
in history from the National Taiwan University and her
Ph.D. degree in history from Columbia University in 1967.
Since 1968 she has been the editor of *Chinese Studies
in History*, an academic journal published in New York.
She is professor of Chinese history at St. John's University
in New York City. Her books include *The Introduction
of Socialism into China* (1970) and *Wu Han chuan*
(A biography of Wu Han, 1973). She edited *Chin-tai
Chung-hua fu-nü tzu-hsu shih-wen hsuan* (Autobiographical
writings and poems of modern Chinese women, 1980),
and coedited with Chang Yü-fa the two-volume *Chin-tai
Chung-kuo nü-ch'üan yun-tung shih-liao* (Documents on
women's movements in modern China, 1975) and the
two-volume *Chung-kuo fu-nü shih lun-wen chi*
(Collected essays on the history of Chinese women,
1981, 1988).

This paper was presented at the Conference on the History
of the Republic of China, held in Taipei, Taiwan, August 24–28,
1981. In 1982 it was published in the St. John's Papers
in Asian Studies series. It attempts to show how tradition has
contributed to changes in Chinese women's status in modern
times.

THE HISTORY of Chinese women has only begun to be studied. I believe that two urgent tasks have to be attended to in this area. One is to gather, sort out, and preserve data extensively, and the other is to achieve sound interpretations. This paper will be concerned primarily with the latter, though previously neglected sources will be utilized in part to demonstrate the richness and diversity of such materials.

Most books and articles on Chinese women share a common feature—sharply contrasted descriptions of the position of Chinese women in the past and the changes that have taken place in the twentieth century. The women of old China are generally described as weak and incompetent, as docile victims of a feudal society and patriarchal system, and as parasitic consumers and men's slaves and dependents. This tends to divide the history of Chinese women into two parts—a pre–twentieth-century history of women's plight, and a modern history of women's liberation. According to these historians, traditional Chinese society consisted of two camps, with oppressive males on the one side and oppressed females on the other. This idea started in the declining years of the Ch'ing dynasty and gained popularity during the early Republican era. It still has a strong hold among contemporary scholars. I myself used to hold this view.

In recent years I have had some second thoughts. Is this conception of Chinese women too abstract, too simplistic? Is it in agreement with the historical record?

Troubled by these questions, I started to explore the history of Chinese women from another angle. There is no question that life was hard for most women, and also most men, in old China. But hardship cannot be equated uncritically with oppression. It is not difficult for the careful observer to find in historical records and literary works a more complex view of diversity among Chinese women. Their capabilities, activities, temperament, and thought were as varied as those of men. That being the case, it is not surprising to find that men and women also held various views about the duties and accomplishments of Chinese women. Their sacrifices and their contributions might be the same thing viewed from different angles. If one says that Chinese women in traditional society were victims of a patriarchal society, one might also describe them as builders of homes and the country.

There is no denying that Western influences played a major role in modern China. Changes in Chinese women's status, however, have had internal as well as external causes; there is both continuity and change. Of course, tradition is linked to continuity, but it is also related to change. Tradition has not only contributed to the evolution of Chinese womenhood; its impact is still being felt today, as will be seen in the following three aspects.

Women's Tradition of Diligence

As stated above, some people have regarded the women of old China as weaklings who lived like parasites from men's labor. Liang Ch'i-ch'ao was most articulate in expounding this view. In 1897 he wrote that women "do not hold public posts or engage in academic pursuits, do not farm or work as craftsmen, nor do they take part in commerce or bear arms. Since ancient times two hundred million women have not received any education. . . . I think the illiteracy of women must be the root cause of our nation's weakness. . . . Two hundred million women are dependents, and none has engaged in any productive labor. Because they cannot support themselves and have to depend on others for a living, men support them as they do draft animals and slaves. Therefore, women are in a pitiful position. However, men are also in an unenviable position because they have to work hard to support their women dependents."[1] This argument gained instant popularity. Ever since, a great many people have been influenced by it, directly or indirectly, in their evaluation of Chinese women.

Liang was a scholar of great erudition, and he sincerely advocated a greater role for Chinese women with genuine patriotic fervor. Yet even such an enlightened scholar failed to give the women of ancient China a fair judgment and instead pointed an accusing finger at them, perhaps influenced to some degree by earlier writers who had for centuries blamed women for the decline and fall of dynasties. Obviously, today no scholar would attribute China's weakness in the late Ch'ing to lack of education for women. If all the women in any country depended on men for support, that country would be paralyzed. No country is wealthy enough to let half of its population remain idle.

The saying that "lack of talent is a virtue in women" was often used to justify opposition to education for women. History, however, shows that a great number of Chinese women did distinguish themselves in the literary world. Works by women authors in ancient China are too numerous to be counted. *Li-tai fu-nü chu-tso k'ao* (Works by women in dynastic China), by the twentieth-century scholar Hu Wen-k'ai, lists more than four thousand women writers.[2] This impressive list is by no means complete. Perhaps no other country in the world has produced as many women writers as China. The best, such as the Sung poet Li Ch'ing-chao, compare favorably with other great poets in China and elsewhere. If the word ''scholars'' refers to intellectuals in general, it would be wrong to say that there were no women scholars in old China. If women had been allowed to take part in the imperial examinations, they would have undoubtedly proved themselves to be strong competitors, for, when given the opportunity in recent times, girls and women have proved that they are generally better performers in competitive examinations than boys and men.[3]

It is also grossly inaccurate and unfair to imply that women of old China did not take part in farming and other productive labor. For thousands of years the Chinese economy has been agriculture-oriented, with 85 to 90 percent of the population living in rural villages, which is to say that as much as 45 percent of the population were women in rural communities. We know that far from being idlers, they played a vital role in economic life. They not only engaged in various handicrafts and such work as picking mulberry and tea leaves, gathering firewood, herding cattle and sheep, tending to domestic fowl, and raising hogs, but also rose early to cook breakfast for the whole family. After the men went to the fields, women did other farm chores, cooked lunch, and brought it to their husbands or brothers working in the fields. In the busy farming season, they often made another trip to the fields to bring the men an afternoon snack. After supper, while the men smoked their pipes or simply relaxed, the housewives did the dishes, darned socks, made cloth shoes, and performed many other chores. In some Chinese provinces, notably Kwangtung and Fukien, women have for centuries worked in the fields alongside men. As Tai Chi-t'ao wrote: "It is wrong to make the sweeping statement that women are idlers without making a survey and gathering accurate statistics. I believe that families with idle women also have idle men, and that women are seldom idle in families whose male members have to work."[4]

It is also incorrect to say that Chinese women of the past had no place in other fields of activity. Both official and unofficial historical records show that some of them were shrewd operators in the business world as far back as the Ch'in dynasty when the First Emperor courted the favor of two women millionaires.[5]

Women in old China also figured prominently in the military field. From the earliest written records, the Shang oracle bones, we learn that Fu Hao and Fu Pin, concubines of King Wu-ting of the Shang, served as commanders of his armed forces.[6] The legalist *Book of Lord Shang* outlined the following military organization of the state: "Strong young men form one army, strong young women another army, and the old and weak men and women still another army. These are the so-called three armies."[7] The First Emperor mobilized a large number of women in his wars against the neighboring states before he unified China, using them particularly for logistical operations.[8] Many centuries later, Princess P'ing-yang contributed greatly to the founding of the T'ang dynasty by leading forces to support her brother, Li Shih-min.[9] Other famous women warriors include Liang Hung-yü,[10] Shen Yun-ying,[11] Ch'in Liang-yü,[12] and Lin P'u-ch'ing.[13] In Chinese fiction and drama, women are also depicted as good fighters. Such names as Hua Mu-lan[14] and Mu Kuei-ying have been household words for centuries.[15]

Traditional China was not lacking in outstanding women in many fields of endeavor. But of course they were the exceptions. The overwhelming majority of Chinese women stayed in the home, performing their prescribed roles of wives and mothers, working long hours without direct financial rewards, like housewives elsewhere in the world. Most seem to have accepted this form of social organization without question. But there were expressions of dissatisfaction, and it is to these that I will now turn.

Reform—A Common Aspiration of Men and Women

Women's lot in old China was undeniably unenviable. "Sad is the position of women. How they fare is determined by men," wrote the great T'ang poet Po Chü-i.

Lack of freedom to choose one's own mate was a common curse to Chinese men and women alike before the twentieth century. Chinese literature abounds with complaints by men and women about the lack of freedom of choice in marriage. The moving narrative poem "The Peacock Flies to the Southeast" has been popular for centuries;[16] many have sympathized with the poet Lu Yu for his unhappy marriage;[17] and the story of Liang Shan-po and Chu Ying-t'ai has been told and retold for over a thousand years because it reveals women's longing for equality in education and young people's craving for the right to pick their own mates.[18]

China once had a real-life Romeo and Juliet, although few are aware of it. The story runs like this. In Fukien during the Ch'ing dynasty, a girl was secretly in love with a young man, but her parents engaged her to marry another man. On the eve of her wedding, the lovers heard of a potion made from wine and the poisonous root of jasmine, which, if drunk in a moderate amount, would make a person lose consciousness for several days with all the appearances of death. Despite the risks involved, the girl drank the potion and, as expected, was mistaken for dead. After her family buried her, her lover dug her up from the grave and eloped with her. But a year or so later, a relative happened to run into the unfortunate young woman and forced her to return home. After learning what had happened, the family of her former fiancé sued the couple. They were arrested, taken to court, found guilty, and severely beaten. The couple thus became victims of free love.[19]

We find many similar tragedies in both historical and literary works. These incidents show that some men in old China shared the suffering of women, and that the desire for a spouse of similar temperament and cultural level was not limited to women. Marriages arranged by parents have as much chance of failure as of success. The abandoned woman has always been a major theme in Chinese literature. When the T'ang poet Yü Hsuan-chi wrote, "It is easier to get priceless jewels than to find a man with a true heart,"[20] she spoke for millions of other women. But men as well as women wrote on this theme, showing that some men were also sympathetic toward women and shared an aspiration for marriage with a congenial mate.

For men in old China, frustration in love or failure in marriage could be forgotten by diverting attention to scholarly pursuits and professional achievements or indulging in carnal pleasures. But, for women, such diversions were prohibited. This did not prevent them, however, from dreaming. Many women lamented that they were barred from the imperial examinations because of their sex. Yü Hsuan-chi wrote: "How I hate this silk dress that conceals a poet, I lift my head and read the names of the successful candidates [of the imperial examinations] in impotent envy."[21]

Nowhere is women's longing for equality with men expressed more strongly than in *t'an-tz'u,* mostly written by women, and as far as one can tell, read by women.[22] One favorite theme of these long narratives of mixed prose and poetry is a girl in man's guise who takes part in the imperial examinations, passes first on the list, and eventually becomes prime minister. A typical example is *Pi-sheng hua* (Flowering brush) by Ch'iu Hsin-ju, which tells the story of a young woman who wins the *chin-shih* degree and becomes an official. After her real sex is discovered, she says in bitterness: "Father gave me the talent. Why didn't he give me the right sex? Now a promising career has been completely dashed after all the painstaking efforts I've gone through. What a waste of talent!"[23] In *Tsai-sheng yuan* (Born again), coauthored by two women, Ch'en Tuan-sheng (1752–1791?) and Liang Te-shen (1771–1847), Meng Li-chun, the heroine, disguises herself as a young man under a false name and not only wins top honors in the imperial examination but also is appointed prime minister.[24]

In his *Lun Tsai-sheng yuan* (On *Born again*), historian Ch'en Yin-k'o said:

> In those times the position of prime minister was the highest goal one could attain politically, and to become a *chuang-yuan* [the top candidate in the imperial examination] was the highest social honor. The road to both honors usually was the imperial examination, which was open only to men. No matter how learned or talented a woman might be, she just did not have the chance to compete with men for the honors and riches that accompanied success in the imperial examination. It is only natural that women who could have competed successfully with men felt very bitter about this discrimination. Tuan-sheng in particular had reason to be angry. . . . Among the descendants of Kou-shan [Tuan-sheng's grandfather, a *chü-jen*], the women were in no way inferior to the men. In such obvious circumstances, Tuan-sheng had a feeling of injustice few others could have shared.[25]

I agree with Professor Ch'en but would go even further. The sense of fair play and aspiration for renown cannot have belonged only to the talented women who put their frustrations in writing. They spoke for many others. No literary product or theme can last long if it fails to strike a sympathetic chord in its readers. Women distinguishing themselves in men's guise is a favorite theme not only in *t'an-tz'u* but also in other Chinese literary works. For me, only one explanation makes sense. In the Chinese consciousness or subconsciousness, women can be men's equals if given a chance. In men's clothing, women can occupy men's roles.

The idea that the real difference between men and women lies in their clothing is clearly shown in the short play *Reading* Li-sao

While Drinking Wine, sometimes called *In Disguise,* by the famed eighteenth-century woman writer Wu Tsao. The plot is simple. Lamenting that she is a woman, Hsieh Hsu-ts'ai, the heroine, puts on men's clothing and paints a portrait of herself, which she hangs in her study. One day, she changes back into women's dress, paints another portrait of herself, reads Ch'ü Yüan's *Li-sao,* the classic lyrical expression of frustrated ambition, and weeps. The play ends with the heroine folding up the portrait and putting it away. The importance of this play lies not in its plot, but in the heroine's indignant statement. When she is wearing men's clothing, Hsu-ts'ai says to herself that she is as talented and ambitious as any man, but unfortunately she has to live like a caged bird because she is a woman.[26] The play was an instantaneous success not merely because of its literary excellence but also because of its strong emotional appeal for freedom and equality for women.

In these works it is clear that clothes make the difference, and that clothing symbolizes not nature but social convention. It is the social order, not nature, that bars women from an official or other male career. Moreover, this idea cannot have been limited to the small number of women who wrote about women with aspirations. A literary work or a drama that gains popularity and lasts over a long period of time must express certain commonly shared thoughts and feelings to arouse the empathy of readers or an audience. Chinese readers and Chinese audiences did not find it preposterous to think of women doing a superior job in male roles. It was as possible to believe in women warriors and women statesmen as in more conventional pale and wan heroines such as Lin Tai-yü in *Dream of the Red Chamber.*[27]

But does this apply to men as well as to women? Were there men who expressed belief in women's character and abilities? It is well known that the rise of Neo-Confucianism during the Sung dynasty was a blow to women's status. The famed philosopher Lu Hsiang-shan had a student by the name of Hsieh Hsi-meng. When Lu learned that Hsieh was frequenting brothels in Hang-chou, he scolded the young man: "Day and night you are spending your time with cheap whores. You're a Confucian scholar—aren't you ashamed of yourself?" Hsieh replied that he would mend his ways. But he soon broke his promise and even built a house for a courtesan. Lu was furious when he learned what Hsieh had done and gave him a severe tongue-lashing. This time Hsieh fought back, replying: "The spiritual essence of nature can be found only in women, not in men." Lu, we are told, was speechless.[28]

The idea that women were superior to men because they possessed the essence, or spirit, of nature, the universe, and so forth was expressed by a number of later writers, too. "The spiritual essence of the world dwells not in men. The field of writing in the universe should belong to women," wrote Ko Chen-ch'i of the Ming dynasty.[29] Ko's contemporary, Chao Shih-chieh, wrote: "The essence of the universe probably is to be found not in men, but in women. What is the essence? It means the beauty of literary products and personal charm."[30] Tsou Chi, an early Ch'ing writer, wrote: "It is strange indeed that the sublime spirit of the universe resides in women rather than in men."[31] In chapter 42 of the novel *Ching-hua yuan* (Flowers in the mirror), one reads, "Men do not possess the sublime. Virtue has long belonged to the gentle sex." Chia Pao-yü, the autobiographical hero of *Dream of the Red Chamber,* says, "Only women are endowed with the sublime qualities of the universe. Men are only dregs and flotsam." In the late Ch'ing dynasty, there was also a popular saying that women are more talented and virtuous than men.[32]

The great iconoclast of the Ming dynasty, Li Chih, formulated a distinctly modern-sounding, universalistic standard of judgment on the issue: "One may say that human beings consist of the male and female sexes. But it would be absurd to classify points of view into men's and women's. One may say that some opinions are good and others are not. But it would be wrong to say that men's opinions are all good and women's are all bad."[33] Li advocated equality of the sexes and freedom of choice in marriage. He was a forerunner of modern ideas in this as in other areas.

Other men of letters in old China who contributed to the emancipation of women include Yuan Mei, who opposed the practice of footbinding, called for the education of women, and himself took women disciples; Yü Cheng-hsieh, who attacked the prejudice against remarriage of widows; Li Ju-chen, who opposed the double standard in judging the chastity of men and women; and Kung Tzu-chen, who also opposed the practice of footbinding.[34]

From this evidence one can see that long before the advent of Western ideas in China, there were many men who admired women's talents and criticized discrimination against women. In other words, the seeds for upgrading women's social position had already been sown in traditional China. They merely required the right climate to germinate. In the next section I shall discuss how the seeds absorbed nutrients from the native soil and grew under the impact of Western ideas.

Contributions of Tradition and Confucianism

A favorite theme among Chinese reformers and revolutionaries as well as many Chinese and foreign scholars is that Confucianism and traditional Chinese society have been invisible shackles on women. But, as the preceding section has attempted to demonstrate, the evaluation of women in traditional society was not uniformly prejudiced.

Confucian philosophy itself was not exclusively antiwomen. It has its favorable as well as its unfavorable consequences with regard to the position of women. There is no need to dwell on the unfavorable aspects; they were of great significance, but they have been expounded by others on numerous occasions.[35] Here I would like to review some Confucian ideas that have helped to improve women's position in modern China. Confucianism did not attach importance to birth or social background. Such ideas as "great generals and statesmen are not born," and "everybody can be a sage" were familiar throughout Chinese society. As optimists, Confucians believed that a person could improve through education and self-cultivation. They also held the view that social order and morality were the result of individuals discharging the duties assigned them under Confucian ethics and playing their respective roles properly, that is, "abiding by *li*" or "living up to *li*." *Li,* commonly translated "rites" or "ritual," is more than simple etiquette or courtesy. It is also the rules of society and human behavior. Confucians had long argued that *li* had first been established by the ancient sages; they were the invention of a certain period in history, not the creation of a divine being. Hence, it made sense that the *li* should not be eternally fixed but adjust to changing times and circumstances. Accordingly, the respective roles of men and women were subject to change as conditions changed.

New requirements of the country and society in modern times have necessitated innovations, which in turn called for adjustments in the roles of men and women. With the rise of modern nationalism, the ultimate purpose of human activities was held to be serving the nation and society. This being the case, because of the Confucian notion that roles were social, not natural, it was easier in China than in many other countries for women to take new roles in national development.

Even the *yin-yang* theory, often seen as detrimental to women, had its positive influence on their position. The cosmology of Confucianism is derived from the *ch'ien* (heaven) *k'un* (earth) theory in the *Book of Changes*. It is a kind of dualism. *Ch'ien* and *k'un* are opposites, but they do not contradict each other. The interaction between the two gives rise to everything in the universe. Among other things, *ch'ien* stands for men, *k'un* for women. Heaven represents men, and earth women. The "Hsi-tz'u" section of the *Book of Changes* says:

> In the family, the proper role for women is in the home and that of men is outside the home. When men and women play their respective roles properly, the great way of heaven and earth shall prevail. The family has its strict monarch in the persons of the parents. If the father behaves as a father, the son as a son, the elder brother as an elder brother, the younger brother as a younger brother, the husband as a husband, and the wife as a wife, the family will function properly. When all families function properly, the country will enjoy peace and stability.

The dualism of *ch'ien* and *k'un, yin* and *yang,* man and woman, is a double-edged sword. On the one hand, it states that "men are in charge of outside affairs while women are in charge of inner affairs." For millennia this argument has been used to justify the idea that men are by nature superior to women, and to restrict the activities of women. Since the late Ch'ing, those who have advocated equal rights for women have rejected this concept without denying that women should be in charge of domestic affairs. In other words, they have favored women playing a dual role, inside and outside the home. But it must also be realized that this dualism acknowledges a kind of equality of importance for women. Even more significant is the notion that men and women are complementary, that neither can do without the other. Since the late nineteenth century, many advocates of a greater social role for women have elaborated on the theory that men and women are interdependent, and that women are the mothers of the nation. A few examples will suffice to illustrate this.

In 1898, K'ang T'ung-wei, daughter of K'ang Yu-wei, published an article entitled "On the Advantages and Disadvantages of Education for Women." The article was written to appeal for the establishment of a new education system for women. "Everything belongs either to *yin* or *yang*," she wrote. "Animals consist of the male and female sexes. Mankind is composed of men and women. There is no superiority or inferiority of the sexes. Regardless of sexual differences the code of conduct for all people is the same." In another passage she said, "According to the doctrines of Confucianism and Buddhism, men and women are equal." Paraphrasing a central idea of the *Great Learning,* she also wrote: "There is no happiness that does not have its origin in the family. The decline of virtue invariably starts in the home." The final objective of education for women, she said, "is to glorify the ways of the [Confucian] sages and revive the ideal of a world community [*ta-t'ung*]."[36] In other words, K'ang, following her father's theories, was promoting sexual equality through Confucian ideas. Other reformists argued along similar lines in calling for the abolition of footbinding and establishment of schools for women. The New Woman envisioned by Liang Ch'i-ch'ao is capable of "assisting her husband, educating her children, making a family happy in the short term, and improving the race in the long run."[37]

Yen Pin, one of the earliest female members of the T'ung Meng Hui and editor of the journal *Chung-kuo hsin nü-chieh* (New women of China), also stressed the importance of mutual help of men and women for the sake of the family and the country. This journal reflected the mainstream of thinking among patriotic women at the turn of the century. Its primary objective was to promote the idea of a "woman citizen." To be a "woman citizen," a woman "must be full of patiotic fervor, regarding the interests of the country as more important than her own life. She does not forget for a moment her own obligations in assisting her husband and raising her children. . . . She also strives to support men when the country is in danger."[38]

The concept of modern Chinese women being "good wives and good mothers" remained strong during the early Republican era. Ts'ai Yuan-p'ei, a firm advocate of liberalism, said:

> The biological functions of women dictate that they must fill the mother's role. In the social structure of our time, a woman must become a wife before she is a mother. Therefore, the principal responsibility of a modern woman is to play the dual role of wife and mother. She is duty-bound to be a good wife and a good mother. Therefore, the major requirement of a modern woman is that she must play both roles well. If a man devoted to academic pursuits or social reform is lucky to have a good wife, he will be able to make greater contributions to scholarship or society, and his wife naturally can take partial credit for his achievements. If a woman gives birth to superior children and provides them with a good family upbringing, they would naturally distinguish themselves in their future careers. Then her contributions to society would be even greater. Therefore, a woman must consider the value of being a good wife and a good mother as equal to that of engaging in academic pursuits or social reform herself.[39]

By this formulation, women's traditional roles were validated in terms of modern nationalism.

During the Second World War, Madame Chiang Kai-shek, who was in charge of women's work, repeatedly stressed the importance of women's assistance to society and the nation. "The women have to assist in upholding the morale of the nation in its gravest trial. . . . The greatest contribution we can make is our strength and determination to make any and all sacrifices for the preservation of the nation."[40] Much like Ts'ai Yuan-p'ei, she wrote: "From time immemorial Chinese mothers have given themselves to the upbringing of their children for the welfare of the nation. . . . The typical and average Chinese mother is the embodiment of the virtues of our race."[41] How widely this idea was held can be seen in an article written in 1942 by Chou En-lai, which expresses the same idea:

> In whatever society, mothers should be good, wives should be virtuous. Likewise, fathers should be good, and husbands should be virtuous. This is universal and unchangeable truth. . . . Mothers' duties constitute the lifeline for the continuation of the biological society, and human society should be even more conscious of the greatness of motherly nature and the importance of mothers' duties. We respect and promote mothers' duties, not from the selfish point of view of male society, but from the point of view of the public interest of human society. . . . Mothers' duties are the most glorious natural duties for women in human society. I feel, generally speaking, there is no other task in the world that is more glorious and enduring than mothers' duties. . . . Women can do anything that human beings can do. However, since mothers' duties are inevitable, natural duties for any woman, in performing mothers' duties, women may do fewer other things. This is not only permissible, but also necessary in the division of labor.

That this notion persists is shown by the fact that this article was reprinted in the People's Republic of China in 1980 in commemoration of Women's Day.[42]

These statements derive from the same idea: The ultimate purpose of an individual's activities is for the good of the family, the country, and society. The Confucian influence here is obvious. The highest goal of the major women's movements in modern China is national rejuvenation and increase of social well-being, rather than the particular interests of women as women. Because of this, men have gladly helped them spread their message and lent them assistance. Due to the same Confucian influences, men's contributions to the elevation of women's position in modern China have been enormous. But it should also be clear that this Confucian idea differentiates the Chinese women's movement from Western feminist movements for full interchangeability of roles.

Conclusion

Tradition has had three distinct influences on women in modern China. One is diligence, which is the biggest asset of the Chinese nation in assuring its continuous existence and a basic requirement for Chinese women to keep abreast of the times. Only a willingness to face difficulties can enable one to survive the challenges of a changing environment and to adapt to new roles in keeping with the needs of the day. The second characteristic is fairness. Despite the prevailing social customs favoring men, it has been generally, if subconsciously, recognized and by some explicitly or implicitly stated that women, if given the chance to develop, can be as capable as men. This awareness is the source of the quest for sexual equality. The third characteristic is the concept of fulfilling one's duties to the family and the country. This is the driving force of the Chinese people and the cohesive element in the mutual help and cooperation between men and women. The improvement of women's position in modern China has been the result of the joint efforts of men and women made for the sake of national salvation and in keeping with the trend of modern times.

For more than a century, China has been buffeted by adversities. This has led to the loss of national confidence and depreciation of traditional values. This tendency to esteem the new and depreciate the old has been reflected in the study of history, including the history of Chinese women. In recent years, for a variety of reasons, aspects of traditional Chinese culture have been reinterpreted in a more favorable light, even though the issue of the relationship between tradition and modernity with regard to Chinese women remains in a placid state. By no means am I a traditionalist, but, as a student of history, I am drawn to the past in the search for the sources of changes in women's status in modern China. In attempting to redress the balance in the study of Chinese women's history, I have thus presented some of the less well-known attitudes toward women, since the better-known obstacles to change and the crucial contributions of the West have been discussed elsewhere. Much research remains to be done in a variety of approaches in all of these areas; the social conditions and conventions that gave rise to the expression of the kinds of dissatisfaction documented in this article, and the ways indigenous trends later combined with foreign influences, are some of the stimulating topics on the agenda for future historians.

Notes

1. Liang's article "Lun nü hsueh" (On women's education) is included in *Chin-tai Chung-kuo nü-ch'üan yun-tung shih-liao* (Documents on women's movements in modern China), comp. and ed. Li Yu-ning and Chang Yü-fa (Taipei: Biographical Literature Publishing Company, 1975), 1:549–50.

2. See preface by Chiang Yü-ching. This book was first published by the Commercial Press in 1944, and reprinted by Tingwen Book Company in Taipei in 1973.

3. See Ch'en Chung-yi, "Professor Ts'ai Sung-lin: From Age of Marriage to Protection of Consumers," *Shih-pao chou-k'an* (China times weekly), no. 183, May 31, 1981. According to this article about higher education in Taiwan, "In 1975 a number of college and university presidents made proposals regarding restrictions on women's education and employment, and there were also suggestions from banking circles to limit the number of female employees. On November 12 of the same year, the Central Headquarters of the Kuomintang convened a meeting to discuss 'the question of young women's school examinations and employment.' " In Taiwan, there are entrance exami-

nations at various levels of school. Generally, female students have had a higher admission percentage than male students because of their higher examination scores.

4. *Fu-nü wen-t'i chung-yao yen-lun chi* (Important essays on the question of women), comp. Propaganda Department, Central Committee of the Kuomintang (1929), pp. 33–34.

5. These two women millionaires are recorded in *Shih-chi* (Historical records), chüan 129. One was named Lo and came from a place called Wu. She had a ranch and was a dealer in horses and cattle. She owned a very large number of horses and cattle. The First Emperor of Ch'in gave her a high-ranking title. The other woman millionaire was a widow named Ch'ing from present-day Szechuan. Her ancestors had discovered iron mines, and the family had been rich for several generations. After her husband died, Ch'ing managed the mines by herself, and no one dared to encroach upon her property. The First Emperor had a pavilion built in her honor.

6. Li Ya-nung, *Yin-tai she-hui sheng-huo* (Social life of the Shang period) (Shanghai: People's Press, 1955), p. 33.

7. Chapter 12, "Ping shou" (Military defense).

8. Yang K'uan, *Ch'in Shih-huang* (The First Emperor of the Ch'in) (Shanghai: People's Press, 1956), p. 117.

9. *Hsin T'ang shu* (New T'ang history), chüan 83.

10. Liang Hung-yü was the wife of the famous Southern Sung general Han Shih-chung. In 1130, she and her husband defeated a Chin army at Huang-t'ien-tang, and they assisted each other in many other battles.

11. Shen lived during the last decades of the Ming dynasty. The Ming court appointed her a general to suppress peasant rebellions.

12. Ch'in Liang-yü (1584?–1648) was from Szechuan. After her husband's death, she succeeded him as a military commander. In 1621, she led troops to resist the invading Manchus, and in 1630 her army guarded the capital. In her later years, she fought peasant rebels in her home province.

13. Lin P'u-ch'ing (1821–1877) was daughter of Lin Tse-hsu and wife of Shen Pao-chen (1820–1879), eminent scholar and official. She assisted her husband in fighting the Taipings.

14. A legendary figure, Hua Mu-lan has been admired by the Chinese through a large variety of literary works. There are no reliable historical data on her real life. According to some, she lived in the sixth or seventh century A.D. According to legend, she joined the army disguised as a man, to substitute for her elderly father, who had been drafted in a war. She was in the army for twelve years, won many distinctions, and was promoted to the rank of general. When the war was over, the court appointed her to a high-ranking official post. She declined the offer, preferring to return to her hometown and to her family. Only when some of her former comrades visited her at home did they discover that she was a woman. The best-known literary work about Mu-lan is "The Ballad of Mulan," translated by Arthur Waley, in *Chinese Poems* (London: George Allen and Unwin, 1962), pp. 113–15.

15. In Chinese literature and drama there are a number of popular tales

about the "Generals of the Yang family," of which Mu Kuei-ying was one of the most colorful. The *Sung-shih* (History of the Sung) records the deeds of a number of the Yang generals, who fought against the Liao in the north in the tenth and eleventh centuries, but it does not mention Mu Kuei-ying. According to popular literature, she was a superb warrior and commander, and moreover a romantic personality who chose to marry General Yang Tsung-pao. Tsung-pao's name is also not recorded in the *History of the Sung*.

16. This poem about a contemporary young couple was probably written in the third century A.D. The husband and wife were very much in love, but she was disliked by his mother, who forced them to separate. Having returned to her own parents' family, the young woman was eventually forced to accept being remarried to another man. On the day of her second wedding, she drowned herself. When her former husband heard of her death, he also committed suicide. For an English translation of this poem, see Arthur Waley, *Chinese Poems,* pp. 89–100.

17. For a description of this tragic romance, see Michael S. Duke, *Lu You* (Boston: Twayne Publishers, 1977), pp. 23–25.

18. The legend of Liang and Chu has appeared in a wide variety of literary and theatrical forms. The heroine Chu, disguised as a young man, goes to a school. There, she falls in love with the hero Liang. Unfortunately, Chu's father engages her to marry another man. Because of disappointed love, Liang falls ill and dies. When Chu goes to visit his grave, it suddenly splits open in a thunderstorm. She leaps into the grave, and the two lovers are transformed into a pair of butterflies.

19. Chi Hsiao-lan, *Yueh-wei ts'ao-t'ang pi-chi,* chap. 17. Chi's story stops at the couple's being sentenced to being beaten 100 strokes, without telling whether they died as a result, which frequently occurred.

20. *The Orchid Boat: Women Poets of China,* trans. and ed. Kenneth Rexroth and Ling Chung (New York: McGraw-Hill, 1972), p. 17.

21. This poem was entitled "On a Visit to Ch'ung-chen Taoist Temple in the South Hall I See the List of Successful Candidates in the Imperial Examinations." The translation is largely based on the translation in *The Orchid Boat,* p. 19.

22. *T'an-tz'u* is a genre of narratives composed of alternating prose and verse. It became popular in the Ming dynasty and is still a form of public entertainment in China today.

23. For an analysis of this work, see Toyoko Yoshida Ch'en, "Women in Confucian Society—A Study of Three T'an-tz'u Narratives," Ph.D. dissertation, Columbia University, 1974, pp. 258–327. See also T'an Cheng-pi, *Chung-kuo nü-hsing wen-hsueh shih* (History of Chinese women's literature) (1935; reprinted Taipei: Ho-lo Publisher, 1977, under the title *Chung-kuo nü-hsing te wen-hsueh sheng-huo* [The literary life of Chinese women]), pp. 438–41.

24. For an analysis of this work, see Ch'en, "Women in Confucian Society," pp. 178–257. Ch'en Tuan-sheng was born into a scholarly family and

married into a family named Fan. She died before finishing *Tsai-sheng yuan,* which was completed by Liang Te-sheng. Liang was born into a famous literary family and married a scholar-official.

25. *Lun Tsai-sheng yuan* (Hong Kong: Union Press, 1959), pp. 75–76.

26. Cheng Chen-to, ed., *Ch'ing-jen tsa-chu erh chi* (1934). For a sketch of Wu Tsao's life and works, see T'an Cheng-pi, *Chung-kuo nü-hsing wen-hsueh shih*, pp. 369–76.

27. *The Dream of the Red Chamber (Hung-lou meng* or *Shih-t'ou chi)* by Ts'ao Hsueh-ch'in and Kao O was written in the eighteenth century.

28. Pang Yuan-ying, *T'an shu,* included in *Hsueh-hai lei-pien* (reprint, Taipei: T'ai-lien Kuo-feng Company, 1977), 6:3.

29. See Ko's preface to *Hsü Yü-t'ai wen-wan,* published in 1632. Quoted from *Li-tai fu-nü chu-tso k'ao,* appendix, p. 44.

30. See Chao Shih-chieh's preface to his *Ku-chin nü-shih,* published in 1628. Quoted from *Li-tai fu-nü chu-tso k'ao,* appendix, p. 45.

31. See Tsou Ch'i's preface to his *Hung-chiao chi,* published in the early Ch'ing. Quoted from *Li-tai fu-nü chu-tso k'ao,* appendix, p. 52.

32. "Hsing nü-hsueh i," first published in *Shang-hai nü-pao,* quoted from *Chin-tai Chung-kuo nü-ch'üan yun-tung shih-liao,* 1:569.

33. *Feng-shu,* chap. 2.

34. Lin Yutang, "Feminist Thought in Ancient China," *T'ien Hsia Monthly* 1, 2 (September 1935): 127–50; Paul S. Ropp, "The Seeds of Change: Reflections on the Condition of Women in the Early and Mid Ch'ing," *Signs: Journal of Women in Culture and Society* 2, 1 (Fall 1976): 5–23; C. T. Hsia, "The Scholar-Novelist and Chinese Culture: A Reappraisal of *Ching-hua Yuan,*" in *Chinese Narrative: Critical and Theoretical Essays,* ed. Andrew H. Plaks (Princeton: Princeton University Press, 1977), pp. 266–305; and Li Yu-ning, "Chung-kuo hsin nü-chieh tsa-chih te ch'ung-k'an chi nei-han" (The reprint and contents of the *New Women of China* journal), in *Chung-kuo fu-nü shih lun-wen chi* (Collected essays on the history of Chinese women), ed. Li Yu-ning and Chang Yü-fa (Taipei: Commercial Press, 1981), pp. 179–241.

35. For example, Ch'en Tung-yuan, *Chung-kuo fu-nü sheng-huo shih* (History of the life of Chinese women), first published in the 1930s (reprinted Taipei: Commercial Press, 1970). Despite its weaknesses, this book remains a useful survey of the history of Chinese women.

36. Originally published in *Chih-hsin pao,* no. 52 (1898); quoted from *Chin-tai Chung-kuo nü-ch'üan yun-tung shih-liao,* 1: 562–66.

37. See *Chin-tai Chung-kuo nü-ch'üan yun-tung shih-liao,* 1: 561.

38. "Pen-pao wu ta chu-i yen-shuo" (On the five principles of this journal), serialized in *Chung-kuo hsin nü-chieh tsa-chih,* nos. 2–4 (1907). The first five issues of this journal were reprinted by Youth Cultural Service of Taipei in 1977. On the women's movement at the end of the Ch'ing, see Charlotte L. Beahan, "Feminism and Nationalism in the Chinese Women's Press, 1902–1911," *Modern China* 1, 4 (October 1975): 379–416.

39. *Fu-nü wen-t'i chung-yao yen-lun chi,* pp. 62–63.

40. May-ling Soong Chiang, *This Is Our China* (New York: Harper and Brothers, 1940), p. 206.

41. Ibid., pp. 277–80.

42. Chou's article, entitled "Lun hsien-ch'i liang-mu yü mu-chih" (On virtuous wives–good mothers and mothers' duties), was first published in Yenan in *Chieh-fang jih-pao* (Liberation daily), November 20, 1942. It was reprinted in *Shang-hai shih-fan ta-hsueh hsueh-pao* (Journal of Shanghai Normal University), Social Science ed., 1980, no. 2.

II

Self-Portraits of Women
in Modern China

8

Opposition
to Footbinding

Chang Mo-chün

CHANG MO-CHÜN (1884–1965), also known as Chao-han, was
born in Hunan. Her mother was well educated and known for her
poetry. Her father was a high Ch'ing official, who in 1901 was sent
to Shanghai to supervise education in the provinces of Chekiang
and Kiangsu. From an early age, Chang had contact with Western
learning and reformist ideas. In 1906 she joined the revolutionary
T'ung Meng Hui, and she participated in the Revolution of 1911.
During the Republican years she had a long and active career
in educational administration.

This brief excerpt from her autobiography, published in Taiwan
in 1953, shows her as an activist at an early age. More generally, it
reveals a variety of attitudes toward footbinding, from popular
beliefs and the resigned suffering of her sister to Chang's
straightforward opposition and the passive behavior of her mother.
One sees how little resistance there was to abolishing footbinding in
some quarters, as well as the kinds of objections raised about
"natural feet."

"Lotus boats" and "golden lotuses" were popular names for
bound feet.

FIFTY years ago, the custom of footbinding was still very strong
in our country, and Hunan Province was no exception. In my

childhood, I used to sleep in the same bed with my oldest sister. One night I was awakened by the sound of chirping sobs; I saw her sitting up with the quilt over her shoulders, holding her feet in her hands and weeping, her face streaked with tears. She looked miserable. I asked her what was wrong. She replied in a low voice, "My feet have been bound by Nanny Ho. Although during the day it makes walking difficult, I can still bear the pain. But at night, my feet get hot under the quilt, and I can't sleep with the cutting pain. What am I to do?" When she finished saying this, she swallowed her sobbing for fear of waking Mother. I leaped up in indignation and wanted to take off the binding. She hastily stopped me, saying, "Don't be in such a hurry. Haven't you heard Mother complaining about the difficulty of changing the evil customs of our country? Haven't you often heard our elders say 'Nobody is interested in lotus boats a foot long, and half a Kuan-yin Bodhisattva just doesn't work'?" I was furious: "I must eradicate this despicable custom that does so much harm; I must sweep away this preposterous idea." I adjusted the quilt so that her feet were outside, and she was able to get some sleep.

At daybreak, I went to Mother's bedroom and tearfully told her about Elder Sister's suffering. I earnestly beseeched her to permit Sister to unbind her feet. I also vowed, "I would rather no one showed any interest in me all my life than try to curry favor injuring the body my parents gave me." I also pointed out, "Among all the portraits of bodhisattvas I have seen, some are walking across oceans barefooted on the waves, some are sitting stately with their feet crossed in the lotus posture, some are standing barefooted holding a fish basket, looking for supplicants and saving troubled souls, and some appear in male form as guardian deities with ferocious, glaring eyes. I have also seen the gigantic stone sculpture of Kuan-yin at the Yun-meng Temple in our district, more than twenty feet high, with natural feet and many hands. It is dignified and extraordinarily beautiful, full of vitality and power. Where in any of these can you see the so-called three-inch golden lotuses? Countryfolk made up the saying about half a Kuan-yin, which only shows their ignorance and stupidity. Why should we worry about what they say?" My mother put on her clothing and got up out of bed. She patted me on the head and said with a nod, "What you say is quite right. Let's wait for the right opportunity."

Two years later, the American missionary Dr. Gilbert Reid founded the Society for Natural Feet at Shanghsien Hall in Shanghai. My father was the first to support this, and he sent us the society's rules and regulations and its literature promoting natural feet. I was overjoyed and begged my mother to print hundreds of thousands of copies to distribute all over. I led my aunts and sisters in liberating their feet, and I never tired of talking to anyone about the harmful effects of footbinding and the advantages of natural feet, as evident in all the advanced countries of the world. In a short while, my clan and relatives followed my example, which became a subject of much discussion in newspapers and magazines, leading millions of women in the southeastern provinces to liberate their feet and becoming a broad movement for natural feet. This eradication of such a longstanding evil custom, which I promoted at a tender age in an effort at social revolution, is worthy of being recorded. At the time, a certain Mr. Liu from a neighboring province, who was a *hsiu-ts'ai* [a holder of the first and the lowest degree in the traditional civil service examination system], wrote and circulated a vulgar poem trying to slander me. It read:

> In Hsiang-hsiang District,
> Among the stately Changs,
> There's a little half Kuan-yin,
> Making a mighty impressive show.

It was absurdly ridiculous.

At that time I was nine years old, and I wrote a poem entitled "On Natural Feet" to indicate my goal. I quote it here, in spite of the crude wording, because of its good intent.

> Sympathy for natural feet has moved
>   hundreds of spirits,

Women can be seen rising from the depths
　of the bitter sea of degradation;
Nature's ways are best after all,
The return to dignity begins with
　emancipating the body.

9

Remembrances of an Elderly Aunt

Ch'en Heng-che

CH'EN HENG-CHE (1890–1976) was introduced in part I (see chapter 4). In the following reminiscence, which recounts how her favorite aunt helped her through a personal crisis, we catch a glimpse of the melancholy existence of an exceptionally talented woman in a society with few outlets for those talents, and we see some of the ways women supported each other in the narrow world within which they were confined. (For ways women support women, see Margery Wolf, *Women and the Family in Rural Taiwan* [Stanford: Stanford University Press, 1972].) We also see some elasticity in the patriarchical family system. When a conflict with her father made home unbearable, the author was able to turn to her aunt for economic and psychological support, and her aunt provided the encouragement necessary for the niece's passage into a world of possibilities that she herself had been denied.

This memoir appeared in Li Yu-ning, ed., *Chin-tai Chung-hua fu-nü tzu-hsu shih-wen hsuan* (Selected autobiographical essays and poems of modern Chinese women) (Taipei: Linking Press, 1980), pp. 511–15.

MY PATERNAL grandparents had twelve children. This aunt was their eldest daughter and my father was their youngest son, so there was a difference in age of twenty years between brother and sister, while she was more than forty years older than me. Not only was she tall and energetic, but she also had an abundance of talents and an outstanding moral character. Whenever we saw her, we immediately felt that she had a talent for leadership and could shoulder heavy responsibilities. Because of the general situation several decades ago, however, her leadership abilities had only been put to use in a few small family matters, like an ox knife being used to hack chickens. Her talent was not limited to the kind associated with so-called talented women, writing poems about balmy breezes and moonlit nights. Besides writing poetry, having a knowledge of history, and being able to write ancient-style calligraphy, she also knew how to write prescriptions for medicine and was an excellent cook. When she was young, she had waited on her mother and father-in-law during the day and tended her children in the evenings; only late at night, when there was no one around and all was quiet, did she study and practice calligraphy, frequently staying up until three o'clock—and then getting up again at six in the morning. Those "talented women" of the beautiful maiden and talented hero types could never have such energy, such fortitude, and such unsurpassed self-cultivation.

When I was old enough to get to know her, she was already middle-aged. She liked me most of all her nieces and frequently praised me to my father, saying that I showed real promise. Then, more than ten years after this time, I fell into a very dark period of my life, because I had refused to marry the man my father had chosen for me to marry. Although my father later forgave me, and I was able to continue my studies in Shanghai, this dark period continued, due to financial difficulties and the lack of good schools in Shanghai. So after a while I ran away to my aunt's home out in the countryside, with the faint hope that some new opportunity would arise that would enable me to pursue my education. Her home was a large and complex household, and life there was a painful thing for me, an incompetent young girl with no rights and no experience in the world. The only ray of light in the environment of thorns and brambles was my aunt's special love.

The place where she lived was a small city not far from

Suchou. There were many clear, beautiful mountains and streams, particularly beautiful when autumn came. She would often send for a small boat, tell one of the elderly women servants to prepare some tea and wine and a picnic box, and, bringing a copy of Tu Fu's poetry and her own recent poems, take me out on the lake to look at the mountains. One time when she had been reading some poems by Tu Fu for over an hour, she abruptly stood up and, holding her hands behind her back, began to pace back and forth in the small cabin, reciting out loud:

If only I had a large mansion with thousands of rooms,
I could shelter and protect destitute scholars and bring smiles
    to their faces.

When she came to these lines, she stopped and stood still, let out a long sigh, and said, "This used to be my dream, but now, I can't even shelter and protect my own son and grandchildren." Her only son, his wife, and their children had all become opium addicts, and it looked like she would soon have to sell her large house and its flower garden, which was in the style of the Ta-kuan-yuan [in *Dream of the Red Chamber*] to an outsider. She had a strong will—though she might sigh, she would never shed a tear. But to me, this sigh was sadder than a whole stream of tears. It was too much for me, and I told her, "But Aunt is sheltering and protecting a suffering child right now."

This perked her up, and she told the elderly woman servant, "Warm up the food, and bring us some so we can drink some wine. Today the second young miss and I are really going to enjoy ourselves looking at the lake and the mountains."

So we talked, ate, and laughed, and we felt happy and relaxed in our hearts.

Once I fell sick with a bad case of malaria. She treated me herself, and, after I had begun to improve, every day she boiled chicken soup for me on a small Western-style stove and prepared delicately flavored and nutritious dishes for me until I had completely recovered. At meals, she always asked me to sit next to her, and I was treated to every single one of the delicacies that the matriarch of the house was served. I slept in her library, a sacred precinct that she had never previously allowed anyone to occupy.

Living like this, under her loving care, made a dark future gradually begin to brighten, turned my feelings about myself from despair into hope, and made me believe that I still had it in me to make something of myself. An uncle who had doted on me in much the same way once told me that there are three kinds of attitude people have about their lives—satisfied with their fate, complaining about their fate, and creating their fate. He constantly encouraged me to take the third attitude, because he believed that I had the substance to create my own fate. The painful experiences I had gone through in those few years, however, had given me serious doubts about myself and made me feel that striving was useless, that life just wasn't worth preserving. Under these circumstances, without the support of this aunt, I might have lost the courage to go on living.

I lived at my aunt's for three years, from 1911 to 1914. In the last year she found me a job as a tutor in the home of a friend, and I taught the children there for half a year. That summer—it was the year that the European war broke out—Tsinghua School suddenly began to recruit women to send to study in the United States. I felt my educational level was too low and didn't dare to try to take the examination; however, I ran to my aunt to talk with her about it. She was very encouraging and urged me to take the examination, telling me I had good reason to be hopeful. Well, I did follow her advice and went to Shanghai and took the exam. After the exam was over, I went back to the family in the countryside where I had been tutoring. Later, she saw my name in the paper and immediately wrote me a long letter. I don't remember what the letter said, I only remember that before I had finished reading it a lake of tears came pouring from my eyes.

This was the darkest, the most painful page in my life; and it was this elderly aunt, with her deep faith and profound love for me, who led me out of the darkness back onto the road to creating my own fate.

10

When I Learned
How to Cook

Ho Hsiang-ning

THREE main themes of modern Chinese history were intertwined
in Ho Hsiang-ning's (1878–1972) long life: nationalism,
socialism, and feminism. Although she did not play a leading
role in any of these revolutionary movements, she was a
well-known figure in all.

Ho was born in Hong Kong, where her father had a prosperous
tea business. Her forebears on her maternal grandmother's side had
been merchants for the Taiping rebels, and in her childhood, having
heard stories about the Taiping women not binding their feet and
fighting in battle, she refused to permit her feet to be bound.
Through a fortuitous set of circumstances, this youthful act of
rebellion became the principal reason for her marriage to Liao
Chung-k'ai (1877–1925). Liao's father, who had run a business in
the United States, and who, like the Taiping leaders, was a Hakka,
had stipulated on his deathbed that his son should marry a Chinese
woman who had natural feet, because this was the Hakka custom
and because foreigners looked down on the custom of footbinding.
Ho was one of the few young Chinese women known to the Liao
family who met this condition, and, after the customary
arrangements were made, she and Liao were married in Canton in
1897.

In 1903 when Ho and Liao were students in Japan, they met
Sun Yat-sen, and two years later both became founding
members of Sun's T'ung Meng Hui (Revolutionary Alliance).
Liao soon became one of Sun's closest aides; Ho's early

contributions are detailed in "When I Learned How to Cook."
Ho had been the first female member of the T'ung Meng Hui,
and in the 1920s she was one of the best-known women in Sun's
reorganized Kuomintang. She was one of only three women
delegates to the First National Congress of the KMT in January
1924, and later she became director of the party's Women's
Department.

She continued to play a prominent role after her husband's
assassination in 1925, being one of two women elected to the KMT
Central Executive Committee in January 1926 (the other was Sung
Ch'ing-ling; see chapter 6). Along with other members of the KMT
left wing, she split with Chiang Kai-shek when he turned against
the Communist Party, and she joined the short-lived left-wing KMT
government in Wuhan. After the collapse of the Wuhan
government, she withdrew briefly from political life but was again
elected to the Central Executive Committee of the KMT in 1931,
and throughout the 1930s she worked with Sung Ch'ing-ling to
promote the civil liberties of opponents of Chiang's increasingly
authoritarian regime. She had little power, however, and much of
her time was spent traveling and painting, an art she had studied in
her youth and practiced throughout her life. During the
Sino-Japanese War, she helped Sung collect funds for relief work,
and after the war she was active in anti-Chiang politics from Hong
Kong.

Following the establishment of the People's Republic, Ho was
elected a member of the Government Council and appointed
chairperson of the Overseas Chinese Affairs Commission. At the
time of her death in 1972, she was a vice-chairperson of the
Standing Committee of the National People's Congress,
chairperson of the Kuomintang Revolutionary Committee, and an
honorary chairperson of the China Women's Federation.

From the standpoint of contemporary Western feminism, it
might seem an anomaly that Ho should portray her entry into the
kitchen as a revolutionary act. But, as she explains in "When I
Learned How to Cook," for a young woman from a well-to-do
family, this was taking on a role traditionally associated with
servants. In addition, Ho's attitude embodies one of the main

themes of modern Chinese nationalism—the primacy of the liberation of the nation over the quest for individual freedom. Again one can see continuity in change; as in the Confucian family ideal, each person's obligations are defined in terms of a proper role within the group. The group, however, is no longer defined by ties of kinship, but by commitment to a new ideal; the family has been replaced by China. In the final paragraph, Ho ties the strands of her life together, arguing that freedom and equality for Chinese women will benefit them as individuals while simultaneously helping to strengthen the nation.

"When I Learned How to Cook" was originally published in Canton in 1938, in a collection of autobiographical sketches edited by T'ao K'ang-te, *Tzu-chuan chih yi-chang* (Chapters of autobiography).

IN OUR China—especially several decades ago—any young woman who was well loved by her parents and enjoyed the comforts of a well-to-do home knew practically nothing about cooking, because that was done by servants. Naturally, I was no exception. My parents regarded me as a precious treasure, so since our family circumstances were good, in our household I never had anything to do with the kitchen. And when I married Mr. Liao [Chung-k'ai], the preparation of all food and meals was done entirely by the servants. When I went to study in Japan, however, in response to a unique responsibility demanded of me, I voluntarily gave up my status as a proper young lady and learned how to cook from a hired Japanese maid. As I think back on these events, I realized that my reflections and memories are well worth commemorating.

When Mr. Sun Yat-sen made his second trip to Japan, the relationships among China, Japan, and Russia were tense. Consequently, the Japanese police surveillance of the Chinese overseas students was very strict and repressive. For some time, the Japanese authorities had already been paying close attention to the voice of revolution that Mr. Sun was raising in those years. Although Sun was using a Japanese pseudonym, Nakano, and living in a hotel, he was conscious of the various inconveniences imposed on his meetings and communications with comrades. At that time, I heard that Mr. Sun had again arrived in Japan and went to pay him a visit. The first time Mr. Sun had come to Japan, Mr. Liao and I had talked with him two or three times. We had then expressed our wish to participate in the revolution, and he had treated us as comrades. From our conversation, Sun had come to know that Liao and I were living in a rented *kashiya* (a Japanese rental house). A year or so later, Sun asked Li Chung-shih (a fine Cantonese young man, a loyal friend, a good comrade—loyal to the revolution—who tragically died early, he left an indelibly good impression on me) to come and talk with me in the hope that I would rent and move into another *kashiya,* located more convenient to transportation. At the same time, he suggested that I not employ a Japanese maid servant. Chung-shih explained that Mr. Sun was planning to organize a revolutionary group, and that the hotel was not convenient for a number of reasons—especially because there was no suitable place to hold meetings. I understood and had no doubt at all that this was for advancing the revolution. But the greatest difficulty that I perceived would be that of meals. Since I, myself, could not cook, how would we manage without a maid? Furthermore, since Mr. Liao, taking advantage of the summer vacation, had already left for Canton to get money for me, there would be no one to go out to help me get such things as food and water—at that time Tokyo still did not have running water. These several problems left me somewhat uneasy. But then I thought to myself: since I do not know how to cook, I should learn, at once, from my servant. Who could object to a lady learning menial work, if it were for the revolution? But food and water would have to be brought in from outside the house, and I had some serious reservations about doing this myself. With this in mind, I replied to Chung-shih, "Moving into another *kashiya* would be possible. But since Chung-k'ai will not return for a while yet, I really don't see how

I could manage without a servant to bring drinking water every day." Chung-shih earnestly responded, "Please find and move into a house as soon as possible. I'll carry the drinking water myself." With this promise from Chung-shih I told him to go and report to Mr. Sun that as soon as a *kashiya* had been found I would move.

As soon as Chung-shih left, I set about planning to move. The first important task was to learn how to cook, to prepare simple meals. Ordinarily I simply ate whatever was put in front of me, never even asking what the servants had prepared. Now it was different. I watched carefully as my servant washed the rice, put it in the pot, added water, and started the fire. I paid close attention to the amount of rice, the proportions of water, how big to make the fire, and how long to cook the rice. As for cooking meats and vegetables, the Japanese method was much easier, and after watching a few times I had learned it. In less than two days I felt that I had grasped it. The servant did not understand why I suddenly took so much interest in cooking. How was she to know that I was intent on learning her skills so that I could then dismiss her?

Originally, I was living in the Koishikawa area of Tokyo. The new *kashiya* had to be in the Kanda area, because many of the overseas students lived in Kanda, and transportation was convenient. The rent on the Koishikawa house was only eleven or twelve yüan; the rent at Kanda was twenty-five yüan for a much larger house of seven rooms upstairs and downstairs. I figured that the number of comrades attending meetings, coming and going, would have to increase somewhat before the space would be all used. It was also sufficient to provide the needed secrecy and concealment. Once the house had been located, I then proceeded to terminate the lease on the original *kashiya,* to dismiss the maid, and to write a letter informing Mr. Liao that I had moved to Kanda. Li Chung-shih aided me with the arrangements.

After moving into the Kanda *kashiya,* on the one hand, I had to attend classes; on the other, I had to manage the daily livelihood myself. I felt rather pressed and harried. Formerly, as a young lady at my father's side, there were people to take care of me. When I married Mr. Liao, I still had two of my maids to accompany me. Suddenly, however, I was leading a double life of student and maidservant, to which I was not accustomed. Ordinarily, I had been concerned only with my own studies, leaving all the other menial and miscellaneous tasks to the maid. Now it was really something! Getting up every morning, I first had to straighten the bedding and even had to fetch my own wash water. Returning after class, I would buy food, make the fire—at that time Tokyo did not yet have gas—boil some rice, and cook a meal. I was busy all the time. After eating, I still had to wash dishes and clean up. In those days, there was no electricity in Japan either, so I had to go through all the mess and bother of lighting kerosene lamps—cleaning and filling them with kerosene. Washing clothes was especially inconvenient. Getting water was a nuisance, too, even though Chung-shih got several buckets of water for me every day. Sometimes I used it all up and had to run down the street to the well and get water myself. I had one belief, however: that the hardships I was enduring were for China's revolution. As I thought about that, whatever the misery or discomfort, I endured it happily and untiringly. At the Kanda *kashiya* the expense of daily provisions, even though many more people visited there, amounted to no more than one-and-a-half hao, and was usually one hao and a few copper cash. I remember that the meals we ate usually consisted of turnips, beef, bean curd, fish, cabbage, and white potatoes. Each time I would buy five copper cash of beef, three coppers worth of fish, two of turnips—at that time two copper cash bought two long white turnips, enough for two meals when sauteed together with beef— or perhaps I would add a little bean curd and cabbage, for one day's meal. No matter who arrived, they ate this sparse fare. When there were a few more of us I simply bought a little more. Sometimes Mr. Sun ate with everybody, but he did not like rice, or at most ate just one bowl. Therefore, I often prepared bread and butter, fried an egg, and fixed a bowl of beef broth for him. It was always the same, and he never complained. At that time I would open a jar of beef bouillion—I forget how many hao it cost—only when Mr. Sun arrived. Since we all thought it too expensive, one small jar probably made soup for seven or eight meals. Before Mr. Liao returned to Tokyo, our life at the Kanda *kashiya* was like this because I really did not have much money on hand then. Even when Mr. Liao returned, our daily life remained quite simple, and we did not buy any fancy food to eat. Mr. and Mrs. Hu Han-min came to Japan on the same boat with Mr. Liao, and when they first arrived in Tokyo they moved into our *kashiya* with Mr. Liao. When Mrs. Hu first arrived in Tokyo, not being accustomed to our bland, simple food—I basically could not cook a real meal—she was at first very polite and swallowed a few meals. Afterward, she gave some money to someone to go out and buy some roast duck to eat. This was also a reflection of the fact that my cooking, apparently, was not very sophisticated at that time.

Mr. Sun often came with Li Chung-shih to my *kashiya* to plan for organizing the T'ung Meng Hui. I joined the T'ung Meng Hui very early—what number on the list I do not remember. The procedure for joining required two sponsors. My entry in the register included only the signature of Chung-shih. Later, when Mr. Sun saw it, he signed his own signature. At that time, I was the only female member of the T'ung Meng Hui, and since I joined very early, Mr. Sun called me "Obasan" [grandmother in Japanese]. Later, all the comrades followed suit.

When Mr. Liao returned to Tokyo from Canton, it was already more than two months since I had moved. He and Mr. and Mrs. Hu Han-min got to the *kashiya* sometime after six o'clock in the evening. After eating dinner, they rested a while; then Mr. Sun and Li Chung-shih talked with Mr. Liao about the organization and principles of the T'ung Meng Hui. Mr. Liao was in strong agreement. That night, around ten o'clock, he too joined the T'ung Meng Hui, with Chung-shih and myself as his sponsors. Liao had been in favor of the revolution very early. Moreover, the first time I met Mr. Sun we had gone [to a meeting] together. Liao had spoken with Sun once more than I had. The reason he was a step late in joining was that he had returned to China at that time; otherwise we certainly would have joined the T'ung Meng Hui at the same time. As for my being one of his sponsors, this was probably at the suggestion of Li Chung-shih. Hu Han-min also joined that night, but he was not able to understand easily or accept its principles, especially those concerning the ''equalization of land.'' He raised some very serious questions and doubts with Mr. Sun, but after Sun had discussed them in thorough detail, sometime after three o'clock in the morning, Hu finally joined the T'ung Meng Hui.

Of the founding members of the T'ung Meng Hui who came often to our *kashiya* I remember Li Chung-shih, Chu Chih-hsin, Hu Han-min, Huang K'o-ch'iang, Chang T'ai-yen, Ku Ying-fen, Chü Cheng, Wang Ching-wei, Niu Yung-chien, Ma Chün-wu, Liu Ch'eng-yü, and Yang Tu. Su Man-shu was also one of the early participants in our patriotic brigade, and we met often. The large founding conference of the T'ung Meng Hui was held later at the Student Association, but when Mr. Sun called a secret meeting of important comrades, it was generally at the *kashiya*. At that time, I felt simply that the comrades who came and went were closer in their relationships than a family of brothers and sisters, with no barriers or formalities separating them. The so-called love and sincerity that is so often glibly mouthed today could not be more truly applicable than to the attitude of everyone at that time.

Mr. Sun was always direct and sincere with the comrades, and toward Mr. Liao and me he was quite without formality. While he was in Japan he lived with us as a member of the family. On occasion, when he needed money and had none on hand, he would come over to me and say, ''Obasan, give me several dollars!'' At that time we did not have much, at most no more than fifty dollars. Sometimes he took ten or twenty dollars. To support Mr. Sun and the revolution, there have been many who spent tens of thousands. I mention this at the risk of making it seem that he was shabby, but I relate it here simply to show the closeness of feelings that Mr. Sun had for us. He was just like a member of the family.

After the T'ung Meng Hui was founded, Mr. Sun appointed comrades to return to China to carry out the revolutionary "movement"—at that time the term "movement" was used as a substitute for "revolution." Mr. Liao was delegated to go to Tientsin to set up an organ, to communicate with the French socialist Boucapaix, and to plan for development of the northern revolutionary forces. Thanks to his earlier years in the United States, Mr. Liao's English was strong. In establishing ties with Western revolutionary leaders, when Mr. Sun was not able to meet them directly, he often sent Mr. Liao ahead to make contact. When Mr. Liao was about to leave for Tientsin, I wrote him a parting poem.

> We still have to avenge the nation's enemy,
>   with no intention of giving up.
> I swallow tears usual at parting,
> Urging you not to spare your life,
> To leave a name in the history of Shina.

The term for China [*Shina*, a Japanese term considered disrespectful by Chinese] was used in the poem, because at that time the overseas students in Tokyo had become accustomed to the term. Besides, we were intent on overthrowing the Manchu Ch'ing dynasty but would not deign to use the words Great Ch'ing. Instead, we used this term, which later, under the Republic, we would never use. To preserve the actual record, I have left the original [term in the poem], without revision.

Thinking back to when I began to learn to cook brings with it associations of a number of past events concerning Mr. Sun's organization of the T'ung Meng Hui in Tokyo at that time. In truth, I dare not assert that my *kashiya* in Kanda was the fermenting ground of the T'ung Meng Hui. But if one were to say that in those days I was a loyal maidservant to the T'ung Meng Hui, perhaps there would be some who would nod their heads in agreement.

At that time in Tokyo, working and meeting together with us were comrades from many provinces of China. Whoever came to my *kashiya* I treated alike, as a member of the family, as a brother. However, since I could not speak Mandarin (the common dialect), I was unable to communicate (except with my Cantonese friends), because our speech was mutually unintelligible. Even when we would have liked to have a long talk, it was impossible. Last year in Nanking, Chang Chi (P'u-ch'üan) and Chü Cheng (Chüeh-sheng) came to see me. P'u-ch'üan said to me, "We have been old friends for over thirty years. During that [early] time in Japan, since we could not understand each other's dialects, although we met often, we said little to each other. Also, because you had natural, unbound feet, whenever we spoke of you, whether to your face or behind you back, we called you Big Feet Ho. Even when you were right there and we called you this, you did not understand." What he said was touching and interesting. Everyone laughed heartily. It was true; among the female overseas students at that time, I was the only one with unbound feet. Two or three years later, I met the heroine Ch'iu Chin, whose feet were still bound.

Time certainly does pass quickly. These events took place thirty-five years ago. In my own life, at my parents' side, I was a young lady; in society, I was able to be a worker. In my home, I could cook and manage all the miscellaneous details of preparing the meals; emerging from the kitchen, I moved into political activities. I have dined on rare delicacies, but I have also been accustomed to coarse, bland fare. I can spend months in quiet, peaceful leisure; but I do not fear difficulty and hardship. I really do not know how wives and young ladies raised in the comfort of luxurious ease and extravagant indulgence can become human beings. And those who have done nothing for the nation but have profited and become wealthy from the revolution must surely be despised by others. Now the nation is in difficulty, and natural disaster strikes. Those who can work should offer their services, and those with money should offer their money. Otherwise, if one schemes only to enrich his own family and clan and to fatten his relatives, he will be criticized by thousands of people, and his luck will not last long.

As for the problem of most women, I believe it should be approached this way: Women themselves should learn a skill to make a living, practice discomfort and hardship, and become involved in the affairs of the nation and society, rather than turn over their own lives to the management of others. And how should the nation treat women? Based on the principle of equality between men and women, it should ensure equal education for men and women alike, and should fully nurture and develop the capabilities of women for social activity and for all kinds of professions. To shut women up rigidly in the kitchen or keep them in the house was already wrong several decades ago. I was an obvious example. There was no uprising of the Chinese revolution in which women did not participate. Nevertheless, even today we still cannot receive truly equal treatment. This is totally irrational—unspeakable. I hope that those who participate in future national assemblies to make the constitution will, in no way, ever again disregard the rights of all women—that they will make detailed stipulations for the full equality of men and women. At this juncture, when we are rescuing the nation from a life-or-death crisis, we must not continue to allow half of all our people to remain paralyzed.

—Written on the anniversary
of the establishment
of the Canton
National Government.

11

Remembrances
of the
May Fourth Movement

Teng Ying-ch'ao

went on the long march

THE MOST important woman in Chinese politics today, Teng Ying-ch'ao (1903–) has become more prominent since the death of her husband, Chou En-lai (1898–1976). Although her name has been inseparable from his, she has demonstrated her own abilities through a long and active political career.

Teng was born in Hsin-yang, Honan Province, where her father was a county magistrate during the late Ch'ing. He died when she was a small child, and she was raised by her mother, who instilled in her the idea that women should strive for independence.

In 1919, when a student at the Chihli First Women's Normal School, Teng threw herself into the May Fourth Movement and organized the Tientsin Association of Women Patriots, which was the most active organization among women students in Tientsin. A forceful speaker with a lively personality, she rapidly became a student leader. In 1924, at the beginning of the revolutionary upsurge that was to last until 1927, she joined both the Kuomintang and the infant Chinese Communist Party. In August 1925, she married Chou En-lai, then deputy director of the Political Department of the Kuomintang's important Whampoa Military Academy and secretary of the CCP's Kwangtung Provincial Committee. Like Chou, Teng was sophisticated and articulate, and she was to show a similar resilience and ability to weather the storms of factional conflicts within the CCP. In 1928 she was

144

appointed director of the party's Women's Department, a position she held on and off over the next two decades. In 1931 she became an alternate member of the CCP Central Committee. Three years later, she was one of only some fifty women who participated in the epic Long March from Kiangsi to Yenan, carried on a stretcher most of the way due to a severe case of tuberculosis. During the Sino-Japanese War she and Chou played key roles in united front liaison with the Kuomintang.

After the establishment of the People's Republic, Teng held a number of important party and government posts. She was elected a full member of the party's Central Committee at the Eighth Party Congress in 1956, and in 1978 she became a member of the ruling Politburo, a position she continues to hold. In addition, she currently is a vice-chairperson of the Standing Committee of the National People's Congress, honorary president of the All-China Women's Federation, and head of the United Front Department of the CCP. Li P'eng, currently premier of the PRC, is the adopted son of Teng and Chou En-lai.

The following article was originally published in *Chung-kuo fu-nü* (Women of China), no. 9 (1959). The translation is based on the version included in *Wu-ssu yun-tung hui-i lu* (Recollections of the May Fourth Movement), compiled by the Institute of Modern History, Chinese Academy of Social Sciences (Peking: Hsin-hua Bookstore, 1979).

AT THE TIME of the May Fourth Movement in 1919, I was just sixteen *sui,* a student at the Tientsin Chihli First Women's Normal School. As today I think back to the events of thirty years ago, since thirty years is not a short time, and since in the twisting complex course of the Chinese revolution many of my memories have already faded, I shall talk here about only those things I can remember.

On May 4 of that year, the Peking students held a demonstration demanding the "indictment of the traitors" and the "abrogation of the Versailles Treaty." In their exasperation the students set fire to the residence of Chao Chia-lou and angrily beat the traitors. The next day the news reached Tientsin and shook the students of all the Tientsin schools into action. Discussion meetings were held everywhere. In response to the nationalistic movement of the Peking students, on the seventh the Tientsin students held a demonstration and very quickly organized the Tientsin Student Union, which, together with the Tientsin Association of Women Patriotic Comrades, led by students from the women's schools, later founded the Tientsin Alliance of All Circles for National Salvation. At that time, reacting with purely patriotic enthusiasm, we shouted slogans that, besides the two mentioned above, included "Abolish the Twenty-One Demands," "Return Tsingtao," "Boycott Japanese goods," "Promote Chinese goods," and "Don't sell out the nation." At that time the Peiyang warlord government adopted a policy of repressing the nationalistic student movement, using all kinds of repressive measures against the students, including the police, bayonets, bullets, fire hoses, fists, and even arrest. The struggle forged and tempered us, gradually raising the level of our consciousness. And then, as both the new thought tide and new culture quickly flooded old China after the First World War, and the success of the Soviet Russian October Revolution began to influence the youth of China, new progressive elements were added to the May Fourth movement, causing it to advance.

The May Fourth nationalistic movement and the New Culture Movement were fundamentally anti-imperialist and anti-feudal in nature, but at that time these ideas were not yet clearly formed in our minds. Not until after the founding of the Chinese Communist Party in 1921 was it clearly pointed out that the Chinese revolution was an anti-imperialist, anti-feudal bourgeois democratic revolution. Only then did our awareness gradually become clarified. At the time of the May Fourth movement we did not know that "the intelligentsia must unite with the workers and peasants." At that time, however, we had attained a kind of spontaneous direct awareness of the fact that in order to save the nation, we must send out a "call to awaken our fellow compatriots." Therefore, we strongly emphasized propaganda work and organized a number of lecture teams. At that time I became the lecture team director for the Association of Women Patriotic Comrades and lecture department director of the Student Union. Our lecture teams went everywhere, on a fixed regular schedule. Tied to the customs of feudal society, the women first could not lecture on the streets with the men but were limited to various meeting rooms, educational facilities, and public auditoriums in the city. Every time we had a large audience we would speak on the need for everyone to stand up and resolve to save the nation with one mind, and to achieve the goal of punishing the traitors. We described the grievous bitterness of the Koreans after they had lost their independence. We demanded the freedom to hold patriotic meetings and opposed the suppression of the students by the Peiyang government. Sometimes tears streamed down our cheeks as we talked. The audiences were very moved. In addition, we also went around visiting homes, often going to relatively out-of-the way places, to the poor districts, to bring our propaganda from door to door. Some received us very warmly. Others slammed the door in our faces or kicked us out the gate. But we were never discouraged by such obstacles and went right on knocking on other doors. I remember that during the summer vacation that year, we once went to the western outskirts of Tientsin. As we were returning we ran into a heavy rainstorm that soaked every one of us to the skin, but none of our spirits was dampened. The next time we went out again, on schedule. On the other hand, we also strongly emphasized the functions of written propaganda and newspapers. The *Student Union Report,* published every three days by the Tientsin Student Union, later became a large-format daily, as large as an edition of the Peking *People's Daily* is today. Each issue was printed in over twenty thousand copies, not a small number. The chief editor of this paper was Comrade Chou En-lai. The Association of Women Patriotic Comrades also published a weekly. These two papers reported the current national and international news, the news of the various patriotic student movements throughout the country, and of the struggle to oppose oppression. It also contained editorials, political and literary essays, and so forth.

Concerning the concrete facts of the students' demands for science and democracy during the May Fourth Movement, I can offer only a few examples from the situation in Tientsin at that time, and from among my own activities.

Owing to the reactionary Peiyang government's toadying to Japan abroad, its harboring of traitors at home, and its unrelenting suppression of the students, we did not have the freedom to be patriotic. Our most pressing democratic demands at the time were the democratic rights to freedom of assembly, association, speech, and publication. For these demands we were suppressed many times and struggled many times. For example on October 10 of that same year, the Tientsin Alliance of All Circles for National Salvation called a conference of all the people throughout the city of Tientsin to continue the demand for the punishment of the national traitors, for the dismissal of Ts'ao Ju-lin, Lu Tsung-yü, and Chang Tsung-hsiang, for tightening the boycott of Japanese goods, and for a demonstration march. We had already heard a rumor that the Tientsin police chief, Yang Yi-te (also known as Yang Pang-tzu) [note: *pang-tzu,* a short length of bamboo or wood for sounding the night watch; also note a pun on *yang,* foreign] was preparing to use armed force to break up our meeting and to stop our march. But we were not in the least frightened. We made preparations in turn to deal with the armed police. It was planned that the meeting place would be set up and arranged such that the townspeople would be standing completely surrounding the speakers' platform. Then a group of students would be organized to form a circle around the outside of the townspeople. Then, around the outside of them, forming the front ranks, would be a circle of women students who would be the first to break through the ranks of the encirclement by the armed police. In addition, each one of us would be carrying a flag, the specially purchased hard bamboo poles that could be turned into weapons should the event turn into a battle.

Before the scheduled time of the meeting, the townspeople and the ranks of students began moving in a mass to assemble at Nan-k'ai Square. As we expected, a large body of police moved in with bayonets fixed on their rifles to surround all of us in the square. We then proceeded with the meeting according to schedule, down to the point where the demonstration march was to begin. At that point we came into conflict with the police. At first we students pushed forward, on the one hand pushing, on the other shouting to them, "the police ought to be patriotic," "do not strike the patriotic students." At the same time, because they were already using the butts of their rifles to beat us—many fellow students were beaten, some had their eyeglasses broken— we also started to defend ourselves with our flag poles, or we would use the poles to knock off their helmets. As soon as they bent down to pick up their helmets we would surge forward through the break in the line. Just as the battle was getting tense, a rank of outside reinforcements arrived—luckily, the Student Union propaganda team arrived, driving their bus into the square. This inside-outside pincer attack opened up a hole and a large column of people broke out following the bus, whereupon the demonstration marched around the city, right up to the police station, where we questioned Yang Yi-te and raised our opposing views with him right through the night until daylight the next day, when we finally dispersed. The incident greatly aroused the indignation of the female students. From this point on they no longer heeded the restrictions of feudal custom. The next day they were out on the streets, stopping at nothing, marching and lecturing on the streets in full daylight, declaiming the beating and wounding of the students by Yang Yi-te.

After the October 10 incident, the suppression became more and more severe. In little more than a month the Tientsin Alliance of All Circles for National Salvation was closed down by the police. Ma Ch'ien-li, Ma Chün, and other leaders, twenty-four altogether, were arrested. Next to be closed down was the Tientsin Student Union; we could not carry out our activities publicly. We moved into the Leased Territory, where the family of a fellow student lent us a small room to continue our work to maintain the struggle. In December, to seek the reopening of the Alliance of All Circles for National Salvation and of the Student Union, and the release of the imprisoned representatives, we organized a large grievance demonstration of all the Tientsin students and surrounded the provincial government offices to demand that the then provincial governor Ts'ao Jui come out and give us a reply. But he would not show his face. We elected representatives to meet with him, but the main gate of the provincial offices had already been closed tightly and was guarded by a large body of military police who would not let the representatives enter. Our representatives—four in all, including Chou En-lai, Kuo Lung-chen (female), and Yü Fang-chou—slipped through a hole under the main gate entranceway, but as soon as they were inside they were beaten and arrested. The large group of students outside became even more incensed and determined not to leave. Near midnight, the reactionary provincial government then put into effect its ultimate measure, using bayonets, rifle butts, and fire hoses violently to force the students to disperse. It was a bloody tragedy. Many students were badly beaten. Blood flowed from broken heads. The seriously wounded had to be taken to the hospital. From this experience we learned to recognize even more clearly the vicious face of the reactionary government. We realized then that patriotic freedom and democratic rights cannot be attained easily, without struggle and bloodshed. During the second year of the May Fourth Movement, the final period of the movement, our work undertook the serious tasks of opposing illegal arrest, of planning to rescue the representatives by demanding that the cases of the imprisoned representatives be presented to the courts for public trial, and of arousing the aid of public opinion. We worked straight through till summer when we finally obtained the release of the entire group of twenty-eight persons.

We were not only affected by the suppression of the reactionary government outside of school. Even within the school, we were suppressed by the school headmaster and the teaching staff who prohibited us from engaging in activities or meetings outside of school. For example, on May 7, 1920, we students at Women's Normal came into conflict with the school authorities when we wanted to participate in a big meeting commemorating the anniversary of the May 7 national humiliation [the day in 1915 on which Japan delivered its ultimatum containing the Twenty-One Demands, which would have given Japan extensive control over the Chinese government]. Although we did finally burst out to attend the meeting, when we returned there was already a notice posted inside the school that announced the expulsion of every one of the more than two hundred students from the school. We were really angry, but not at all intimidated. We were certainly not going to submit. Without a thought for food or sleep, we worked into the night putting together our luggage and moved out of the school together. But the school authorities had locked the main gate and would not allow us to move out. They had also locked the telephone room. The whole school rocked to the racket we made that night. When morning came, the entire student body was still resolved to move out. Eluding the surveillance of the police, we moved to an area in the botanical gardens outside the school where we called a discussion meeting and maintained the struggle for a week. In the end, with the assistance of our families and public opinion, the school authorities were forced to rescind their order. Not until after they had removed the public notice expelling us did we all return together to the school in victory.

Although at that time we still did not know about serving the people with one's whole heart and mind, our breasts were filled with patriotic fervor. This revolutionary spirit of total commitment gave us the courage to sacrifice everything for the salvation of the nation, for national independence, for the struggle for democratic freedom against the forces of feudalism.

Along with the development of the May Fourth patriotic movement emerged the movement for the liberation of women. This was also one of the important elements of the May Fourth democratic movement. It raised such issues as "male-female equality," "opposition to arranged marriages," and the demands for "public social intercourse," "freedom to love," "freedom of marriage," "admittance of women to the universities," and "employment of women in all institutions." In Tientsin, we first of all merged into one the separately organized men's and women's student unions, and worked together. At first there were obstacles to putting this into practice. There were some women students who did not agree; some were concerned that public opinion might disapprove; some were afraid that after uniting, some people would make jokes about the free mixing of men and women. But the positive, progressive elements among both men and women students were extremely natural and open. In our tasks, mutual equality was respected, and everyone worked together with one heart and aim of saving the nation, and for the common struggle. The women competed with the men in all tasks, and women students did not want to fall behind others. The positive elements among the women clearly understood that they themselves were pioneers, that they must not become the laughingstock of society, so as not to block the road for others coming afterward, that they must work conscientiously and create the model for others to follow. The positive elements among the male students at that time, under the flood tide of the new thought that had dealt a severe blow to the idea that men were superior to women, were very respectful of their women fellow students. Everyone shouldered equally the work responsibilities. In each department of the Student Union, for each man in a position of responsibility there was also a woman. The Student Union advisory council also had one male and one female chairperson. The status and function of the Tientsin Women's Normal students in the Student Union were absolutely the same as those of the Nankai students. The men's and women's student associations of Peking united later than did the student associations of Tientsin. They were very envious of the union of our Tientsin Student Union and of the good results of our work. At that time the most obstinate element obstructing the union of the men's and women's student associations in Peking was the Student Union of the Women's Normal College, which was under the control of T'ao Hsüan, who later threw her lot in with the reactionary Kuomintang.

As the influence of the October Revolution of Soviet Russia and the new thought tide swept into China, the New Culture Movement gained increased momentum along with the development of the May Fourth nationalistic movement. This was the primary content of the May Fourth "Science" slogan. Periodicals such as *Hsin ch'ing-nien* (New youth), *Shao-nien Chung-kuo* (Young China), and *Hsin Ch'ao* (New tides), published in Peking, were widely read and appreciated by large numbers of students. To raise our practice of the new culture, the Tientsin Student Union held weekly academic lecture meetings to which progressive professors from Peking such as Comrade Li Ta-chao were invited to lecture on opposition to classical Chinese and the eight-legged essay, on advocating the use of colloquial Chinese, on how to practice writing in the colloquial, and on the use of punctuation symbols. From the vantage point of today, these seem rather common and ordinary. But at that time these were extremely fresh and important problems.

At the end of the May Fourth summer, some twenty of us male and female students who were relatively progressive and positive elements felt that we needed a body that was organized a bit more tightly than was the Student Union, that would be more capable of doing some scientific and new thought tide research, so we organized a small group—the Chüeh-wu She (Awakening Society). The members of this group often discussed and studied the new thought tide together. At that time I was the youngest and did not participate in formal discussions frequently, but I often listened to the male and female members who were older than I discuss socialism, anarchism, guild socialism, and so forth. No one had a fixed faith as yet; nor did any of us understand communism. We had only heard it said that in the most ideal society it was "each gives according to his ability" and "each receives according to his needs." We knew only that Lenin and the October Revolution of Soviet Russia had succeeded; we knew only that their revolution had liberated the oppressed majority, that they wanted to realize a classless society, and that these attracted our sympathy and admiration for the October Revolution. At that time we still could not obtain individual works on these problems! The Awakening Society did not last very long—only a few short months. After the unfortunate incident of the surrounding of the provincial offices mentioned above, a number of the society members were put in jail (including Ma Chün and Chou En-lai). Some members left for other places upon graduation, leaving only a few, and they could not undertake any activities because of the severely adverse circumstances.

In the summer of 1920 one group of our members, including Chou En-lai and Kuo Lung-chen, emerged from jail and soon went with Liu Ch'ing-yang and others to France to further their studies. I and other society members also graduated and left to work in various places. Our little group ceased to exist. But we were in touch frequently, and some kept in contact by mail. By 1920 there was a Chinese Socialist Youth Corps (which later became the Communist Youth Corps). After the founding of the Chinese Communist Party in 1921, more than half of our twenty-member society sooner or later joined either the party or the youth corps. Some constituted the earliest members in the organizations of the party or youth corps in various places.

The Tientsin Socialist Youth Corps was founded in early 1924. Later, the party organization was established. By this time we already knew clearly what the proletariat was, that we must struggle for the benefit of the proletariat and the working people, and we had firmly resolved that the objective of our faith and struggle was communism.

The twenty-odd members of the Awakening Society have changed much in the past thirty years. There are those who were early deserters from the revolution. There are those who pursued only their own personal pleasures and did not follow politics. Some fell to run over to the reactionary Kuomintang camp. But there are those who have upheld the revolution throughout and are continuing the struggle today. Some courageously sacrificed themselves as honorable Communist Party members. Comrade Ma Chün (a Moslem) at that time was one; he was the finest student leader, and in 1927, when secretary of the Peiping Municipal Committee of the Chinese Communist Party, he was arrested and murdered by Chang Tso-lin. Comrade Kuo Lin-i was another; she was arrested at Tsingtao in 1931, and upon release went to Tsinan where she was killed by Han Fu-chü. Both these persons when arrested shouted loudly, sang the international anthem, and met their deaths with honor. Comrade Yü Fang-chou, who was a member of a small group of progressive students of Tientsin, during the time of the land revolution led an uprising in Yü-t'ien (about 90 km northeast of Tientsin) and was sacrificed. In speaking of them, I cannot repress a feeling of sadness and respect that I feel for them, and for other countless revolutionary martyrs. At the same time I am filled with hatred for the enemy. We must certainly march forward on the bloodstained path of the revolutionary martyrs, to carry out the revolution completely.

12

The Family Prison

Hsieh Ping-ying

THOUGH known primarily as a writer, Hsieh Ping-ying (1906–) has also had successful careers in journalism and university teaching and represents in many ways the courage and independent spirit of the new Chinese woman in the twentieth century. In her youth she was a rebel; she refused to bind her feet, was expelled from school for organizing demonstrations against Japanese imperialism, joined the National Revolutionary Army during the Northern Expedition against the warlords, fled an arranged marriage to pursue her own career and find free love, and was arrested in both China and Japan (where she was studying) for political activities. During the Sino-Japanese War she organized the Hunan Women's Battlefront Corps, which worked with the wounded at the front. From 1940 Hsieh alternated between editorial work at several newspapers and teaching. She was a professor of Chinese literature at Taiwan Normal University from 1948 to her retirement in 1971. During this period she collaborated in translating the Confucian *Four Books* and the best-known anthology of classical prose masterpieces, *Ku-wen kuan-chih*, into modern colloquial Chinese.

Hsieh's writing career spans over half a century, and her works continue to be widely read. Her first book, *Ts'ung-chün jih-chi* (War diary), published simultaneously with an English translation by Lin Yü-t'ang (see chapter 3) in 1928, is in its nineteenth printing, and her best-known work, *I-ko nü-ping te tzu-chuan* (Autobiography of a woman soldier, first published in 1936) is in its twenty-fifth printing. The latter, translated into English (along with excerpts from her war diaries) as *Girl Rebel*, was published in the United States in 1940 and has recently been reprinted by Da

Capo Press. There have also been French, Russian, Japanese, Korean, and Esperanto editions, as well as a film version.

Hsieh's appeal to readers comes largely from her frank and vivid portrayal of her personal experiences and emotions. The following excerpt from *Girl Rebel* is an excellent example of her talent for rendering her own experiences as both uniquely personal and representative of her times. Through the description of her struggle against an arranged marriage, she dramatizes the conflict between the old and the new in a manner that resonated in the minds of her readers. The issue is not solely the manner of selecting a marriage partner, but individual freedom versus absolute subordination to traditional authority. This excerpt begins with the twenty-one-year-old Hsieh returning home after having served in a propaganda team during the Northern Expedition in 1926–27, and it ends with her being confined by her conservative parents. "The Family Prison" is not merely metaphorical. Following the dispute described in these pages, Hsieh was held captive by her parents and forced to go through with the marriage they had arranged. She was eventually able to escape from her new "home" to Shanghai, where she managed to scrape out a living through writing until financial support from her sympathetic elder brother enabled her to attend the National Normal University for Women in Peiping, and thus begin a new life.

Two thin little sedan-chair carriers carried me step by step nearer to the home that I had left two years ago. My heart was feeling heavier and heavier.

"We are nearly there, Aunt Ming," Hsiang shouted to me from her sedan chair.

I did not want to meet people whom I knew and hid my head between my shoulders.

We passed the tea pavilion, and half a mile beyond stood the large, newly built house that was my home. Looking at the new house for the first time, I heard a faint sorrowful voice whispering in my ear, "This is the prison you are going into!"

But I was not afraid; I had made up my mind to come back, and I believed I should be able to break out of this prison even though it was so strongly built.

Home again! My mother, sister, sisters-in-law, and many children came to receive me. Their faces were beaming; they held my hands tightly. The children pulled at my dress and said, "Remember me, Auntie?" My white-haired grandmother was so glad that tears stood in her eyes.

"You are much thinner, dear," she said. "You must have suffered much."

Mother was wiping her eyes with her sleeves, and Sister's eyes were moist. But little Yunpao pulled my hand and asked, "Did you bring me a doll, Auntie?"

I went into the main hall, and there I saw all kinds of furniture painted red and green, shining, glittering. I knew these were part of my dowry, and I felt sorry for Mother for wasting so much money.

After lunch they took me through the new house. The rooms were big and high and sunny, though quite old-fashioned. There was plenty of light and the good country air of the village. Mother said the original plan had been to make two main houses and two annexes; but when they finished the main houses, they had already spent three thousand dollars. The bricks, the stones, the wooden beams could not have been stronger. I was sure this home would remain intact after three thousand years—if no imperialist came to bomb it. I did not feel much concerned about it because I did not intend to stay in this little town. I should not have felt like living here if it was as spacious and magnificent as a cathedral.

"See what your mother has done for you!" said Mother. "During the two months they were painting the furniture I hardly slept. On windy days I was afraid the dust might stick to the golden foil, and I came and covered up the pieces with oil cloth. In the daytime I was afraid the children or the sparrows might dirty them. And then I had to watch the workers every day, or it might not have been finished in two years. Now they are all painted, all thirty of them. The bedding, even the mosquito nets, all are ready. We were just waiting for you to come home to make the dresses." She said it all in one breath, but I did not answer a single word. I bent my head, and she thought it was girlish shyness, and continued happily:

"It is really the Buddha who sent you back. After I learned that you had become a soldier, I washed my face every morning with tears, worrying that you might be in danger. I prayed and burned much incense for you. When I heard that you were fighting I fainted three times. I was unconscious for fully an hour! The Hsiao family was anxious too, and constantly sent people to inquire about you. They thought they would not have the luck of having you as their bride. Now, thank Heaven, you have come home safe and sound."

I did not know how to begin all I wanted to say. It was better not to say anything about the engagement before Father came back. Mother was a stubborn woman, and it was no use talking to her. I passed two days like a dumb person. But in the village news spread faster than by the radio. The Hsiao family knew I was home. Chulin, the uncle of my fiancé, wrote a letter to our family asking for the wedding date. Elder Brother showed me the letter.

"How are you going to answer?" he asked.

"Ask them to wait till Father comes."

But how was I to settle the problem? The wedding date could not be put off too long. If I did not hurry to break the engagement it might be too late.

It so happened that Father returned that very night. After reading the letter he came with Mother to ask me what I thought would be a suitable date.

"Father, I have come home especially to settle this matter," I began. "You must remember the letter I wrote you. I cannot possibly live with Hsiao-ming. We are not even fond of each other; indeed, we feel absolutely nothing toward each other. His ideas, his interests, differ altogether from mine. I cannot understand his character, I just do not understand him. How can I be his wife?"

"You don't want to live with him? Do you mean to say you wish to break the engagement?" Father shouted and banged on the table.

"Yes, I have come back to break it off," I replied calmly.

Mother angrily shouted, "You can't break the engagement unless you leave this house and never come back. Now that you are here, do you suppose you are going to escape from marriage by running away? No matter what you do, you can't escape." She raised her hand as if to strike me. Father left the room puffing with anger, and I could not go on, and went to my bedroom and wrote a five-thousand-word letter explaining why I did not want to be married.

The next day, to my surprise, Father did not seem to be a bit touched by my words, but, with a severe countenance, started berating me.

"Your reasons for breaking the engagement are evident in your letter. First, no love, second, difference in ideas. Let me answer you: As to your first reason, love exists only between husband and wife. Love begins after marriage, and not before. You are not married to him yet, so of course you don't love him. As to your second reason, the question of 'ideas' comes up only between revolutionary comrades, not between husbands and wives. If you two are united, you will make a 'husband-sing-wife-accompany' sort of happy couple, and you will give birth to sons for the ancestors. Then you will be a model of the 'clever wife and wise mother.' You are not going with him to join the revolution. Why should you need the same ideas?"

"Father," I replied, "love after marriage is your philosophy, a strange symptom of the old society. Nowadays man and woman become husband and wife through different stages of emotion. First they know each other as friends and the affection of friends develops into true love. And when love reaches its highest peak, they unite and become companions for life. That is what marriage means. As to having the same ideas or beliefs, that is even more important. Two persons whose ideas differ could never be friends. How much more should this be true of marriage which should be the basis of happiness for a lifetime! If their ideas are different and each goes his own way, love will not last. Modern marriage differs entirely from that of older times. The purpose then was simply to make a happy family. Today when two persons are married, they don't strive only for selfish happiness. The chief thing is that they must work together for society. They are sincere friends and faithful comrades, as well as husband and wife. Hsiao-ming's ideas are utterly different from mine. The first fundamental for a marriage with me is lacking."

"Hunh!" my father exclaimed. "Idea? What need has a woman of such dangerous revolutionary ideas? Of course, you have had several years of education and you will be allowed to be a primary school teacher after marriage. I don't think he will object to that."

"Don't argue with her any more!" Mother burst out. "She is not even human! We are her parents. How dare she oppose us?" Turning to me, she went on, "When we sent you to school, we were hoping that you might learn social manners and a sense of honor. We did not expect you to turn out to be a beast. You don't even care for your parents! This engagement was made when you were still suckling at my breast. Are you so shameless as to break it and ruin your parents' name and disgrace your ancestors?"

She quoted an old verse: " 'A good husband and a good wife are predestined.' No matter what kind of person you are engaged to, you've got to marry him. Besides, the Hsiao family has a large property and a good name; Hsiao-ming is a good young man. He is not blind or crippled. You know it is said that 'a thread of romantic destiny can unite a husband and wife a thousand miles apart.' Marriage is something already settled in your previous incarnation. How can you oppose it?"

I listened without a word, without even a sneer, for I knew before she spoke all that she was going to say.

"I realize," said Father, "that in these times we cannot force you to 'follow a cock if you are married to the cock, and follow a dog if you are married to the dog.' But Hsiao-ming is a nice fellow; you can marry him in any case. Read his letter to your third brother. It is clearly written and well-worded." At this I almost laughed. As a matter of fact, Hsiao-ming could not write an ordinary, clear letter. I remembered that a certain teacher in the primary school had said, "What a difference there is between you and your fiancé! Your work in school is at the top, and his, I am afraid, is at the bottom." Later I had several letters from him, and his ability was really as the teacher had said. How could I be married to a man with such a simple and vacuous mind?

Mother was scolding again, saying that she had not thought I would disappoint her thus after sending me to school for so many years. She said she was not going to let any of the daughters of Elder Brother and Third Brother go to school anymore. I was worried for the children who were now in the fourth grade. After this, they would certainly never go to school again. Would it be my fault or that of society?

Absorbed thus in my own thoughts, I suddenly heard Father renew his curses. "What kind of witch house is the school! Every girl comes out of it bewitched and demands the breaking of the engagement her parents have settled! She has to break it, however good it is."

"Of course," I said. "How can parents know what kind of husband or wife their child should have? Marriage is a great part of life. Everyone has to choose for herself if marriage is to be successful."

I knew these words would provoke them more than ever, but if I did not say them, my head would burst!

"Outrageous! A young girl picking a husband for herself!" Mother cried. "The Hsiao family has high standing. Hsiao-ming's third uncle was once a member of the provincial assembly and very well known. The Hsiaos have all studied in the cities. And I have received so many presents from the family! Last year your fiancé even came to congratulate me on my birthday. Now you are creating this scandal. How can I ever face them? The proverb says, 'A good horse will never turn round to feed on past pasture; a good girl will never marry twice.' Do you remember the story in the *Book of Heroines*?"

Father interrupted. "Do you think she reads the *Book of Heroines* any more? She reads only new novels of free love, newspaper stories about how a girl committed suicide because she could not have freedom in marriage, and how a boy broke with his family because he hated the old conventions. She is affected by all this and is turning against her parents, against the conventions."

"The old conventions were set by the sages thousands of years ago." Mother's tone became more and more severe. "And you, a girl, dare to defy them! Don't you know how chastity monuments were built? Even girls of twelve know the importance of chastity. And I am afraid your group, who talk about freedom, won't pass a New Year's with a husband even if you marry twenty-four times a year!"

I realized that it was completely useless to argue with her. The only way was to fight it out, not to give in until I had broken the engagement.

She went on, "The Hsiaos own a lot of property and you can earn money too. You will set up a home and build a fortune. You will become rich with land and fields! You will have a very comfortable life!"

These words hurt me deeply; I considered them insulting. She belittled my sense of honor. Fundamentally she did not understand what kind of person her daughter was. She thought I feared poverty and worshiped wealth and was trying to tempt me.

"Don't talk of these things," I cried with visible annoyance. "I'd rather marry a poor man I love than a rich man!"

"What do you want then?" Mother banged on the table.

"She wants to break the engagement," Father answered for me.

"What will she do if she can't break it?"

"In her letter she said she would commit suicide!"

"All right! Let her do it! I have brought her up and sent her to school in vain. Perhaps I owed her a debt in the previous incarnation, and I am asked to repay it now!"

Mother burst into tears and struck her head against the wall.

Afraid that she might be hurt, Father went to her and held her, and my sister and sister-in-law went to her too, and while they were thus occupied, I slipped away and went outside to walk.

The sun was warm, but my heart was sad and cold.

I saw a man in a long white gown approaching and recognized him as my eldest brother. He asked me what I was doing out there alone, and I told him the whole melodrama that had just been enacted. He paused and knitted his eyebrows and said, "You ought not to have come home. Now that you are at home, I think . . ."

"What are you thinking?" I interrupted. "Do you want me to sacrifice myself and marry Hsiao-ming?"

"I—that's what I mean," he said slowly.

"No, I cannot; I will fight to the end!"

"Mother is worse than any despot in history," said Eldest Brother. "You remember how she made me kneel down for two hours with a basin of water on top of my head, when she blamed me for being disobedient to my parents and listening to my wife. And your second and third brothers and your sister have suffered very much in their marriages, yet no one has dared to mention divorce. You are stronger than all of us, but although you might fight outside, you cannot rebel at home." He smiled a little, but I was serious and said:

"Don't be sarcastic and don't think too little of me. To tell you the truth, I knew that I would be either shut up or forced into marriage. But if I don't break the engagement legally, I cannot marry anyone. The Hsiao family would always bring out the letter of engagement and create endless trouble. Because I don't want this future trouble and because I want to declare war formally against the old society, I have decided to fight it out."

Poor Elder Brother was looking around every minute, afraid to be seen talking to me. He said, "I am going now. If Mother should find out that we are talking here, she would think I am conspiring with you."

"All right, you go back. I don't want to get you or anybody else involved."

"I wish you success, fighting single-handed!" he said, and went away with a cynical smile.

I wandered back and forth through the fields for some time before I went home. I did not take any supper, for I was afraid to see the cold faces of my parents, and went to bed as soon as night fell.

My sister and sister-in-law came in to see me but they did not dare to talk much, or too loudly, for Mother could hear everything. They whispered in my ears not to be too downhearted. They still put too much oil on their hair, and the unbearable smell almost choked me. I thanked them but secretly wished they would not come to my room at all.

My mother's second sister was living in the old house. Her husband was a doorman, earning six dollars a month. Her two sons were in the army, the younger as a corporal, but the elder, a minor officer, had been discharged for disobeying orders and had completely disappeared. She had another son and a daughter, but they had both died in the last year. She was an absolute believer in fate; she believed that everything was predestined before birth. Even more superstitious than Mother, she prayed and said religious chants and ate only vegetables. Nevertheless, her ideas were not so conservative as Mother's. She had permitted her son to marry as he wished; her little girl who died at ten was not yet engaged. She often said to Mother, "The world has changed. You must not be too severe with your children. They can read and write, and want to accomplish something in this world. Don't control them too much."

Mother, on the other hand, rebuked my aunt for failing in her duties as a parent. "No matter how the world changes, parents are still parents. If you can't make your own children obey you, how can you control others?"

This aunt came to my room and sat for a long time before she said a word. Only when she heard Mother talking with a laborer did she whisper to me, "Mingkang, you had better yield a little; you know your mother has a temper. Marriage is predestined. Your husband is not so clever as you are, but you can come down a little to him. In the future they will say you were a good wife and your name will go down from generation to generation."

But I asked her only to leave me alone, saying, "None of you understands my difficulties."

That day I began my life as a prisoner.

13

My Escape from Hardship
to a Free Life

Hsiu-ying

THE NEXT four selections are taken from a large number of
autobiographical sketches published in *Fu-nü tsa-chih* (The ladies'
journal) 10, 6 (June 1924), which had been chosen from
manuscripts sent in by readers in response to a public solicitation
by the editors. Each of the four is translated in its entirety. Since the
editors did not supply any additional biographical facts, these few
pages are all we know about the authors, some of whom omitted
surnames or used pseudonyms and were not specific about where
they lived.

Hsiu-ying and Lu Lan vividly describe the misfortunes that
could occur to a young wife as a result of an arranged marriage.
Both seem to have come from families that, by village standards,
lived comfortably, and both suffered economic hardship as a result
of the irresponsible behavior of fathers and husbands. Lu Lan's
insistence that women must learn that not all males are dependable
is another way of saying that not all fathers or husbands lived up to
their Confucian responsibilities. Profoundly unhappy in their
husbands' families, both women derived psychological satisfaction
as well as financial rewards from getting and holding a job. Indeed,
they do not separate the two. It should be noted that both found
employment in the new industrial sector, in light industries, which
typically used cheap female labor. Yet they do not complain of
exploitation, but rather communicate their sense of pride in having
successfully acquired the skills necessary for their jobs and a sense
of dignity gained by earning their own living and becoming

independent enough to plan their own futures. Hsiu-ying's use of new terms, such as "authoritarian family system," "freedom," and "humanism," and the perspectives from which each analyzes her life, reveal how the new ideas of May Fourth Movement were spreading and creating new aspirations.

Courage is a theme in all of these autobiographies, and it is central to Fu I-hsing's chronicle of her transformation from a timid, passive young woman to a self-assured and energetic proselytizer of the new culture. Village schoolteacher was another new role women began to fill in large numbers in the 1920s and 1930s. Yet, although the content of the education and the sex of the educator are new, the intensity of dedication to education as a moral mission goes back at least as far as Confucius, as does the idea of being flexible to meet students' needs, and many parallels to Fu's commitment to social reform through education could be found in the biographies of model Confucian teachers and local officials in traditional times.

The fourth and last sketch in this group records the proud successes of young women entrepreneurs and managers. Perhaps the most remarkable element in Hung-ying's story is the note of subdued self-confidence, which helps add conviction to the message that women can handle any task once they put their minds to it. Though, as will be seen, discrimination against women in the business world was far more prevalent than Hung-ying's experiences might indicate, it is also imperative to keep in mind that many women did achieve success in various enterprises, especially, as in this case, on the local level.

How I Came to Go to Work

OVER a decade ago, my parents were reasonably well off, because of the inheritance my father got from his father. Every year we had more than enough grain to meet expenses, and in May and June, after all the surplus grain was sold, we had at least one or two hundred dollars left over. Sometime later, when my father thought about how much money we had and couldn't figure out any way to put it to use, he started to spend it on having a good time. There was only my elder brother and I. He had already graduated from upper-level elementary school, and I was just starting school myself, when suddenly he got a severe case of dysentery and before the week was out closed his eyes and, without bidding farewell to his family, left us forever. By this time my father had mastered the art of having a good time—gambling, prostitutes, and that kind of thing—and when my brother died he stepped it up something terrible, so that we began to fall into debt. My parents felt very bad about my brother's death. My mother couldn't eat a thing; she forgot about everything else and spent the whole day crying. My father, however, although he felt extremely bad about my brother, didn't forget any of the skills he had learned, and went out to have a good time every few days.

After my brother's death, I became more important in my parents' eyes, and they gave me all kinds of treats. By this time I was in second grade, and my teacher took notice of me, because my parents asked him to do his best with me. Another year passed, and things at home began to get more complicated. My father hadn't gotten rid of his itch—he was actually spending more time with the prostitutes—and our family prosperity was crumbling down. The signs of our former prosperity were all gone, and we were heavily in debt. Meanwhile, I was exceptionally quick to learn and making good progress in my studies, and my teacher was quite fond of me.

By this time I was twelve [*sui*], and my father began looking around for a husband for me, and engaged me to a young man named Chou whom I had never even met. Although I was still pretty young, I knew a thing or two, but I was afraid of making a fool of myself so I kept my ideas about marrying this unknown man to myself and didn't dare say a word about it to my father. So everything was settled. In the winter of my second year of upper-level elementary school, our family debts had piled up so much that we were put through the grinder. [This is a rural term; when a debtor pays back a percentage of what he owes his creditors to clear up his debts it's called putting him through the grinder.] We had almost nothing left after clearing up our debts, and that winter it was very dry. There was no rain for a really long time, so that everything dried up and there weren't vegetables to eat, even in the villages. Then, one evening one of our neighbor's children was careless and started a fire. Our house was very close by, and this disaster wiped us out. No use mentioning no warm clothes or food; we didn't even have a place to live. That was in December. The very next month my father married me off. I thought that I could help by lightening some of the burdens on my father at least a little, so the only thing to do was to go off to the Chou family.

Well, when I got to the Chous I found out that my husband had been married once before. But because she didn't get along with her mother-in-law—I heard that they quarreled a lot, that there was a shouting match between the two of them at least once a day—her mother-in-law eventually forced her to leave. She had gone straight to Ch'ang-sha and then to Yuan-ling, where she married another man.

The first year at my husband's was all right. I did whatever my mother-in-law told me to do. I never saw my father-in-law because my mother-in-law had kicked him out and wouldn't let him live at home. Later he went and got a job at the Ch'a-ling Iron Works, and the same year my husband went to Yi-yang to work. In 1918, about the time Chang Ching-yao* entered Hunan, my mother-in-law went to visit her family. There were only four of us in the family, but we were scattered all over. Later, my mother-in-law returned, and I lived with her for half a year or so. She had a really big mouth and was always talking about something or other, or cursing someone, or muttering about this or that all the time. Gradually she began to curse at me, and sometimes when I couldn't take it any more and answered her back, she'd say that she would tear out my mouth, and sometimes she beat

---

*Chang was a militarist of the Peiyang clique, who in March 1918 invaded Hunan under the orders of the Peking government.—ED.

me. I just had to put up with it. I don't know how many tears I cried all by myself, probably enough to fill a whole lot of grain baskets. At home I had never done any real heavy work, and I got married right after we went broke. At my husband's, every morning I had to go out to the hills to gather firewood for cooking and cut fodder for the hogs. Fortunately for me, I don't have bound feet, so I could do it. Even when it rained my mother-in-law sent me out to do these things. One year she went to spend New Year's with her daughter's family. She locked up the grain bin and told me not to open it, left just a few piculs of rice in the rice cupboard, and, without any further explanation, took off. When all the rice in the cupboard was done, I opened her lock, measured out a few pecks of rice grain, and milled it to prepare for New Year's. When she found out after she got back from New Year's she gave me a real beating. I thought about killing myself, but I couldn't bring myself to leave my father and mother so I didn't do it.

In 1919 my father made a little money in some business dealings, enough to meet family expenses. In July I heard my husband had gone to Ch'ang-sha from Yi-yang, so after talking it over with my father he lent me enough to go to Ch'ang-sha. On September 2 I packed everything I had and, without saying goodbye to my mother-in-law, took the boat to Ch'ang-sha. When my husband saw me, the first thing he said was, "What are you doing here? Did you come to make trouble, you good-for-nothing bag-of-bones?" Afterward, my husband and some others worked out a way for me to learn a job, and I went to learn how to weave foreign socks at Ma Heng Chi.

My Life at Work

When I started in the foreign sock plant, every day I sat in front of a machine. At first I messed up quite a few needles, which cost sixty cents a piece. I worked hard, but I could only do about five dozen a day. At a hundred cents a dozen, that came to five hundred cents, which left about three hundred after deductions for room and board. Afterward, when we got only seventy cents a dozen, there wasn't even that much left over. There were five women workers there. After a whole year of very hard work, I was able to save less than twenty silver dollars. Later, thanks to a recommendation from an influential man in a government office, I got a job as an apprentice at a company that manufactures cotton textiles, working in the reeling section. After just two months as an apprentice I was able to work by myself. As an apprentice, each day's wages went to the master, but after I left the master to work by myself, I received all my own wages. There are about five hundred to six hundred women and about two thousand men working in the factory, all from different counties in Hunan, except for a few from other provinces. We get Sundays off, but except for that we have to work days and nights. There are two shifts. The day shift lasts from 6:00 in the morning to 5:40 in the afternoon, but we can leave the factory at lunchtime, and we get about half an hour for rest breaks. On the night shift you work from about 6:00 in the evening to 5:00 the next morning, though there is more time for rest breaks on the night shift and everyone gets an extra eighty cents snack money. The day and night shifts rotate, so if you work the day shift this week, you have to work the night shift next week. There are foremen and supervisors, and you aren't allowed to ask the foreman for time off unless you are really sick. If you take too many days off, they let you go. Every man and woman has to wear the emblem of the workers' association to make it easier to get in and out of the factory. Nobody, no matter who, is permitted to smoke on the floor. The wages in the reeling section, the spinning section, the fly section, the cotton fluffing section, and so forth are based on the type of work you do. Subtracting for raw materials and deducting the salaries of workers and other employees, the factory makes about three thousand dollars for each day's production. Workers are paid in cash regularly twice a month, and every worker gets a dollar bonus at summer and winter vacation time. The women all work in the reeling and picking sections, and most live at the factory. The dormitory for women workers is especially strictly controlled, and we aren't allowed to have anything to do with the people who live nearby. There are eight of us in one room, all from the same local area. Most of us have some education and can get around all right.

When I work days, I set aside some time in the evening to read. The electric light in our room is on all night long. And when I work nights, I set aside some time in the daytime for reading, washing, and other things. Every Sunday I spend the whole day reading. My books all come from a younger male cousin on my mother's side. My life at work is truly happy— compared to all the humiliations and hardships I had at home, it's like I'm in some kind of a fairyland.

My Hopes for the Future

How is a woman like me, who has gone through all the things I have and who has had so many things go wrong, qualified to hope to become some kind of a human being? Nevertheless, I still want to go back to school. I've decided to take the entrance exam this summer vacation and to take a review course to brush up on the science I learned in elementary school. Maybe I'll go to a teachers college or a vocational school; the two hundred dollars I've saved up can go for tuition and expenses. I don't have any children to hold me back, so I'm free to move on, and later I should be able to attain economic independence. After graduating from teacher's college I might become a teacher or maybe study medicine. Of course this is only a fantasy of mine, and whether or not I'll be able to reach my goal it's hard to say. I'm one of the most unfortunate of women, but I have the willpower and I'm going to give it a try. For many thousands of years Chinese women weren't even thought of as human beings. They lived in submission, under the authoritarian family system without any freedom. Lots must have lived under conditions very similar to mine, so my own history can't be considered unusually pitiful. If a woman can obtain economic independence she can be a human being. And if you want to gain economic independence you have to have some kind of a job. If you have a productive job, then you can attain a position of economic independence, and you don't have to depend on a man and submit to the power of a man or the head of a family. You can get away from mistreatment forever and have a really enjoyable life like a human being. That's not only happiness for women, but also the realization of humanism.

14

Sorrows of a
Factory Worker

Lu Lan

I SUPPOSE you could call me a person who has suffered a lot. For several years now I've been living at my maternal aunt's, and I don't know how many times I've talked about my troubles to her and her daughter. But for all I've said over and over again, only the two of them have heard. I'm very grateful to them but, although they constantly comfort me, I still feel I haven't poured out everything. Sometimes I think that all the talk is of absolutely no use, and that all I can do is to endure my suffering alone, by myself.

My maternal aunt's husband feels sorry for me. Last year he got me a subscription to *Fu-nü tsa-chih*. "When you're feeling bad you can read it," he told me. Only after I began getting this magazine did I realize how many women suffer hardship, and that there is a way to pour out your troubles. So, I have often thought of writing something about my troubles and sending it to *Fu-nü tsa-chih*. If they published it, all the readers would know about my troubles; I would have poured out my heart, and I also think that it might very well be of some use to others, and afterward I would be able to stop annoying people.

One day my cousin came in with the latest issue in her hand and a big smile on her face. She opened it to page one and said, "It looks like you've got qualifications to submit a manuscript. Why not write about all the things you've told us about in the evenings and send it to *Fu-nü tsa-chih*?" My heart beat faster as I looked it over carefully. For several days, awake and asleep, I thought about my plan of writing this manuscript and wondered whether or not this would be right for the essay topic being solicited. I don't know how many times I thought it over in my mind, but tonight I finally got enough courage to write it all down. I know that I haven't always kept to the subject, but I just can't leave out things that have been on my mind, so I want to inform the editors beforehand that not every sentence sticks to the theme.

At the age of eight *sui*, I began my education under a tutor at my maternal uncle's house. At fourteen, I had to put aside all the books that I had laboriously studied for six years, because my mother wanted me to learn sewing under her. Luckily, I still know 70–80 percent of the words I learned, and I still remember the rudiments our teacher taught me and my younger male cousin. Ever since coming to my aunt's, every afternoon after 5:00 when my cousin comes home from her school and I've come home from work, she goes over her lessons and I study along with her. The only subject I really like is Chinese literature. It's been three years since my reunion with the books that I had parted with for eight years. As for my technical skills, they are about average. From the time I got married until my husband died, I didn't have one day's peace. Following my aunt's advice, I went to the Prosperity Hosiery Factory to learn how to knit socks, which for the first time gave me a gleam of hope. That about covers my early life and career.

I am employed as a female worker at the Prosperity Hosiery Factory, which is at Ch'ing-chiang-p'u [near Shanghai]. There was no pay for the first three months, which was a training period, but after that was over I began to receive wages. At first I couldn't knit more than a half dozen a day, but gradually the number increased so that by the time I had been working for eight or nine months I could do a dozen a day, about the average for workers in the factory. The rate paid for each pair of socks is three and a half cents, or forty-two cents per dozen. If you calculate on the basis of a dozen every day, you can earn twelve dollars and sixty cents a month, which is roughly what my monthly income amounts to. Living at my aunt's, I don't have any rent to pay. The only monthly expenses I have, besides the four dollars I contribute toward food, are for clothing and various minor things for my child and myself, about four dollars in an average month. So, if I don't miss any days, I can save about three dollars a month.

Since at the factory you're paid for what you get done, and the factory allows a great deal of freedom, workers' work time differs as much as two to three hours a day. I work seven or eight hours a day. I've been there for over three years, and, except for times when I or my child have been ill, I have in the main kept to this schedule. After a while it becomes a habit. I have only one child, and I have my maternal aunt to take care of things, so there is little interference with my work schedule, which makes me a little better off than most of the twelve other workers.

I haven't learned very much, you could almost say nothing at all, since starting work. But from my training period to the present, I feel I've gradually become more proficient and deft. I do believe that, as the common saying goes, "familiarity makes for skill."

I am a woman who has been saved from a living death! I feel that, compared with the past, when I had no life at all, the fact that I am alive today is a source of considerable happiness, so that I don't have any particular feelings or aspirations about my occupation. I'm not very strong physically, so I can't work much more than seven or eight hours a day. But I do hope I'll be able to stay at this job long enough to save up four hundred to five hundred dollars so that my child can go to school and leave me. Then I could leave my maternal aunt. They say the wages at the Kiangnan Hosiery Factory are better than here, enough to pay for food and lodging. I would like to move there.

Now that I've gotten this far, I can't restrain myself from pouring out my sorrows. It's been over three years since I came with my child to my aunt's. Besides her, I have no one else to rely on for help. My parents had only me and my younger sister,

but she died years ago, and I was the only one surviving. My
father earned a living by tutoring. He died a year before I married. After the funeral, mother and I had nothing left. We depended entirely on sewing and embroidery to get by, and it was
difficult to make ends meet. My wedding expenses were entirely
paid by my aunt. My marriage had been arranged when I was
very young. At the time, he was only nine years old and was said
to be a very bright young boy. He was an only child, and although his parents weren't particularly well off, with such a
small family it looked like the future would be reasonably comfortable, so my parents settled my future when I was only seven
years old. When he was fifteen, I began to hear unpleasant things
about him, and there were more and more as time passed. My
mother and I would sit facing each other under the lamplight and
cry. Sometimes we would try to comfort each other, but we could
never set our minds at ease. By the time he was twenty, his
parents realized they couldn't handle him and got the idea that
marriage was the only way left to control him, as if women have
some great ability and can manage to discipline a son the parents
haven't been able to. They didn't give the slightest thought to
ruining an innocent person's life. My mother couldn't think of
anything to do, so she let the marriage take place. From the
moment I entered his house, every single thing I had heard about
him took place right before my eyes, and I also saw some things I
had never heard about. But he was my husband, and I don't want
to wash dirty laundry in public. Let me just say that in our three
years of married life, I never saw him do one decent thing or earn
a single cent. All I saw was him asking his parents for more
money, and people coming to collect debts at the end of the year.
Sometimes he even took clothes and jewelry from my dowry, so
you can tell what kind of a person he was. My only instinct was
to cry; I had no way to keep him under control. And not only was
he nasty to me all this time, but my father-in-law and mother-in-
law would reproach me as if they had every reason in the world
to complain. When he saw that I didn't have anything left for him
to squander, and my parents-in-law saw that I couldn't discipline

their son, they all began to feel I was an extra mouth, and that it would be better to do without me. Perhaps if they no longer had a good-for-nothing like myself they could find someone worth something to them. So I was like an affliction. His parents didn't pay any attention to his bad points, but I had to put up with this jail-like existence because I had to eat and didn't have parents to help—my mother had moved to her sister's after I got married—and to go work as a servant would just have been too humiliating.

In the spring of the third year of my marriage, my mother-in-law died, and that autumn my father-in-law died. My husband inherited some land, a little over fifty *mou*. At that time there were only the two of us. If he had had a change of heart and we had been thrifty, we would have had no difficulty getting by. But unexpectedly, just a few days after my father-in-law's death, his "bell debts" were all disclosed one after another. [A "bell debt" is an agreement between a debtor and his creditors whereby when the debtor's parents die, the creditors, hearing the bell announcing the death, come to take the inheritance for the debts.] They came to more than a thousand dollars. The creditors all came to the house—they ate, they drank, and they argued all day long. My mother asked her sister's husband to come to discuss things with my husband. He said that in a few days he would be able to explain everything. But unexpectedly, a few days later I heard that he had sold all the land for something over fifteen hundred dollars. After paying off his debts, there was only three hundred or four hundred dollars left. My mother tried to talk to him several times. All she asked was for him to give me two hundred dollars to live on. He not only refused to acknowledge anything but said a lot of senseless things. My mother wasn't very well to begin with, and after all this strain she died less than six months later at my aunt's.

I figured there was only one road left for me to take—to follow my mother! I thought about suicide a number of times, but I've always been weakhearted, and I just didn't have what it takes to do it. Also my maternal aunt kept comforting me, "As long as I'm around, you'll have nothing to worry about," so I stopped thinking about suicide. However, she didn't want to take me home to live, because she didn't want to break up the marriage, and I didn't want to be dependent on others. After my mother-in-law and father-in-law died, I had a hard time getting enough to eat, while he was a lot looser than he had been in the past. He left early in the morning and didn't return until night-time, often with the smell of alcohol on his breath. Within three months everything was gone. Naturally, no one paid any attention to him when he tried to borrow money. But he still didn't repent. One day he would sell one thing, and the next he would pawn something else. In addition to things in my room, whenever he found something he could exchange, he would immediately start to negotiate with me about it. But his dissipation had gone too far, and he grew weaker and weaker with each passing day. By the time everything had been pawned or sold and there was nothing left, he was so sick he couldn't get out of bed. I worked as hard as I could for him, I pawned everything I had for him, I prepared meals and medicine for him, hoping that once he recovered he would remember all the things I did for him and would change his ways. But unexpectedly, after three months of untold hardship, he passed away. From the time we married to his death was only a little over three years. I went through all kinds of misery, and the only thing I have to comfort me is this little tot. The child was born three months after my husband died. A month after I gave birth, my maternal aunt asked me to come live with her and, knowing that I didn't want to be dependent on others, encouraged me to go to the Prosperity Hosiery Factory to learn how to knit socks. She told me that once I had learned I could contribute four dollars a month from my pay to help pay for food. I've been living at her home for over three years now. She often tells me that she puts the money I give her for food into savings for my child's education. Though I would rather she didn't do this, I am very grateful for her kindness.

I haven't said all there is to say about what happened in my family, but I have poured out my troubles and told quite a bit about my past. I hope my women readers will realize that not all men are dependable. If you have no special aptitude so that you can earn your own living, and you should get married to an undependable man, even if you don't die of starvation or frustration, what kind of life is it if you're always feeling sad and bitter? If I had learned some craft before getting married, afterward would I have had to put up with so much misery and hardship? When he died, leaving us completely destitute, if I hadn't learned a skill right away, but just sat at home depending on a little sewing and embroidery, that wouldn't have been enough to live on, much less to take care of raising and educating my child. It's true that I had relatives I could count on, but to be entirely dependent on others gives you a bad feeling. Well, now I have described a lot about my family situation. My women readers, if you can sympathize with me for my sufferings, you will see that having an occupation is an absolute necessity, that you can't put off preparing for. My women readers, if because you feel sorry for me and wake up and think of yourselves, and make up your minds to learn an occupation, then my pouring out my sadness can be said to have been of some use to others. Well, now I have poured out all the sorrows in my heart, and from now on there'll be no need for me to mention a word to anyone ever again.

15

A Village Schoolteacher

Fu I-hsing

IT IS unfortunate to be born a woman, and more unfortunate to be born a Chinese woman. For several thousand years we've been secluded within the family, fettered by Confucianism (*li-chiao*). When we were young, we were daughters; when we grew up, wives; and when we got old, mothers. These three stages are all natural duties we ought to have, but all are a kind of parasitical existence, with no truly human life to speak of. If you look for the root cause, it is that women are not economically independent. And our only road to economic independence is getting jobs. If we want to gain a human existence, we must work to seek our economic independence.

I am a woman with a secondary education, and also a person who has been oppressed under the double standard. Many times I thought of leaving my jail-like existence, but I didn't dare because it would have been impossible for me to live independently. But later, with the help of a recommendation from a school friend, I did enter a school with a half-work, half-study program. However, in this kind of arrangement it isn't really possible both to work and to study. My wages at this school weren't even enough to cover my living expenses. Half-work and half-study is just too far-fetched an idea. With a lot of effort, I managed to work and study for a year, and later, through the recommendation of a fellow student, I came here to take a position in the local elementary school. Let me tell my sisters what has happened since I started this job.

This school is located in a remote rural area, not only cut off from the city, but six or seven *li* [about two miles] from the local market town. When the school first opened its doors, it was completely free—no tuition, book charges, or other fees—and therefore the number of students steadily increased. About 95 percent of the students come from peasant households, and, although they understand the importance of going to school, nevertheless, in terms of immediate material benefits, it can't compare in practical importance with gathering firewood, reaping the rice, shepherding, and so forth. So, frequently about half the students skip school. Fortunately, there are no fees, otherwise the number of students would certainly not get better.

Last autumn when I arrived here to take up my duties, I carefully observed local conditions and looked into the number of children of elementary school age. I felt that under this kind of economic organization, it would be impossible for all the children to come to school every day. And it's also impractical to ask children to find time from their busy schedules to appreciate juvenile literature. So the standard kind of rural school regulations—"first semester," "second semester," "junior high," "senior high"—just can't be applied in an inflexible way. What's important is to have the children come to study when they have spare time. That's enough—we shouldn't bother about a fixed schedule. Accordingly, I divided the students into two groups. Those who only occasionally miss classes have a curriculum about the same as ordinary elementary schools, while those who regularly miss classes have a reduced curriculum and, in addition, specially prepared educational materials that emphasize practical everyday reading and writing. During the months when agricultural work is slack, after the autumn harvest and before spring planting, the daily hours of instruction are extended. After doing this for about half a year, I feel the results show significant improvement. The peasants didn't use to give this school much credit, but now I have gained the trust of some.

Now, let me say a few words about education, and then about society.

Education. It takes a lot of effort for one person to manage a school. You have to get up about 7:30 in the morning, and, after taking care of various little things, you begin classes about 9:00 and go straight through till noon before you get any rest. From two to four in the afternoon you go without a break, like a puppet on a string. All this lecturing and demonstrating takes a lot of physical effort, though psychologically it's really very enjoyable.

Society. "To the People!" Down to the dark villages, far from the centers of civilization, deep into the rustic countryside of our ancestral land. When we go to the people, educate their children, raise their youngsters, take care of their aged and infirm, and pay attention to their endeavors, we must speak in a gentle voice and be amiable and sincere. If we thus arouse the masses and awaken the Chinese people from their slumber, China will be saved!

In addition to educating children, in my spare time I have been doing the following two things.

1. Eradicating superstition and inculcating scientific knowledge. Although China has no religion like the Christianity of Europe and America, superstitious belief in gods and Buddhas exists all over South China. Just think of what a huge obstacle to the peasants these preposterous superstitions are! After class and during vacations, I frequently visit students' homes to chat, and I take advantage of the opportunity to tell their families about simple, easy to understand scientific knowledge. Although for the moment it's no easy matter to shake their beliefs in deeply rooted superstitions, I think it has had some effect.

2. Reforming customs and spreading the new thought. Rotten customs, blind, unreasonable habits, and Confucianism, which eats people, are all thriving and spreading. In Shanghai and Kiangsu, I had never heard of the custom of "wife grabbing" and so never expected it would be so common here. Last winter it happened twice in neighboring villages. In one family, the daughter ultimately cut her own throat. Later, the groom's side spent several tens of yuan to settle the matter. Such customs that kill people are genuinely alarming, especially since we women bear the brunt. So I have exerted myself to expose and destroy the darkness these people live in and to destroy its hiding places.

I propagate the new thought to build new customs and new habits, and I show them the bright promises that lie ahead and the road to the future.

At present, I'm working hard at my rural movement. So far the results have been meager, but if in the future I have better results I shall once again report the facts to the readers.

16

Scientific Entrepreneurship

Hung-ying

THE SOUND waves from the cries of "women's liberation" are almost enough to break the eardrums. However, since we have attained liberation, how should we go about putting this word into practice? It would be painfully distressing if, several thousand years of continued ironclad moral teachings for women having been overthrown, we would behave like birds who have escaped from their cages or horses without bridles, unable to avoid impulsive feelings and misunderstanding the true meaning of liberation. This would give the opponents of reform a good excuse. Liberation means demanding equal treatment with men, and so obviously genuine liberation means thoroughly fulfilling obligations the same as men. Men have occupations, and so women should also have occupations. At present, not many occupations have been opened up to us women; with the exception of a handful of jobs women are forced to take to avoid cold and hunger—in textile mills, sock factories, silk mills, and so forth. Among the educated class, women can get a foothold only in hospitals, schools, and a small number of banks.

When I graduated from high school, friends urged me to go on to normal school. But because I felt that the dull and lonely life of a schoolteacher didn't suit my personality, I took the entrance examination for a sericulture school and passed. At that time I had already set myself the goal of managing my own business. Little did I know that after graduating I would feel bewildered because I couldn't find a job anywhere due to lack of experience and ability. Under the sponsorship of my alma mater, graduates were sent to a silk mill for training. I had no place to go, so I went along and enrolled at the mill. Having been a student, suddenly to have to put in long hours of labor naturally made me feel I was putting up with a lot of physical and mental hardship. But the others who had come to the mill frequently encouraged one another with the common saying, "Only by bearing the hardest of hardships can you rise above others." After a while, it became natural when I got used to it. When we left the mill the silkworm season had just begun, and with the help of an introduction from my alma mater I got a temporary job as a supervisor in charge of silkworm cultivation in a silk mill. After that job ended, I returned to the school as an assistant in silkworm studies for more than two years. Although I can't say that I became experienced, at least I felt slightly improved from when I graduated. So, last spring, my friend Ch'iu-lien and my father's sister P'ei-ch'iu (both silkworm school graduates) and I got together and organized our own silkworm business in the Nan-yuan District of Su-chou. It hasn't been easy getting to where I am today, but if you put forth effort you get results. The earnings are meager, but it's very enjoyable work. Now, let me say a few words about my current occupation, experience, and circumstances.

Preparations for Managing a Business

In the autumn of 1922 we purchased an old-style house, added windows along the ceiling for ventilation, and had wooden flooring installed throughout the silkworm rooms so that the floor would be elevated and dry. But no matter how painstakingly you build things up, you're never completely satisfied. We also installed implements for silkworm cultivation and other miscellaneous items. We had already made arrangements for the rest—workers, mulberry leaves, etc.—the previous year. And before setting up the business, we had also decided how to divide the tasks among the three of us.

The Situation Last Year

At the present time, when education is not yet universal, many people say, "What's the use of going to some school to learn how to raise silkworms? It all depends on the blessing and protection of Heaven." This kind of talk is ridiculous. Our silkworm business is close to Nan-yuan. Although it is within the city limits, it's in a splendid rural landscape, right next to farmland, with mulberry and hemp trees growing all around. The local people are all in farming. When we are raising the silkworms, we let them come and see, and tell them, "We don't avoid verbal or personal taboos in raising the silkworms." (The country people are full of superstitions and, at this time of year, aren't supposed to utter any unlucky words or let strangers in to see.) "Please watch whatever you want. If there's anything you would like to adopt for yourselves, please do so, and if there's something you don't understand, please don't hesitate to ask us." When it was time to pick the cocoons and they saw how big and fat our cocoons were, they were full of praise: "The foreign way of cultivating silkworms is after all very different." (The country people are stuck in their local way of raising silkworms. From what they said, it sounded like they hadn't believed that our methods would work, but when they saw the big, fat cocoons they gradually became convinced.) At that time I told them, "Our techniques for cultivating silkworms are different from yours in a lot of ways. The silkworm rooms must be kept neat and clean, and the right temperature must be maintained so that they are kept at a consistent warmth and grow uniformly. All the eggs produced by each mother moth have to be kept in separate lead enclosures, and each enclosure designated by a number on a label. After each mother moth has been examined under a microscope, all the eggs of any diseased mother moth must be discarded. That way, the silkworms next year will all be unadulterated and of excellent quality. In addition, the rooms and the implements must be decontaminated the following year before using them again. There are several methods of decontamination, such as a lime mixture, hot steam, and liquid disinfectants. Anyway, you should destroy any germs from the previous year or germs that have been brought in adhering to something, so that they won't infect the current year's silkworms. Decontamination is what you have neglected most." I told them a great number of things, which they were able to understand. While it is impossible to make them apply scientific methods in silkworm raising, we hope to enable them to see the benefits of improving silkworms.

Although we hired several people for the silkworm raising season, during the busy period we always worked along with them. Afterward, however, we all were worn out and listless. So, if you're cultivating silkworms on a large scale, those in charge should only supervise; otherwise, they'll work too hard and are bound to overlook some things, and the losses will outweigh the gains.

Expenditures and Revenues

Because we want to augment our joint capital each year, we don't have fixed expenditures and revenues. At the outset we spent about 1,500 yuan. This year, we acquired several new things. In addition, because the house is low-lying, damp, and small, and not really suitable for raising silkworms, we have been thinking that in the next six months we should reconstruct the silkworm rooms. We want to have more complete equipment, so we'll have to increase our capital investment. After we have purchased and installed all the equipment we need for raising the silkworms, each future year's labor costs, mulberry leaf costs, and other expenditures such as silkworm paper, moth bags, charcoal, firewood, and pesticides will be fairly low. When we first began the operation, we felt that it was very difficult not only in economic terms but also because of our inexperience. But the second year was easier than the first; last year our silkworms weighed three *liang* (silkworms are weighed right after they hatch). Due to problems in marketing our silkworms, we produced only slightly over a thousand sheets of eggs. The remaining cocoons, altogether approximately three and one-half piculs, we sold to cocoon shops, and we got a good price because the quality was rather high. After the silkworm season, in our spare time, we made silk floss from the empty cocoons, but because we didn't have much, it was quickly sold out. For beginners in managing a business, we can't say we were dissatisfied with last year's results.

After the Silkworm Season

Because the three of us are partners in the silkworm business, we form a small household. We also have two young sisters—one motherless orphan, and the other an adopted daughter who was abused. We took the two of them in to support them. In addition, we hired someone to prepare meals and also to cultivate the mulberries (last winter we leased a ten *mou* plot of mulberry land). In the mornings, after we help the two girls get ready for school, we work on the silk floss. In our leisure time, we go home to visit relatives, or go for a walk in the mulberry land. When the girls return home from school, we go over their lessons with them, tell them stories, and sometimes take them down to the river to fish under the shade of the willows along the bank. If we happen to catch a small fish or two, we carry them back home and feed them to the cat. The girls are so delighted they jump and dance around and play on their harmonica, though they can't make a tune. So our lives are very free and happy.

The thing that pleases me most about our business is that we benefit others as well as ourselves. When you look around the country at present, quite a few places are using improved methods of silkworm cultivation. If every household that raises silkworms can be converted to using improved silkworms, and they get rid of their local superstitions and take the enlightened path, sericulture will prosper, and that will be the dawn of a bright future for the Chinese silkworm industry. So I hope that my sisters in the silkworm business will not shrink from the task for fear of the difficulties or because the earnings are meager, or achievements are remote. So long as we are willing to make an honest effort, remembering that it's difficult at first but a lot easier later, we are bound to grow and expand. There's no need to worry that we women can't do anything. Don't we also have the responsibility to develop industry and commerce? My sisters! No matter what our occupation is, we must strive to do our best. If we want to have equal status with men, shouldn't we also fulfill our obligations?

17

Struggling Against Discrimination in Business

Anonymous

THE FOLLOWING three accounts of women's experiences at work have been selected from a group of seven that appeared in the second issue of 1935 of *Fu-nü sheng-huo* (Women's life), a leading women's magazine in the 1930s. All were written down by one of the editors at a meeting with the seven women held in Shanghai in early 1935.

The editor describes Ms. A as youthful-looking and energetic. The main theme of her tale emerges quite clearly from her businesslike description of her experience: entrepreneurial energy hampered by the prejudices of male businessmen. Ms. E, a clerk in a department store, described as seventeen or eighteen years old, straightforward and frank, reports other forms of prejudice that she encountered from customers and male fellow employees. Being the butt of unpleasant jokes by customers and male colleagues was a frequent complaint. Women found the charge of being a "flower vase" (meaning a woman hired for her good looks who does little or no work) particularly annoying, since the image ran counter to a major goal of women, the self-esteem earned by doing a good job and contributing one's fair share. Ms. F's story has similar themes—sexist attitudes in the bank where she worked and the sense of injustice that ability and enterprising spirit would not be rewarded with salaries or promotions equal to those of male colleagues. She gives no indication of discrimination either in hiring or in the lowest stages of a banking career.

What these sketches from the 1930s show is that new problems accompanied new opportunities. Some of these problems were the manifestations of old prejudices, but Ms. B, another of the seven women interviewed, was surely right when she attributed the accusations of being a "flower vase" to deep resentment and a desire to squeeze women out of their jobs.

Ms. A: IN 1929 I broke up with my husband and escaped with my four daughters (the eldest was then fourteen and the youngest seven) to Shanghai. My spouse not only didn't give the five of us one single cent of support, but on the contrary did his utmost to spread rumors everywhere he could, trying to make our lives impossible. Under these circumstances, I resolved to fight to the end in order to earn a living as well as to provide for my daughters' education and their future, and to find a way out for myself, and thus I made it by struggling my utmost. Since I had some business experience in the family, friends urged me to try my hand at business. So I made plans to operate a factory manufacturing spindles of cotton. The capitalization was twenty-eight thousand yuan, of which over ten thousand I was to raise in the Southeast Asia, and the rest was to come from friends buying shares in the company. Now let me tell you a little about what happened when I went to Southeast Asia to raise the capital.

All I had were a few letters of introduction from some friends, but filled with hope I went to Southeast Asia. However, while overseas Chinese businessmen there found it amusing to hear that a woman wanted to run a business, they were very skeptical. In the end, a few finally purchased some stock, out of consideration for their connections with the writers of the letters of recommendation. But in their hearts they thought of me as a not altogether honest woman with shady ambitions. To my face they were pleasant and encouraging and praised me in the highest terms; but behind my back they said all kinds of things, calling me a swindler and a scoundrel and spreading harmful and untrue stories about me, such as that I had had [sexual] relations with this man or that.

After I returned to China, amid a lot of talk I succeeded in getting the factory started, and the business got underway. There were no problems at all with manufacturing or making purchases; the difficulty was in marketing and sales. In marketing and sales, if you get someone who turns out to be undependable, this can easily give rise to abuses and malpractices, resulting in losses to the factory. For this reason, at first I took personal charge of marketing and sales.

I soon discovered another difficulty I had never thought of. Whenever I went to some factory or business office, while I was in the reception room requesting to see the manager, all the office workers looked at me as though I were some sort of weird creature. They stood around in small groups viewing me suspiciously and making surreptitious comments. When I did get to see the manager, not one ever treated me in a businesslike fashion. They were unstinting—in their lack of trust, in their disrespect, and even in their insults. That kind of attitude, along with unusual actual difficulties, made it clear to me that if I wanted marketing and sales to go smoothly, I would have to give the other party some extra favors, i.e., a little sex. So that was it; I had to hire a male employee to take care of marketing and sales, while I spent all my time taking care of things within the factory.

I feel that you could call our factory the best and largest model of its kind, but, alas, the January 28 incident soon occurred, and we were completely wiped out.* But I think that, even without the January 28 incident, it would have been difficult for me to last much longer, for the following three reasons:

1. The factory equipment, wages, and working conditions were all above average, and hence our expenses were especially high.

---

*On January 28, 1932, the Japanese landed seventy thousand troops in Shanghai to bring a halt to the Chinese boycott of Japanese goods that had begun in reaction to the Japanese occupation of Manchuria the previous year. There was considerable fighting and much destruction of property. In May, an agreement ended the boycott.

2. Since I was rejected, even insulted, by society, marketing and sales were completely in the hands of someone else, and accordingly the factory suffered large direct and indirect losses.

3. This is the most important factor. Women's standing in society is very low. Capital expansion was extremely difficult, and the financial community was particularly unwilling to give us credit or any kind of financial assistance, which made problems in our cash flow, on top of the general slump in the market and the lack of opportunities for Chinese industries.*

Ms. E: I worked for over a year at a store that sold only goods made in China. The store was only a temporary arrangement, organized by joining several shops and companies, so each section had its own boss and different salaries. Later, when the store went out of business, I went to the department store where I work now. The procedure to get a job at this store is that you have a recommendation and there are some simple tests—an oral examination and tests on writing and arithmetic.

I work from 9:00 A.M. to 8:30 P.M., and my salary is nineteen yuan a month. (The starting salary was eighteen yuan, but this year it was raised one yuan.) They provide for meals but not lodging. If you're late for work or leave before quitting time, a deduction is made from your salary according to the amount of time lost. Every half-month, however, we can leave early for a total of six hours. Sometimes some of the men employees offer to give me a break and let me leave a little early. But I don't do it. Why should I let anyone say I'm a "flower vase"? Although I'm not tall, I always get things from the top shelves myself and never ask any of the men for help. In every respect I want to show that we women can handle things ourselves, that we weren't hired just to be "flower vases."

We women clerks have a lot of problems with customers.

---

*Chinese-owned and operated enterprises were at a disadvantage in competing with foreign enterprises, which benefited from privileges granted under extraterritoriality provisions of the "unequal treaties" that China had been forced to sign with the powers since the Opium War.

Most well-off married women and young ladies look down on us and don't even give us a passing glance, as though we were some kind of vile thing beneath their dignity. It's very difficult to deal with this kind of haughty arrogance. Then there are those rich playboys and troublemakers who spend their time making fun of female clerks. They're even more difficult to handle. They pretend to be buying something just to have an excuse to make fun of you. If you don't know how to cope with them, they can give you a real hard time. They write letters to the manager, and they make up all kinds of stories about you and false accusations against you.

But I really do like the people who are like us—average people, men and women—they chat with you while they're buying something, and they say things like "I'm putting you to a lot of trouble," or "You're very polite." That makes me feel good. It's true, I have quite a few friendly customers, men and women, who always buy from me whenever they come to the store.

Among the women employees, there are some good ones and some bad ones. For example, some really do come to be "flower vases." Every day they dress up like goddesses and just sit there acting like they are really something. When a customer comes in, they don't pay any attention at all. And when there's anything to do, they're only too eager to get someone to help them or to do it for them. It's no wonder people call them "flower vases," and they ruin the reputations of the rest of us. In some cases that's just the way they are, but some actually aren't there to work for a living but took the job so they could behave that way to attract attention, or because they have something else in mind. In our dealings with the men employees we have to watch our step, too. You can't get too familiar with any of them, because if you do, the rest will immediately spread all kinds of rumors; but you can't be too aloof either, because then they'll give you a hard time.

The raises we women clerks get are very much connected with the kind of patronage we have. When "Miss Glamour Girl" first came, she got the same salary as the rest of us, eighteen yuan.

Now she makes thirty yuan. When you've made a name for yourself, the store is afraid some other place will draw you away by offering you a lot of money, so they give you a raise right away to hold onto you. On occasion, people have asked for my photograph to publish in the newspaper to help me publicize myself. But I won't do that kind of thing. I know that the higher you climb the harder you fall, and that it would do me no good and a lot of harm.

As for marriage, I'm not fond of the idea. To have to depend on a man for your daily existence, what kind of life is that? I'm an independent person.

Ms. F: Most people believe that women who work for the post office, or customs, or a bank, have it pretty easy. From my own experience, although you make pretty good money in these places and your life is more or less stable and comfortable, all too frequently when your life gets too comfortable you wind up no longer seeking to improve yourself.

To get this job, you have to pass a test. But, like the customs service, the bank doesn't solicit applications publicly. You have to be recommended by someone at the bank or by an intermediary, and, when you take the exam, you have to have a guarantor. They solicit for two kinds of job grade, trainees and assistants-in-training. The qualifications are that a trainee must have graduated from junior high school, and assistants-in-training must have graduated from senior high school. But, although this is the rule, college graduates and students who have studied in the West or Japan also take the exam.

As far as salary goes, trainees get between ten and twelve yuan a month and assistants-in-training get sixteen to eighteen yuan, with raises up to thirty yuan. You're not considered a regular employee of the bank until your salary reaches forty yuan. Work hours are 9:00 to 12:00 in the morning and 1:00 to 4:00 in the afternoon, but we can't leave until 5:00 because between 4:00 and 5:00 we have paperwork to take care of. The bank gives us an allowance for food, lodging, and transportation, and a bonus at the end of the year, to a certain percentage of your annual salary. If you regularly do a good job and don't take time off, the bank also gives you an additional reward, which can amount to four months' salary and is at least one month's salary. They don't give you this in cash; they only give you a savings book with the money in a ten-year long-term deposit in the bank.

We get a month's vacation a year; women who give birth get one month for maternity leave plus an additional twenty days of regular vacation.

Among the women employees, some are very conscientious, but some spend all their time making connections and scheming. When there's something they don't feel like doing, they use little tricks, like playing the spoiled young lady, to get a male colleague to handle it for them. The end result is that most of the latter kind get away with quite a bit, while the former, who bury their heads in their work and work hard, don't get very much for it.

When we first began working at the bank, men and women both had to take the test and got the same salaries, as if everyone was equal. Afterward, however, it's easy for the male employees to get promotions, and it's possible for them to become directors or vice-presidents of the bank. But we women? The best we can hope for is a salary of thirty or forty yuan a month; there's nothing beyond that. The explanation that the directors give is, "What use would you women have for such a high salary?"

18

Shen-shen

Hsiang-ts'un

FOR SOME, the disjunction between the new ideals and current
realities was a challenge, a stimulus to pursue a career or
participate in political activities. For others, it could be
traumatic, crushing, and destructive. The next two women are
representative of many who were unable to cope with the world
around them. The unnamed young woman in the first account,
which appeared in *Chia* (Family), Shanghai, no. 21 (October
1947), pp. 372–73, had the opportunity for self-development
provided by the new higher education, and she seems to have
flourished while she was away from home at a local university.
Her marriage to a mediocre young man, arranged by her father to
maintain a tradition of family connections (a not uncommon
occurrence), brought an abrupt end to what must have seemed a
bright new life. The young woman's rapid descent into a state of
dejection and torpor, told with sympathy by a relative of her
husband, provides the background for understanding her short
letter to her father, the spiritual autobiography of a young
woman whose life was shattered not by cruelty or poverty but
because her dreams were so out of joint with ordinary life.
Although few women went to the extreme of leaving society and
becoming a Buddhist nun, many suffered a similar agony due to
the disparity between the new ideal of marriage for love and the
realities of arranged marriage. This topic was a frequent theme in
the writings, fictional and nonfictional, in the years following the
May Fourth period. The author's pseudonym in this piece
translates as "Village," and the title is the term for the wife of
one's father's younger brother.

DURING the four or five months Shen-shen was married into our family she never ever showed the slightest trace of a smile. Her face was dark and expressionless, as if it had been dusted over by a heavy frost. And, although none of us ever saw her cry, from observing the rings around her eyes sink deeper and deeper, we all could tell of her silent grief.

Shen-shen never did any knitting or sewing, nor did she attend to any household chores. She kept apart from all of us and never had anything much to say to anyone. If she wasn't sleeping, she was reading, day in and day out. So, none of us ever developed a friendly feeling toward her. When she wasn't around, Grandmother frequently complained about her in all sorts of ways. "Taking a fine hussy like this into the family is eighteen generations of bad luck," she would say. Sometimes, when my fifth aunt would try to make trouble because she was envious of Shenshen just sitting there reading without doing any work, Grandmother would give a cold smile and say, "Well, who are you to compare yourself with her—she is a young lady scholar."

In some ways my uncle really did love Shen-shen, but he wasn't very pleased with her attitude. However, he was afraid of her, terribly afraid. She never paid much attention to anything he said, so naturally he didn't dare utter one word of reproof. For this Grandmother frequently bawled him out, "A really stupid ass—completely useless—can't even control his wife." My uncle would just stand there with a sad smile on his face, not uttering a word in reply. Sometimes, when she scolded him too strongly, he would be so hurt that he would start to cry, just like a child.

It was said that before her marriage, Shen-shen was an exceptionally bright and clever, and very lively, young woman. So, after the engagement, my uncle went around beaming smiles from being congratulated for getting such an excellent wife. Only after they were married did this pleasure begin to be qualified. Of course, in her looks and her education, there was nothing to make Uncle displeased; but Shen-shen's personality and attitude shattered his fond dreams.

There's an old saying in the countryside—"There're eighteen ways a woman can change after the wedding." Other young women change for the better, but, in our eyes, Shen-shen changed for the worse. We all knew perfectly well that she was very dissatisfied with Uncle. To be quite honest, although Uncle wasn't all that bad-looking, in every other way he fell far short of her. He had attended school for seven or eight years, but even the most ordinary letter was filled with miswritten words. He had very limited experience of the world, and it was only in our local area that he was shown any sign of respect, and that was because of his family background. In contrast, she had studied in the provincial capital and graduated from teachers college. In her student days, she had made quite a name for herself and was pretty good at writing and speaking. Hence, after she graduated, Grandmother hastened to conclude the marriage because she was afraid that the engagement might be broken off. We heard that Shen-shen was strongly opposed to the match, but that her father had tricked her into returning home and then forced her to agree, partly by persuasion and partly by fatherly advice, and then shoved her into the wedding sedan-chair so as to continue the three generations of friendship between the two families.

The only member of the family that Shen-shen got anywhere close to was my mother. Father was still away on business, and Mother was as kind as a wooden statue—she wouldn't offend anyone. She stood outside the whirlpool of open and veiled squabbles in the household. Perhaps this was why Shen-shen liked to be with her. Every few days, she would go to my mother's rooms in the evening to sit a while. Mother wasn't much of a talker, and she made no great effort to be a hostess, so whenever Shen-shen came for a visit, all she would do was offer her a cup of tea and a bowl of melon seeds, and then go over and sit by the stove. Mother never said very much, and Shen-shen said even less, so a solemn and respectful atmosphere lingered around them. From time to time, Mother would ask her about something or other—how things were going, what it was like in the provincial capital, was she getting used to living with us;

sometimes she would answer a sentence or two, and sometimes she would just bluntly reply: "Sister-in-law, please just let me sit here in peace for awhile! The more questions you ask the worse I feel." Mother had been thinking of saying a few words to help her take her mind off things, but after an answer like that, she would just sit there quietly without saying another word.

Once, Mother told her how much she regretted not having a formal education. Shen-shen let out a profound sigh and said, "Having no formal education is a blessing. The only result of a formal education is that your body is in one world while your mind is in another. Spirit and body are out of joint, and you spend your whole life in pain and suffering." And at that the tears poured from her eyes.

Whenever she cried or sighed, Mother would say a few words to comfort her. But the more she tried to comfort her the worse she cried. After she had cried to her heart's content, she would give a long sigh and say, "You have no way of understanding how I feel."

When she went to my mother's rooms to sit awhile, sometimes she would stay for a long, long time, and other times she would leave after only a few minutes. It all depended on how she was feeling. When she left, she never said thanks or goodbye, but, as if she had suddenly thought of something she had to get done right away, she would stand up and quietly depart. Mother always accompanied her to the door and said, "Come again and sit a while when you have nothing else to do." She always nodded, and even might say, "After I sit here with you for a while, I do feel greatly relieved."

One day, early in the morning, Uncle came rushing in very agitated and told Grandmother: "I can't find Shen-shen anywhere. I don't know where she's gone. She's not in the house, and no one has seen her." Grandmother was very angry. She figured Shen-shen had slipped out and sneaked back to her parents' home. She told Uncle to bring her back, and while he was there, to ask his father-in-law to come over and give her a talking-to. So Uncle set out amid Grandmother's angry curses of "This is outrageous! This is outrageous!"

Along about evening, Uncle returned with a panicky expression on his face and told us that Shen-shen hadn't gone back to her parents. That upset Grandmother, and everyone else too. There was a general flurry, and Grandmother issued an order mobilizing every adult in the household to go and make inquiries everywhere. In the middle of the night, Shen-shen's father came over to find out about the whole affair. The entire family was completely occupied with trying to find Shen-shen for two whole days and nights. On the third day, Shen-shen's father sent someone over with a letter and told us we could stop looking.

The letter was in Shen-shen's own hand, and since it was so very short, I can give it all here without leaving out a single word.

Father!

Your daughter is gone!

If you want to know your daughter's present circumstances, she has cut her black tresses and put on Buddhist vestments, bowing before a dimly lit figure of the Buddha and reciting sutras.

Perhaps you know how much I have suffered, perhaps you don't. Your daughter does not harbor any resentment against her father, or anyone else; she only resents having been born to be a sacrificial victim caught between two eras.

Father! Please don't blame your daughter. She has already been sacrificed for the sake of a family reputation of having three generations of friendly relations in your feudal society. Nor should you feel sorry for your daughter, because the person who has cut her hair and shaved her head and donned Buddhist vestments is not your daughter— your daughter died a long time ago on the day she was married.

Your daughter doesn't want any relative to know where she is, and doesn't want anyone to come to see her. And if you won't let the mortal remains of one who has died a hundred deaths drag out the rest of her life in the only peace she can find, your daughter knows she would not have the slightest hesitation to put an end to it all.

19

Problems Confronting
an Ideal Couple

Ah-jung

AH-JUNG (in all likelihood a pseudonym) begins her story in an almost opposite vein. She and her husband met and fell in love when they were university students. Her pointed reference to the "congratulatory voices of our friends" when they married, along with the absence of any mention of relatives on either side, imply that the two married without their parents' consent. A network of friends seems to have replaced, at least partly, the more traditional family networks as a source of psychological and financial support. But the modern economic sector, symbolized by the great metropolis of Shanghai, was not adequate to sustain their modern marriage, and eventually economic difficulties eroded their happiness. It is noteworthy that although the author focuses on her small family's economic problems, she also introduces the theme of the obligation of educated women to make a contribution to society.

The story was published in *Fu-nü yueh-k'an* (woman's monthly journal), Nanking, 5, 4 (January 1947): 67–69.

IN THE EYES of our friends, my husband and I were a perfect couple when we got married. That was three years ago; he was a promising young university student, tall and robust, whose conversation was lively and engrossing. From every point of view—academic achievement, character, health, family background—he appeared to be an ideal husband.

At that time I was an attractive young woman, slim, pretty, and graceful, with beautiful limpid eyes; such a splendid young woman naturally had plenty of admirers running after her. Perhaps it was fate. I got to know him by chance, prodded into an introduction by some girlfriends. In a very short time we became friends and then rapidly went beyond that—like the talented young man and the beautiful young woman in the old romances.

Our university was located in a small, out-of-the-way town, on the banks of the Chia-ling River, which flowed peacefully by. Not far from the university in a peaceful spot there was a small, charming stone bridge that everyone was fond of and that you never could forget. The gentle willows on both sides of the bridge wafted in each passing breeze and provided abundant shade. The stream beneath the bridge was not four feet deep; in the clear and transparent water, delicate water grasses evenly grew. The meticulously tended flowers and shrubbery on the university grounds diffused a rich, sweet fragrance. When you had some spare time, you could stand on the bridge and watch the sun setting in the distance, enveloped and caressed by the crisp, cool air emanating from the water, which carried a wisp of flowery fragrance from afar. The tiny bridge, the flowing stream, the fragrant vegetation, and the haze all fused to make a picture of quiet beauty. Living in this lovely natural setting gave you the feeling of being in a fairyland paradise.

When the spring was at its most gorgeous—when the azaleas were in full bloom—we would walk side by side along the quiet secluded path on the university grounds, talking in low voices about our innermost feelings. On a bright moonlit night, we would stroll along the stream or the tiny bridge, prisoners of love, deeply, devoutly extolling the god of love's great gift. We lived in this lovely, tranquil, and contented atmosphere.

The golden days of university life quietly slipped by, and we graduated. Looking forward to a bright and successful future, and as an expression of our faith in love, our new married life began amid the congratulatory voices of our friends. In those early days, life was so much fun and we were so happy; even today, when memories of those days come to mind, I still can't bear to talk about them. Our warm and tender care for one another, our sweet whisperings, nourished the seedlings of love, making our love thrive.

New misfortunes began to befall us. My husband had majored in engineering, and after graduation he held a job as an engineer in a factory. Following the victory over Japan last year, his factory announced it was closing. The shadow of unemployment fell over him, and the hateful problem of money, which followed closely on the tail of unemployment, threatened us again and again.

Thanks to the kindness of friends, we accumulated a not inconsiderable sum of money for travel expenses, and, after careful consideration and reconsideration, my husband and I and our baby set off on the arduous road of demobilization.

At dusk one evening we arrived in bustling, noisy Shanghai, which we had yearned for for so long. Dusting ourselves off, carrying our meager luggage, our hearts filled with joyous feelings, we walked along the brilliantly lit streets to the home of a friend we hadn't seen for a long, long time. All along the way our eyes met brightly colored advertisements, enticing one to purchase all kinds of products, and the dazzling array of department stores that lined the streets. From every direction came the sounds of melancholy, tempting songs. It all made us suddenly realize that we really had arrived in this nightless metropolis of the East.

After a series of entreaties and ceaseless scurrying here and there, my husband was lucky enough to find a job in this city filled with masses of unemployed people. Of course, present reality didn't turn out to be as perfect as our ideal. Although he was trained as an engineer, he wound up in a clerical job that didn't have anything to do with engineering. Perhaps you can imagine the hardships and financial difficulties of living in Shanghai, where everything is so expensive, entirely dependent on a small salary.

Displaced from his professional goals and interests, in dire financial straits—one blow followed another, and he grew thinner and thinner. The plumpness left his face and his lively smile disappeared, dimly recollected only in my dreams. Under economic pressures, I longed to take a job to lighten our burden. But, looking at our young baby in my arms, I remained silent. For me, a job was only a beautiful dream.

Because of the problem of finding a reasonable solution to the problem of bringing up their children, thousands and tens of thousands of capable, educated women have lost the opportunity of having a job. From the perspective of the individual or of society, this unquestionably is lamentable. Since the end of the war, due to the initiative and leadership of progressive women, the number of child-care centers has steadily increased, but there are still far too few. And they are so expensive you want to wring your hands in despair. For ordinary, impoverished government employees, the costs are so high they can't even afford to think about it. Except for educated women who are content to be supported by their husbands, most women are willing to work and share the burden of household expenses with their husbands. But when you look around at those scarce, upper-class day-care centers, and then look at your own darling child, the hope of getting a job is just that, a hope and nothing more. The establishment of day-care centers has a tremendous bearing on the individual and society. After more than ten years in school, once a woman gets married, because of the problem of bringing up her children, she has no opportunity to devote herself to society and benefit others. That the incalculable sums of money spent by the nation and the painstaking instruction of teachers to train young talent should have this outcome truly makes you feel sad and indignant. Men often find fault with women for sitting idly at home and enjoying the fruits of their husbands' efforts without producing anything, but at the present time when day-care centers are not widespread, all a wife can say is, "What can I do?"

We've been here in noisy, bustling Shanghai for exactly three months, and due to economic pressures our little tranquil family has been ruined. I am convinced that there may be all too many like me in our country. The direct advantage of establishing day-care centers would be that they would enable educated women to obtain employment so as to make contributions to society and prevent families from sinking into poverty. Indirectly, that would benefit social order and prosperity enormously. Having suffered deeply myself, I ardently hope that leaders of the women's movement will please rapidly establish a large number of day-care centers. And it is especially important that every effort be made to make them less expensive. If at all possible, the best would be a government subsidy to cover all expenses, so that day-care would be free. Otherwise, only the better-off women, who are only a small, prosperous proportion of the populace, will get any actual benefit.

Outside the window, the autumn wind is rustling. Pushing the shutters open and looking into the pitch-black darkness, I hear the plaintive chirping of autumn insects in the withered grasses. How painfully sad and mournful! A whole series of events from the past suddenly come surging into my mind. The happy atmosphere when we were first married, and our present poverty-stricken circumstances; my husband's bright laugh, which has long disappeared without a trace, replaced by a chilly expression on his face and gloomy talk. When, alone in the desolate autumn wind, these cold thoughts come to mind, my hair bristles and my body shudders. Please, please, build many day-care centers, as quickly as possible. Amen!

—November 11, 1946

20

Mother's Books

P'an Ch'i-chün

A PROLIFIC writer, P'an Ch'i-chün (1917–), known by her
pen-name, Ch'i-chün, has published several dozen collections of
stories, essays, and sketches. Childhood memories of life in her
hometown of Yung-chia in Chekiang Province provide many of her
favorite themes, but both in style and subject matter, she also draws
on the classical literary tradition, which she studied in her youth
and majored in at Chih-chiang University in Hangchou.

    The following memoir (from *Liu-yü t'a-nien shuo meng-hen*
[Vestiges of dreams saved for future conversation] [Taipei:
Hung-fan Bookstore, 1980], pp. 1–7) is typical of the warmth with
which she evokes the everyday life of ordinary people. It is
included here as a reminder that, for many women, growing up in a
traditional family environment was a positive experience. For,
although the title indicates that the subject is her mother, the author
herself is also present throughout, both as the growing daughter
under her loving mother's care and as the mature, reflective writer
whose appreciation of her mother's influence on her own
development pervades the memoir. The result is a depiction of a
mother-daughter relationship very different from other
autobiographies in this collection; the contrast with Hsieh Ping-ying
(chapter 12) is particularly striking. In keeping with the best in the
Confucian tradition, Ch'i-chün's mother educates her by being the
role model of a proper mother and wife, and a moral human being,
as well as by transmitting what she believes to be practical
knowledge. Character is central, for the mature author no longer
shares many of her mother's beliefs and values; her modern
education has taught her to be more skeptical, and to know that the

"rubber paper" her mother prized so highly can be explained in more accurate, scientific terms. Yet this education has not distanced her from her mother, for she values the sincerity and earnestness with which her mother held her beliefs, and the respect for learning and books that she so lovingly conveyed to her young daughter. Ch'i-chün thus highlights humanistic aspects of Chinese culture, and depicts family life in a far more sympathetic vein than most reformers and feminist critics. In the process, she suggests an interpretation of the family as sufficiently flexible to adapt to change, and to provide the emotional support needed in a period of instability and transition.

AFTER a busy day cooking meals, washing clothes, and feeding the pigs, chickens, and ducks, my mother would call to me, "Hey, Little Spring (Hsiao-ch'un), go and get Ma's book and bring it here."

I would answer, "Which book, Ma?"

"The one with the rubber-paper pages."

I knew that this evening Mother was happy and would keep me company in the library, would light an oil lamp and embroider a pair of slipper faces for Daddy.

Not a single word was written in this rubber-paged book. It was indeed a "tabula rasa" into which were stuffed an assortment of red and green silk threads, design patterns cut from white paper, and a pair of aqua satin slipper faces that Grandmother had given to Mother, that had never been made into slippers but which Mother had kept pressed between the pages of the book for nearly ten years. Grandmother had died long ago, but the cherries embroidered on the aqua satin still looked bright red enough to pick and eat, and there was a pair of tiny embroidered magpies, one with its beak open, the other with its beak closed. Mother had told me that the one with the open beak was the male, and the one with the closed beak was the female. She said that, like people, magpies were differentiated by male and female sexes. Each time Mother opened the book she would turn first to this page, which was stuffed the fullest. She would examine the pair of magpies for a long time, the corners of her mouth seeming to smile without smiling, her eyes fixed in thought as if in profound contemplation or appreciation of some important event. Afterward she would turn to another page, carefully select some threads, and begin to embroider, as if this pair of cherry and magpie embroidered slipper faces were Mother's eternal model, from which the design and colors in her mind seemed to evolve.

Why did Mother call this the book with the rubber-paper pages? Because the material from which the pages of the book were made was both thick and rigid, the color of bark. I do not know what kind of material it was, but the pages were extremely sturdy and durable. No matter how many times they were turned they would not tear, and because they also repelled water, Mother gave them a new name—rubber paper. Actually it was some kind of extremely old paper that my maternal great-grandmother had bound with her own hands for my grandmother, who had then handed it down to my mother. The book pages were double-layer bound, accordion style, and in between the two leaves of an individual page were often secreted Mother's most precious possessions, Father's letters from Peking, the real book within the book without words. Mother never pulled these out or reread them in front of me, but when she tired of embroidery, when the flame of the lamp burned low and weak, when I, exhausted from reciting the *Analects* of Confucius or *Mencius,* fell asleep at the desk, she would silently pull out one of these letters and recite in a low voice the words from Father, far away across a thousand mountains and ten thousand rivers.

There was another book my mother loved that left an extraordinarily deep impression on my memories. That was the fascinating, startling, *Shih-tien yen-wang* (Ten palaces of the king of death), printed on rough yellow paper with simple pictures depicting the ferocious visage of the king of death in his ten palaces in hell. He had the head of an ox and the face of a horse, and was accompanied by ghosts and spirits of all shapes and descriptions who, depending on their good or evil merits when alive as human beings, received different rewards or punishments. The most fearsome forms of punishment included climbing a knife-edge mountain, falling into a cauldron of boiling oil, and being chased and caught by wild beasts. Afterward, emerging from a complete cycle of the wheel of transmigration, some would rise as great officials or wealthy gentry, others would become beggars, and still others would fall to the status of pigs and dogs, ducks and chickens, or insects. Mother never seemed to tire of looking at these pictures. Sometimes she would point to them and say to me, "The difference between life and death, the world and hell, is but one breath. The living still have this breath. You must be a good person, do good things." An admonition that Mother liked to repeat often was, "Do not lie; beware the plucked tongue that plows the fields." The "plucked tongue that plows the fields" was a picture in this book that portrayed the disheveled head and wild hair of a female ghost whose tongue was plucked out, pierced with a hole, stuck onto a plow handle, and dragged by an ox to plow a field. This was the most extreme punishment for lying, so Mother often brought it out to warn us. Grandfather said that the *Ten Palaces of the King of Death* was the work of someone's imagination, but that there definitely was a law of retribution, of cause and effect, as clearly explained in the Buddhist classics.

Another book that throughout her life never left Mother's hand was the almanac. In the drawer of a small table at the head of her bed, and also in the cupboard drawer in the kitchen, were separate copies of the almanac which she might pull out to consult at any time, to find out what kind of a day it was that day. Whether the day was good or bad was extremely important to Mother. She was meticulous about everything, and everything required a calculation of the auspicious omens: buying suckling pigs, repairing the ox fence or pig pen, transplanting the rice seedlings, and harvesting the grain all required selecting a good day. For making wine and steaming rolls for the winter sacrifice, this went without saying. The only thing for which Mother could not choose the proper day was when the hen would hatch her nest of little chicks, but Mother would still have to consult the almanac, and if it fell on a highly auspicious day she would be very happy, thinking that this brood of chickens would grow to maturity very smoothly and easily. If it was not a very good day she would tell me to be especially careful walking, not to step on one of the little chicks, and to keep the hawks away from the courtyard. Once a big hawk flew down and Mother set down the cooking spade and rushed out to chase away the hawk, which still made off with one little chick. Mother was running so frantically that she was not careful and stepped on a chick, breaking off its little wing under her foot. The chick chirped out most pitifully and the mother hen flapped around and around us, cluck, cluck, clucking mournfully. Mother bent forward and almost fell down. I helped her sit down on the bench. In the palm of her hand she was holding the wounded chick. At the same she was worried about the chick carried off by the hawk. Her tears fell in a stream, and I wanted to cry too because the little chick was covered with blood and the whole scene was really tragic. Grandfather immediately poured some sesame oil and rubbed the wound. The poor chick; its pitiful chirps became weaker and weaker and finally stopped. As she wiped her tears, Mother recited an incantation for the dead. Grandfather said, "It's for the best. Of the six cycles of transmigration, these two little chicks have already turned one. If their sins are expiated a bit sooner, then they will be able to enter the world as humans sooner." I again thought of the picture in the *Ten Palaces of the King of Death*; in my little heart I suddenly felt the sadness that everything in this life is beyond our control.

The twenty-four seasonal celebrations of the year in the almanac Mother had memorized thoroughly. Each time she opened the almanac to find out the day of the next upcoming celebration, she would always recite from the very beginning up to the celebration of that current month. I recited them with her: "First month: beginning of spring (about February 5), the rains (about February 19); second month: insects awaken (about March 5), spring equinox (about March 20); third month: pure brightness (about April 5), grain rains (about April 20). . . ." But every time we recited down to the white dews (about September 8) and autumn equinox (about September 23) of the eighth month, I don't know why, but I always sensed a feeling of cold and chill. Though young, I responded to the sigh of "the year passes quickly and again the autumn wind blows." Perhaps it is because the eighth month contains the Midautumn Festival and there are so many poems describing the Midautumn Festival. The Midautumn Festival is supposed to be a time of homecoming and family reunion, but year after year Father and Eldest Brother tarried at Peiping and did not return. Furthermore, my tutor had taught me the poem "The Rushes" from the *Book of Poetry* (*Shih ching*): "Thick grow the rushes, white dew turns to frost, where is that man? Somewhere along the river bank, I follow upstream, but the way is long and difficult, follow back downstream, there he is in midstream." At that time I did not quite understand "there he is in midstream," and furthermore it seemed a bit facetious. I liked best the first two lines. "White dew turns to frost" reminded me of "hair tinged with frost." My tutor had taught me that that was a metaphor for white hair, and I frequently looked up to see whether or not my mother's hair on the temples was "tinged with frost."

Of course, Mother also had many other books, such as *Ming-hua pao-chuan* (Tales of famous flowers), *Pen-ts'ao kang-mu* (Encyclopedia of plants and herbs), *Hui-t'u Lieh-nü chuan* (Biographical sketches of famous women), *Hsin ching* (Heart sutra), *Mi-t'o ching* (Amida sutra), and other classics. The ones she treated with most reverence were the Buddhist sutras. Every day she lit incense and knelt on the grass mat to recite the sutras, turning page after page. Sometimes she finished reciting a whole sutra volume and I had not seen her turn the pages; she had long ago memorized it. I would sit at a desk in the left corner of the temple room and intently listen to her recite the sutra, the tone of her voice suddenly high then low, slow then fast, each word distinct and clear, proper and exact. Seeing her close her eyes in reverent concentration, I sat in silence, not moving a muscle.

After finishing reciting the sutras she still had to recite a few lines resembling a benediction, the last two lines of which were, "Forty-eight vows to save all people, nine grades of merits to carry the soul to the other world." After finishing these two lines, a light smile floated upon the composed face of my mother as if she had already left her body and crossed over to the other side. I watched the flickering of the candle flame and the thin taper of smoke and felt that for the two of us, mother and daughter, to be alone in the empty temple room was rather lonely.

The *Encyclopedia of Plants and Herbs* was Mother's book for scholarly study. So many of the characters in it had wood or grass radicals; mother could really recognize only a few, but she placed this book squarely on the table at the head of her bed. Occasionally she opened it and would explain something from it clearly and logically. Actually her explanations all came from the mouth of Grandfather, who was a country physician with a knowledge of herbal medicine. Mother knew only that the sources of this knowledge all derived from this book.

Mother had never attended school or studied formally, but in my eyes she was a person of broad and extensive learning.

21

Why I Parted with T'ang Na

Chiang Ch'ing

CHIANG CH'ING (1914–1991) is probably the best-known woman in modern Chinese history. She is included here not in any of her later roles as the wife of Mao Tse-tung, leader in the Cultural Revolution, or member of the "Gang of Four" denounced by the new leadership after Mao's death, but as an example of the kinds of conflicts that occurred between men and women who professed little or no allegiance to the past.

Chiang Ch'ing was born Li Yun-ho in a poor family in the city of Chu-ch'eng, Shantung Province. Her brutal father died when she was a child, and she was brought up by her mother, who worked as a servant to put her through junior high school. Drawn to the glamour and fame of the theatrical world, she became a film actress in the early 1930s, with the professional name Lan P'ing. In 1935 she began an affair with the film actor, writer, and leftist critic T'ang Na, and in April 1936 they were married. Her explanation of the failure of the marriage is the subject of "Why I Parted with T'ang Na," which was published in 1937 in *Lien-hua hua-pao* (United China pictorial), Shanghai, 9, 4 (June 5, 1937). (Reprinted in *Ming-pao yueh-k'an*, Hong Kong, no. 166 [October 1979], pp. 41–48.) Written as a response to the publication of T'ang Na's version of the same events, the essay is noteworthy for its remarkably frank account of the relationship between a husband and wife, rare in China even in modern times. It is also a valuable source for understanding the most influential woman in modern Chinese politics before prominence placed her behind the veil of official news releases and hagiographic stories. The author vividly conveys the emotional turmoil that many Chinese women (and men) experienced in the freer atmosphere of a cosmopolitan city like Shanghai, in which the boundaries of new freedoms and the allocation of new responsibilities were undefined, while not far beneath the surface traditional attitudes were still very much alive. Between the lines, one can see that even among those who had adopted modern ideas about the selection of a spouse, older expectations about the proper role of a wife still prevailed. The tensions that Chiang Ch'ing portrays were to continue into the future.

For a biography of Chiang Ch'ing, based both on written sources and extensive interviews with Chiang Ch'ing herself, see Roxane Witke, *Comrade Chiang Ch'ing* (Boston: Little, Brown, 1977).

RECENTLY various small publications have carried a number of news items concerning T'ang Na and myself. These stories mainly say that I jilted T'ang Na. Originally I thought that I would just remain silent and let this affair pass. Because this is how it could have been, T'ang Na and I had had no contact for some time, and he had no reason to come and bother me over and over again. However, since various publications have published inaccurate stories unfavorable to me, to make everyone understand clearly, I am no longer willing to endure this in silence.

Let it explode! This frustration long accumulating in my mind! I've lived with this destructive frustration for over a year, and during this long, sad year, except for a very few friends, most people, including a number of friends, have been saying, "T'ang Na loved Lan P'ing so madly and passionately, but Lan P'ing's affection for him was capricious." Implicit in these words is a lot of dissatisfaction and blame.

I really cannot take it any longer, even though average people who have serious business to attend to would consider this kind of nuisance quite senseless, hardly worth wasting their breath on.

But since there are some who are quite willing to waste their breath in this way, and have taken such great pains to devise ways to bear this heavy "responsibility," it wouldn't be appropriate for me to disappoint all the rest; moreover, I hope that most people will understand the facts. That's why I have to speak out.

What I want to explain is the way T'ang Na loved me, that his way was to love someone else at the same time he was deeply in love(?) with me! That was when I was working for the Tien-t'ung Movie Company, before I fell in love with him, when we were good friends. Everyone knew (company colleagues as well as his friends) that at that time he was in love with a young woman (in order not to drag others into this, I would rather not mention her name here). Later, after he fell in love with me, I asked him about this affair, but he said that it was a smoke-screen because he was afraid of letting others know that he was chasing me. I had never suspected that someone who loved me would lie to me, so this simply flashed across my mind like a shooting star, and I completely forgot about it.

Last year, however, on International Women's Day (March 8), we were very short of money and I was sick. But for an entertainment at the Young Women's Club, I ran out on that cold day with my illness and went on stage sick. Because of a small misunderstanding, none of my friends had time to help out, and things got even more complicated. Feeling really miserable, I carried through with this strenuous task. Through the efforts of several friends, the entertainment finally ended. But it ruined me! With a very high fever and a head so heavy that it felt like it had been filled with lead, I went home by myself in a rickshaw. At the time we lived on Nanyang Road. When I got home, I forget what I was looking for, but among a stack of books on the table, I discovered a love letter he had written to another woman (the one he was after when he worked for the Tien-t'ung Company) and a love letter from that woman to him. Ah! Heaven! Can you imagine how painful that was? A misunderstanding with my friends, sick, and on top of that the man I loved was unfaithful, all melted together into a huge iron club that came crashing down on my head! When I came to, I was still Lan P'ing. Lan P'ing is the kind of person who didn't give T'ang Na any trouble at all, but just simply wrote him a note and left. Having nowhere to go, I ran over to a hotel room that I rented for rehearsal during the day, because I knew that my friends from the club would come, and that they would help me think of something.

After a while, the door opened, and in walked T'ang Na. He wanted me to return, but I said that things had already reached the point where it would be impossible for us to be together again. But he started to cry, sobbing very sadly! He said that even if something had happened we could go home and talk it over before parting. At that point I was afraid of creating some kind of disturbance in the hotel, so I went back with him. But I told him that there was no way we could continue living together, and that I would leave in the morning. Ah! I shall never forget the pitiful way that he cried! Later, he tried to make me say that I forgave him, but I said nothing, and he turned around and walked out. Because he was in such a terrible state when he left, I jumped out of bed and discovered the note he had left on the table in the other room, the gist of which was that he wanted to die. I was very alarmed, and, collecting all my strength and energy, I ran after him and asked him to come back. But he asked me whether or not I loved him, whether or not I would forgive him. Good lord! What was I to say to someone who wanted to die! I said that I loved him, that I forgave him! Thus, from that day on, I was fighting a temperature of about 40°C (104°F), I was delirious, and I was pounding the bed and cursing people. I was going crazy! I am grateful to T'ang Na for looking after me so well. Because we were poor, he took me to his home, and I stayed in bed at the home of one of his relatives in Suchou for nearly two months.

He had talked of marriage earlier, but only then did I finally agree. However, I told him very clearly that this ceremony was not to restrict anyone, but merely to solve our financial problems, since by marrying he would receive a little money from his family with which we could pay back the debts incurred due to unemployment and illness. Thus, during the ceremony, among the three couples,* we did not sign a marriage certificate because we clearly understood that if one day we no longer loved each other, the marriage license would not be of any use, and neither he nor I took this ceremony seriously.

To return to what I was saying. Although at the time I said that I forgave him, every time I recalled that night and those two letters I suffered as if my heart had been dashed to pieces! I had told no one about this affair, because it hurt my poor self-respect (I thought about it a lot, and I felt that the affections of someone who really loved me could not possibly change), but most important was that my Ah-Q temperament made me feel that I should not make a fuss because of my jealousy. So I just repressed it, deep in my heart. In a state of mind like this, which could erupt over the slightest provocation, it was easy to get into squabbles. Since we frequently had fights, added to which was the fact that, owing to a misunderstanding, friends were put off, and also that in my career I could see no clear road ahead, I went back to the North.

After he attempted to commit suicide in Tsinan, I returned there. The main thing I wanted to do was to have a frank, face-to-face talk with him, to urge him to respect himself and not to act this way again, after which we would again separate. But when I saw how miserable he looked, how shameful! My heart softened incredibly, to the point that I totally forgave his faithlessness. I felt that everyone makes mistakes, and that if one simply admitted and corrected one's mistakes that would be enough.

Out of a sense of sympathy and pity, I did the most humiliating thing in my whole life—I returned with him to Shanghai. At the time, however, I really thought that he and I would build a new life. But not long after we had settled in Pihsun Road, inside a book I found a poem cut out of a newspaper. Because I was still

---

*Three couples were married at the same ceremony, witnessed by Cheng Chun-li and Shen Chun-ju. They were Lan P'ing and T'ang Na, Chao Tan and Yeh Lu-ch'ien, and Ku Erh-i and Tu Lu-lu.

so weak from my illness, my whole body began trembling and I collapsed in a heap on the floor. It was an ardent love poem to a woman in Japan, written when I had returned to Tsinan (the woman had then already gone to Japan). I sat on the floor staring numbly, like an idiot, at the tree branches outside the window quivering in the wind and the clouds in the deep blue sky. Ah! I shall never forget those white clouds rushing by. I wanted to kill myself. Because I didn't have the courage or strength to leave a second time, my physical condition deteriorated terribly. Furthermore, there was no one I could tell my troubles to. Those thoughts of suicide were written in my diary. (T'ang Na stole this diary from me at six o'clock in the afternoon on the twenty-seventh of this month when I wasn't home.) However, I had already promised Mr. Ts'ai Ch'u-sheng that I would act in *Wang Lao-wu,* and a sense of responsibility was at the same time a thread of hope that made it possible for me to continue living. However, I had already fallen into a very serious depression! I frequently beat myself on the head and hit myself.

Later, once I joined Lien-hua Movie Company and had a job, thanks to Mr. Fei Mu who gave me a part, I shifted all my attention to my work and forgot a lot of my worries. Following the filming of *Wang Lao-wu,* I acted in *Storm* [by Alexander Ostrovsky]. Because I had a job and because I had more contacts with friends, I stopped thinking about dying, and I just wanted to get it settled once and for all! Thus it was that we started living apart.

While we were living separately, I talked things over with friends, my very closest friends—even including some friends of T'ang Na. They all feared that an abrupt, total break would be too much for T'ang Na, that he would attempt to commit suicide again, and that the only thing to do was to adopt a more gradual approach. If he were given a hope so that he could work hard, write, and study, later there would still be a chance for mutual love. On the other hand? If thus spared a severe blow, under the encouragement of friendship, he could certainly exert himself, and so long as he exerted himself his life would certainly become fulfilling, and then a blow like this would not make him want to commit suicide. However, he could not stand this, nor did he have the determination to change himself. (Even if he had changed I could not have loved him; I could never have loved him again, because scars in my heart from the past can never be erased.) Thus, he again wanted to commit suicide, and it was only due to the urging of myself and three friends that he didn't go through with it. But at that time I told him that if he did try to commit suicide again, it would only strengthen my determination to live on, and with a heart of steel I would simply wait for the press reports and all the accusations, because in my heart I knew that I had nothing to be ashamed of and that I had treated T'ang Na fairly and decently.

At the time, he said that he definitely would never attempt to commit suicide again. I never hated him—even today. Although I no longer love him, we can still be good friends. He has a strong sense of friendship toward all his friends, and I certainly cannot obliterate his good points just because of this affair. In this way, we continued to see each other, but it was quite clear that we would not interfere with each other.

But one day he suddenly came looking for me to talk, saying that to go on like this was too aggravating for him, that he wanted to settle it once and for all. He also showed me a torn letter—the letter was from that woman who had returned from Japan, ending their relationship and demonstrating his fidelity to me. However, I no longer loved him, and I asked him, since he wanted to terminate our relationship completely, if he wanted to put a notice in the newspapers announcing our separation. He said to go ahead and do it if I wanted to, but that it was not necessary for him. Of course I needed it even less. Thereupon he decided to leave Shanghai.

Later, I fell in love with someone else. Under such circumstances, my loving someone else was none of his business, and he had no reason to concern himself about it, and even less reason to make me take him into consideration. However, when he returned and found out about it, the first time he came running over to my place, he reproached me in a threatening manner. I don't know what words he used that made me start to cry! But I turned my head aside so that he wouldn't see how badly I felt. Because not long before I had been acting in *Storm* during the day while filming *Wang Lao-wu* in the evenings, I was in poor physical condition, and in particular my heart was very weak. The day that he came was also just when I had been filming at night for two days in a row. Again I fell ill.

The second time he came, he started upbraiding me the moment he entered the door. I asked him to leave, and when he refused I called my maid to come up, but he locked the door to the room, leaving the kindhearted servant outside, crying anxiously. And I? I was very calm. I knew that he was suffering greatly, so that it might be a good idea to let him rant and rave and get it out of his system. But, good lord! How he ranted and cursed! Never in my life have I been so insulted. He accused me of playing around with men, of being weak-willed, of using men to help me get ahead, and of cheating him. He also mentioned the hope I had given him when we were living apart. But he himself had not wanted this hope; he had been finished with me! Even after he and I were finished, was I still not supposed to love anyone else? Even if we were not totally finished, I still have the right to love someone else!

I endured his ranting in silence. When he was finished he left, but I swore to myself that I had taken it once, twice, but would not take it a third time, that if he came again I would teach him a lesson, not because I feared him but because I pitied him, and moreover, I should maintain my own self-respect.

One night he came again, and this is what happened. I hit him and he hit me. We closed the door of the room and did not open it to the knocking of the servant and friends. I was hurt. I never screamed so loud. He took with him every one of the letters he had written to me, and he said that he was going to put a notice in the papers announcing our separation, though he didn't do it.

Other than one small paring knife and a pair of scissors, I have no weapons in the house at all. Don't be afraid, come on! I'm certainly not hiding. As for the "news tactic," I'm not going to be like Yuan Ling-yü [a famous movie star] and kill myself because I'm "afraid of what people might say." Nor will I retreat. I'll just wait without moving a muscle, wait for them to curse me in large bold type.

T'ang Na stirred up trouble over and over again, and his friends are trying to deal me "damaging blows," all because of that marriage ceremony, because in this society, this ceremony— even though there was no marriage license—is considered by the average person to be a binding agreement between the sexes. Of course, this sort of thing is quite common. And it is even very common for those self-appointed superior people to use it to attack others. First of all, I did not want to make a public statement simply because I did not want to make a noisy row over such a senseless affair, nor did I want to make things even more aggravating for T'ang Na, because all along I have continued to feel sorry for him. But now, since he has acted like this, am I just supposed to be a pitiful little bug and let others trample all over me whenever they feel like it? No! Lan P'ing is a human being and will never retreat, especially in the face of such shameless tactics. Since in his eyes I have already turned into such a shameful female, there was certainly no need for him to pay attention to me anymore, and I in all good conscience did not worry about him. From that day on, I have no longer been concerned about him. Moreover, except for a few close friends, I haven't thought of discussing this with anyone, because I do not want people to say that I was begging for sympathy. Furthermore, there was no need to discuss it. Because I had nothing to apologize for to T'ang Na, or to myself, I am not afraid of anything, and I am adamantly going to go on living. Now, however, I have no choice but to speak out; otherwise people will say that I was in the wrong and will humiliate me even further.

On the twenty-seventh, I returned from the countryside to discover that he had left a note and a fountain pen. Furthermore, he had stolen both volumes of my diary. Because he had said that he would never again try to commit suicide, it never occurred to me from those vaguely worded lines that he would try to kill himself again. But he did. Before he committed suicide, there was one group of friends who, I do not know whether they did not know about the state of our affair, or whether it really was out of true friendship for him, or perhaps . . . , but I do know that they expressed their displeasure toward me. I did not know about T'ang Na's suicide. It was only from a good friend who was also a good friend of T'ang Na—he really understands T'ang Na's personality and our conflicts—that I learned something about it. At the same time, I heard that T'ang Na's friends were going to use force in dealing with me. Ha, ha! Good heavens! If they would be so brave in fighting against XX [Japan], then, really, China couldn't ever be defeated! Unfortunately, to use it against one young woman, that's laughable.

I simply wish to explain the facts, and to make clear to everyone my attitude toward T'ang Na. Other than this, I have no other designs. Having made this explanation, I don't want to waste any more mental effort and ink on this senseless affair, or to waste valuable space in the papers. I don't feel like carrying on a long-winded discussion over such a senseless affair. I need to protect my self-respect, and I want to devote all my time to my career.

—May 31, 1937

Oh yes, today's papers say that T'ang Na did not commit suicide, that it was a rumor. I sincerely hope so. (The End)

22

My Life in the Imperial Palace

Li Yü-ch'in

IMPERIAL consorts in traditional China were, like government officials, reticent about their private lives. The innumerable women who served as consorts of various ranks over the course of the two millennia of China's imperial age left only a small number of poems, which, for the most part, express the same thoughts and sentiments as the many poems in the voices of imperial consorts written by male poets. The poignancy of literary imaginings about these women and the rarity of actual accounts enhance our appreciation of the following memoir by Li Yü-ch'in (1928–), the last consort of the last emperor of China, P'u-yi (1906–1967).

Although P'u-yi abdicated in 1912 following the creation of the Republic of China, he continued to live in an imperial style in the Forbidden City in Peking. In December 1922, Wan-jung (1907–1946) was made his empress and Wen-hsiu (1909–1950) his imperial consort. Both women came from the former Manchu nobility. Wang-jung's jealousy and P'u-yi's neglect made Wen-hsiu so unhappy that she attempted suicide several times. Eventually, in 1931, she was able to divorce P'u-yi, the first imperial consort in Chinese history to obtain a legal divorce. Rather than remarry, she established a primary school with funds from her alimony and ran it herself as principal. Wan-jung had a sadder fate. In 1935 she gave birth to a baby daughter by another man, and P'u-yi had the baby killed. She fell into disfavor, developed an opium addiction, and became mentally unbalanced. In 1937, P'u-yi, who since 1932 had been head of the Japanese puppet state of Manchukuo, took T'an Yü-ling (1920–1942), also from a Manchu noble family, as his consort. P'u-yi apparently loved T'an, but she fell ill and died five years later. Later, P'u-yi stated his suspicion that the Japanese doctors who tended her during her illness had deliberately killed her because of her anti-Japanese sentiments. Shortly after T'an's death, P'u-yi's Japanese advisers suggested that he take another consort, and he selected Li Yü-ch'in, a fifteen-year-old Chinese schoolgirl, from a photograph the Japanese showed him. Li's life with P'u-yi, from February 1943 to August 1945, is the subject of the following memoir, which was published in the Hong Kong magazine *Kuang-chüeh-ching*, March 16, 1980.

Li Yü-ch'in's autobiography is valuable not only because of its uniqueness, but also because she conveys so well the changes going on around her. She vividly describes both her living conditions as imperial consort and her feelings as a young woman torn between two forces, her yearning for freedom and genuine affection and the necessity to submit to strict confinement and strict orders. Surrounded by suspicion and mistrust, she had neither security nor privacy, even though she had an abundance of material comforts. Her description of P'u-yi is on the whole credible: vain, egotistical, insecure, and suspicious, yet not altogether unreasonable. He was not a husband to her in the physical sense, but he seems to have had some feelings for her. For reasons not entirely clear, perhaps to avoid embarrassing her, he only briefly alluded to her in his autobiography, *From Emperor to Citizen* (Peking: Foreign Languages Press, 1964–65), without mentioning her name. Li's memoirs thus also serve to add another dimension to our understanding of P'u-yi.

At the end of World War II, P'u-yi was captured by Soviet troops and imprisoned in Manchuria. Though not formally tried, as the consort of a war criminal, Li Yü-ch'in was socially ostracized. She was still young, but her parents advised her to wait for P'u-yi's release. With no economic resources of her own, she alternated between living with her parents and with P'u-yi's relatives. In 1955, when she had a temporary job in a nursery, she learned that P'u-yi was in a prison in Fushun, Liaoning Province. With hard-saved and borrowed money she made several trips to visit him, bringing him small things he needed, such as sweaters and socks. But his coldness and his indifference to her hardships freed her of any lingering sense of obligation, and, after a period of deliberation, she decided to live a normal life and have a family of her own. In 1957, P'u-yi consented to her request for a divorce, and a year or so later she married a radio broadcasting technician. She gave birth to a son in 1962. At present she lives in Ch'ang-ch'un.

P'u-yi was released from prison in December 1959. In 1962 he married a young nurse named Li Shu-hsien, in Peking, where he died five years later. Li Shu-hsien currently lives in Peking.

I WAS BORN in 1928 in the countryside near Ch'ang-ch'un [Kirin Province in Manchuria], the sixth child of my mother.

When I was six or seven *sui,* the entire family moved from the country to live in the city. Later I entered the first year of the Nan-ling Girls Academy, equivalent to a higher elementary school, where I was deceived into entering the puppet imperial court.

One day in February 1943, the Japanese school principal, Kobayashi, with the woman teacher, Fujii, went around to each of the classes to select three or four students from each class, a total of some ten students, who were then taken to a Japanese photographer's studio to have a four-inch-square photograph taken of each. Some three weeks later, Kobayashi and Fujii came to my house and Fujii said to me, "Your photo is excellent. The emperor has issued an order that you be selected to come to the palace to study."

I was taken directly to the home of the Japanese military officer Yoshioka Yasunori. Yoshioka had a position at the puppet court of "attaché to the Manchukuo Imperial Household" and was a special agent of the Japanese government attached directly to P'u-yi. Yoshioka scrutinized me from head to toe and said, "Excellent!" He then asked my age, how many people were in my family, what my father did, etc. Later we went out and took a car straight to my family's home. At the time my family was just in the process of holding a family conference, including my father, my three married older sisters, and my older brother who had returned, as well as the landlord. They were just discussing with concern what to do about me. Yoshioka entered the room and said to my family, "The emperor has issued a command that the best students be selected to study at the imperial court. The emperor will confer his pleasure upon those who study well and select consorts from among them." Mother asked whether or not I would still be allowed to return home, and whether or not they would still be allowed to see me. Yoshioka replied, "That can be arranged. Her photo is the best; it pleased the emperor greatly." As he said this he took out more than a hundred four-inch-square pictures and showed them to us, saying, "She can return home. You may also come frequently to the court to see her. There is a great deal of money that is given just to those who enjoy the imperial favor."*

At the time, I thought that being able to go study without spending any money was something I greatly desired. My mother took out for me a quilted jacket made of black silk with yellow flowers and had me put it on. This was my only article of good clothing. Father and Mother also urged me to study hard and not waste my time playing. Just before leaving, my eyes filled with tears, I comforted them, saying, "If it's good there I'll stay, if not I'll come home."

---

*About Yoshioka's functions in Manchukuo, P'u-yi wrote in his memoirs, *From Emperor to Citizen,* 2:292: "If one compares the Kwangtung Army to a source of high-tension electric current and myself to an electric motor, then Yoshioka was a wire of high conductivity. He was a short man with a small moustache and high cheekbones, and he never left me during the ten years from the time he first came to the palace in 1935 to the Japanese surrender in 1945, when he was captured by the Soviet army at the same as time as I was. In those years he rose from lieutenant-colonel to lieutenant-general. He had two posts: one was as a senior staff officer in the Kwantung Army and the other was 'Attaché to the Manchukuo Imperial Household.' This latter was a Japanese term, but it does not describe his real function. He was the wire through which the Kwantung Army transmitted its intentions to me. The excursions I made, the visitors I received, the protocol I observed, my admonitions to my subjects, the toasts I proposed, and even my nods and smiles were all under Yoshioka's direction. He decided what meetings I was to attend and wrote out my speeches in his own Japanese-style Chinese."

That evening I was sent to the home of Fujii, where she prepared a bath for me and gave me a Japanese meal. That night I could not sleep at all, thinking of many things.

The next day, after eating breakfast, Fujii took me to a hairdresser and then to a large hospital for a medical examination. From the hospital she took me to the Yoshioka residence. Yoshioka's wife brushed my hair, straightened up my clothes, and then took me by car to the house of P'u-yi's second younger sister, Yun-ho.

At the time, Yun-ho was called the "Second Royal Sister." She was a full-blood younger sister of P'u-yi, and the wife of Cheng T'ui-ai, who was a grandson of Cheng Hsiao-hsü. She told Yoshioka and Fujii to return and she took me by car directly to the inner quarters of the palace. Before leaving she said to me, "Upon meeting his majesty, you must kowtow to him, and you must be certain to address him as 'Your Majesty.' You cannot say 'you' this or 'you' that to him." Upon getting out of the car, several men came out to greet us. One of them sprayed her all over with a sprayer. She even held up her arms and extended her legs forward and back, turning around several times. He also sprayed me front and back. Only later did I realize that everyone entering the palace had to be fumigated, to avoid bringing any contagious disease inside. Yun-ho then took me up to P'u-yi's residence. It was a two-story building, surrounded on all sides by one-story buildings. P'u-yi lived on the west side of the second story. On the east side resided the Empress Wan-Jung, who was also called Ch'iu-hung. Her English name was Elizabeth. The west side of the first floor, which had been the apartments of the deceased T'an Yü-ling, was now vacant.

P'u-yi Tells Me to Sleep in His Bedroom Chambers

When we got upstairs, Yun-ho took me into a room. In a few moments a man entered who seemed to be not yet thirty, and the Second Sister, with both hands on her knees, bent down in ceremonial greeting, telling me at the same time to kowtow. I knelt down and kowtowed three times. P'u-yi then said, "Stand up, stand up!" and pulled me up. Discovering that my hand was feverish, he hastened to ask whether or not I was feeling well. I said that my head hurt a little, at which he touched my forehead and took out a thermometer to take my temperature, telling someone to get some medicine to reduce my fever. In the room was hung a painting of P'u-yi, and he asked me whether or not it was well painted. I looked at the painting, then boldly looked at him and said that the painting did not much look like him. At this he broke into hearty laughter. I asked P'u-yi whether I had been summoned there to study. He said that it was indeed to study. I again asked, "Why just me alone?" P'u-yi laughed and replied, "I don't like a crowd. When there are many people, the feelings are badly dispersed. One came a few days ago, but I wasn't pleased with her so I told her to go back home." In a little while a meal was served, four entrees and a soup, as well as steamed bread and rolls, and a dish of dessert. I asked, "Are these bought outside?" Laughing, P'u-yi replied, "They're not bought outside. They're made in the imperial kitchens." I wanted him to eat with me, but he said he would eat in a while.

After I had eaten, P'u-yi picked up a string of Buddhist prayer beads, saying that he was to pray for the victory of the Japanese Imperial Army so that we would live a good and happy life. This seemed very strange to me. I had never heard anyone say they hoped for the victory of the Japanese. Later I asked him why he had said this, to which he replied that he was afraid that I might be a special agent sent by the Japanese and had therefore said this intentionally. In actuality he wanted to read the Buddhist sutras.

After the meal, I took some fever-reducing medicine, and P'u-yi told me to sleep in his bedchambers. I did not accept this offer. Later it was decided to let me live in the T'ung-te-tien (Hall of Common Virtue). The T'ung-te-tien was on the east side of the Ch'i-hsi-lou (Tower of Brilliance), separated by a courtyard with a beige-colored wall. It was a newly constructed building.

The extreme east wing of the upper floor of the building was a large room that served as my living room, from which there was a connecting hallway to my bathroom and toilet room, and another room that was my bedroom. When we went over to it, the bed was already prepared, a double bed made of wood with gold-plated, brass-inlaid flowers. That evening P'u-yi was especially happy and had dinner served in my new chambers. He then said, "Serve the meal." Within a short time a table was laid, including altogether ten entree dishes, each placed on the top of a vessel five or six inches tall. Each dish was covered with a lid. The food was placed inside in a very deep plate warmed by hot water in the vessel so the food would not get cold. The serving vessels were yellow with colored designs, bearing the inscription "Long life forever." P'u-yi picked up a kind of pastry called *cha-p'ai-ts'o,* telling me to taste it. I replied that I was quite full and declined. He laughed and put it down. Only later did I learn that when his majesty offered you something it was called an "honored present" and you had to accept it immediately, kneel, and kowtow, thanking him for the present. If it was something to eat, you had to accept it and eat it whether you were hungry or not. After talking for a while he then returned to his quarters. The impression he gave me that first day was that he treated people very amiably, without any overbearing affectation. Actually this was just for my benefit, because he was very pleased that day.

He Gave Me a Great Heap of Playthings

The next day after finishing breakfast, I wanted to go down into the garden to walk around, but the old servant woman said, "Miss, you cannot just walk around here." Not only did they tell me not to go walk in the gardens, every step I took they all followed me. There was no one else there, just two servant women, and they did not speak to me. If I asked them a question they always said they did not know the answer. In the evening, about six or seven o'clock, P'u-yi arrived. I asked him when was he going to call me to study, and why was there just me? He stopped a moment and then replied, "Later you'll be allowed to study, don't worry about it. I like you by yourself and have chosen you to enter the palace to wait on me. I don't like many people." So saying, he again looked at me and laughed. P'u-yi then said, "In a day or so the Second Sister will teach you the rules of etiquette, and then later we'll pick a good day to give you an 'investiture' ceremony." I did not really understand what he was talking about. I truly did not know what kind of game was meant by 'waiting on' him or by 'investiture.' I asked him why I was not allowed to go outside. He said that I could, but that I had to tell the servants and order them to chase anyone else out of the gardens before going out to walk. He also said I must be terribly bored, so tomorrow they would set up a radio receiver for me. The third day, a three-foot-high radio was indeed brought in, together with a phonograph that changed records automatically and could also record. Being very fond of music, I bought many records and in my free time listened to songs and music. P'u-yi came every evening, and then after spending a while with me he left again. He said that he was busy during the day and could not come then. After another two days, P'u-yi again gave me a great heap of playthings.

After a few days I began learning and practicing the aristocratic style of life and the etiquette and ceremonies of the aristocracy.

In greeting someone there was the two-legged greeting, also called the kneeling greeting, a ceremony of the aristocracy. For women there was only the full curtsy. With the waist straight, one knelt down on the left leg, maintaining one's balance while the right leg swept back half a step until it was lower than the left leg, the knee going down, and both hands placed on the knee. I practiced it for a month or two until both legs hurt from kneeling. At that time, whenever I saw P'u-yi, I only bowed to him each day, giving him a full curtsy only when I had not seen him for several days. When the servants met P'u-yi, unless it was during the New Year festival, they did not go through any ceremony but just uttered the phrase, "Blessings on the Ten Thousand Year Master!" The servants called him the "Ten Thousand Year Master" or the "Old Master." One also had to kowtow to General Kuan Yü in front of Buddha. If it was the anniversary of the death or birth of one of the imperial ancestors, we had to light incense to them, and P'u-yi had to kowtow to them himself. The color of my clothes meant various things. In mourning the dead, one wore plain clothes and did not eat meat; for a birthday one wore flowered clothes and a bouquet of flowers in the hair. For the commemoration of a death, singing and listening to music was also proscribed that day. On the New Year, I had to kowtow to the ancestors, to the Buddhist masters, to Kuan Yü, and even to the deceased T'an Yü-ling, and also to P'u-yi. In the so-called Great Ceremony of Ruler and Ministers, everyone, no matter who they were, had to kowtow to him. On my own birthday I also had to kowtow to him, and of course again on his birthday. His birthday was called "Ten Thousand Happy Years," while my birthday was called "A Thousand Autumns."

When I ate alone I usually ate fairly well. When our life-style reformed we ate Western food. Sometimes P'u-yi gave feasts that were parties for the civil and military officials. At these parties, he ate food prepared in the imperial kitchens, while the dishes for the puppet officials were prepared by a chef brought in from the "Great Harmony Restaurant." Each time I was given a plate. The first time that I ate Western food was the time P'u-yi taught me how to use a knife, fork, and spoon. There were many ways of stuffing sweet dumplings, rice cakes, and moon cakes. There were also the sweet cakes to be eaten in the ninth month, candied apples to be eaten in winter, fresh lotus seeds to be eaten in the fifth month, arrowroot, water chestnuts, and so forth.

Investiture as the "Fortunate Noble Lady"

After I had been in the imperial palace for something over a month, P'u-yi selected a propitious day for my investiture ceremony. What good name should precede my designation as a noble person? P'u-yi said, "You have the appearance of someone of very good fortune, so let's call you 'Fortunate Noble Lady.' Later should you run into some unlucky happenstance, your good fortune will be able to overcome it." Before me, P'u-yi had had three women. The first was Empress Wan-jung. The second was Imperial Consort Shu [Wen-hsiu], and later the already deceased T'an Yü-ling, who had been invested as the Luck Noble Lady and upon death had been canonized as the Wise and Virtuous Imperial Noble Consort. At my investiture, P'u-yi received congratulations for the occasion from many outside the court, for whom a great feast was prepared. To those not qualified to participate, P'u-yi sent some foreign delicacy. From then on, I was no longer called "Miss" but was called "Noble Lady." That day, with Second Sister's help in combing my hair and make-up, I wore a dress of gold velvet, the outfit having been designated by P'u-yi himself. The Second Sister was the master of ceremonies, but out of fear of saying something wrong she could not help laughing. P'u-yi was in a particularly good mood that day and had a smile on his face. This time, after I knelt before P'u-yi and presented to him a *ju-i* [an ornamental object, usually made of jade, a symbol of good luck] and he gave me another one, while the Second Sister stood at our side offering blessings of good fortune, I performed the full kowtow ceremony of three prostrations and nine knockings of the head. After the ceremony was completed, P'u-yi stood up and started laughing heartily. The Second Sister also laughed aloud. I did not really laugh. Following this P'u-yi took me to kowtow before the imperial ancestors. He told me that my status as a noble lady was not high enough to kowtow with the emperor to the imperial ancestral line, but that this time he was making an exception by going with me to kowtow to the ancestors. But we could not actually kowtow together, so he told me to stand back half a pace. After this was completed, it was my turn to be honored. There were only a few younger people and servants who kowtowed to me. This too had been the Second Sister's idea, that since I was quite young, I should be somewhat humble, so that she could avoid kowtowing to me. At mealtime Second Sister and a dozen or so women ate in the T'ung-te-tien, the women servants all wearing purple silk flower-patterned vests and a bouquet of small flowers. That day my picture was also taken outside the main gate of the T'ung-te-tien, which they said would be sent to the Empress Dowager of Japan, together with some small gift that would be sent to her in my name.

I Swear Before the Buddha to Be Faithful until the Sea Dries Up and the Rocks Melt

Several days before my investiture, P'u-yi summoned me to him. He told me to copy in my own hand a draft of a kind of contract that he had prepared for me as a "covenant" of my faithfulness to him. It was what might be called an oath, of some ten articles. Its main content was that I would obey him absolutely, that I would submit to him even in my thoughts, that I must resolutely carry this out, that I would absolutely never do anything that he opposed my doing, that if he told me to go east I could not go west, that if he told me to go south I would not go north, and that to do otherwise would be to be unfaithful to him, that I could not ask for an official position for any member of my family, or for money, and that I would not be allowed to return home. In brief, I was to have no freedom whatsoever, and I would be able to do nothing without his approval. When I heard these articles, I was extremely unhappy. I picked up my writing brush and doodled on the paper, not copying a word from the covenant. I do not know how I finally wrote the word "death." When P'u-yi saw it, he became furious. "All right! Now you're so young and you won't listen to me, what will you be like in the future? My fondness for you has been in vain. I had even planned to ask you to stay with me for life. How would that be? You're not happy. Fine. Tomorrow I'll send you back home. Don't think it's just you. Everyone has to listen to me! You've never heard the saying, 'When the ruler tells his minister to die, the minister dares not not die'? I haven't demanded anything of you, and you're unhappy. It looks like I've wasted my feelings on you in vain!" As he said this, he appeared to be very hurt and angry. I was frightened and immediately blurted out, "Don't be angry, Your Majesty. I made a mistake. I'll write this." I had no choice but to pick up my brush and start copying those articles. P'u-yi then added, "To show your sincerity, burn it as a vow before the Buddha. Let the Bodhisattva be your witness." So I knelt before the statue of the Buddha in the Ch'i-hsi-lou and burned the contract. This time P'u-yi was pleased and said, "I knew you would listen to me. You are a sensible person."

From that moment on, I started to live the wretched life of that so-called Fortunate Noble Lady.

The Wretched Life of a "Noble Lady"

I lived within the palace for two and a half years. During that period, the only men I met from outside the palace were the doctor who came when I was ill, and the Japanese, Yoshioka and Umezu [Yoshigiro],* whom I met once. Aside from these, I did not meet a single other male. The women with whom I had regular contact were P'u-yi's second sister, third sister, and fifth sister, and they did not come frequently. There was also P'u-chieh's woman, Saga Hiro, who came only at the New Year Festival, bringing with her women of close relatives of the imperial family, who had been students before their marriages. They included P'u-chien's wife, Yeh Nai-ch'in, whose official title was the Sixth Madame Chien [Chien Liu nai-nai], P'u-ying's wife, Yeh Hsi-hsien, Yü-yen's wife, Ma Ching-lan, Yü-t'ang's wife, Yang Ching-chu, Yü-hen's mother, and so forth. Aside from these there were P'u-yi's wet nurse, Erh-ma, and the servants, totaling no more than twenty persons. When I was really terribly bored, I would go over to Erh-ma's apartment to play, which was the only place I was allowed in. Erh-ma gave people a really good feeling. She also told me some of the rules and regulations, and stories of past events. I also played cards with her.

Every day after the noon meal I would rest a bit, and then at

---

*Umezu was the commander of the Kwantung Army and the fifth "Ambassador to Manchukuo."

about two o'clock the women of the court, who were students, would arrive. After the usual formalities, the studies would begin. Everyone would come into my study, and if they wanted to practice calligraphy we would practice calligraphy, or we might read some from old books such as the *Tsa-tzu* (Miscellaneous characters), or from the *San-tzu-ching* (Three-character classic). Sometimes we would take out some classical essays or poetry and discuss them. P'u-yi sometimes talked to us about essays, poems, and even the Buddhist sutras, at which times we would go over them again. Afterward we would go into the courtyard to play, or if the weather was bad we would go downstairs and play ping-pong, or play the piano. We would also sing songs, and occasionally play mahjong. As practical activities, the women did needlepoint and embroidery, knitted sweaters, and so forth. I had learned embroidery at home, and I learned how to knit from Sixth Madame Chien. We also frequently told stories or listened to the radio. Later I sometimes cooked my own food, taking some to P'u-yi. Every time he ate some of my food he always said it was delicious, which encouraged me to want to cook for him even more. He even kept some sea slugs and prawns that had been given to him by Chang Hai-p'eng at my apartments so that I could fix some for him to eat. Later, when he became a vegetarian, I would fix him vegetarian dishes. In the T'ung-te-tien quite a few little garlic plants were growing. I would cut the young garlic shoots and use them as leeks, mixing them with eggs and wrapping them as dumplings for P'u-yi. He liked them very much.

In the puppet court they also occasionally showed movies—rarely of fiction, mostly news documentaries and propaganda of Japanese power. I attended musical concerts only twice. The puppet court had its own orchestra that sometimes gave concerts for P'u-yi. I had always loved songs and dancing music, but P'u-yi did not want me to listen to them, saying that while Japan was at war there should be fewer recreational activities. I had no recourse, so I did not listen to them. I also played in two movies. They were not very good, and I do not know where the films went. Other events such as plays were never performed. There was no stage in the puppet court, so there was no place for performances. Furthermore, P'u-yi did not like them. In the courtyard I once learned how to ride a bicycle, but unfortunately I was not allowed out on the streets, so I could only ride around the courtyard.

As regards my relationship with P'u-yi, considering the fact that he was the emperor, he treated me fairly well. The demands that the various little forms of etiquette placed on me were not very severe or strict. Sometimes I made mistakes at which time he would correct me and forget about it. He also expressed to me that his feelings for me would "not waver until the sea ran dry and the rocks melted." He even said that we would "share together good fortune and bad." When the planes of the Soviet Union bombed the Northeast, at the first sign of the warning siren he would drag me to the air-raid shelter. However, his expressions of favor toward me could only be shown under certain specific conditions. First of all, I had to be 100 percent subservient to him. How was I to demonstrate this subservience? He frequently told me, "My entire day is taken up with troublesome business and no pleasures at all. I am only happy when I come here to see you. Thus you should think of more things that will make me happy when I see you. Don't do things that won't please me. And you should not talk to me about unpleasant things. This is what your duty is."

My Only Duty Is to Be His Play Companion

The only duty that P'u-yi gave me was to be his play companion, to make him happy. As soon as he arrived at my apartments he would say he was tired. He would lie down on the bed and have me sing to him, tell him stories, or talk of some happy thing that would make him happy. He would always say, "Use that lively vitality you had the other day and make me happy!" But when I too was sometimes unhappy and was not in the mood to sing to him, he was displeased. What really annoyed me the most was that he would lie down on the bed, a cigarette hanging from his lips, in a state between listening and not listening to my singing.

Later, aside from telling me some moralistic sayings and proverbs, he would lecture on some Buddhist sutra. Without any regard for how much content it had, he would both read and expound at the same time, and then tell me to expound in reply immediately. The Buddhist sutras contain a lot of unfamiliar vocabulary, but I dared not say that I could not reply. Thanks to the fact that I was young, I learned fairly quickly, and with effort I was able to give a reply. But if I made a mistake, he would be annoyed, or he would turn out the lamp and tell me to join him in sitting in quiet meditation for an hour or two. The servants would certainly think that we had gone to sleep.

Upon becoming a noble lady, I was torn away from my own family and relations. During the two and one half years that I was in the puppet court, only my father and mother were allowed to come see me, an event that was called "meeting one's relatives." The first time I saw them, I started crying. I saw that they had gotten thinner, and with great anxiety I asked, "How come you've gotten so thin?" My father replied hastily, "Not at all. We've not gotten thinner." To one side there was an attendant observing us closely. In a low voice my mother said, "During the first few months after you left, we received no news or word of you at all. Everyone in the family was terribly worried. We were afraid that the Japanese had hurt or killed you." The first time they came, they stayed for only an hour or two and then left. Each time they came to see me, my father sat down for a short while and then left before my mother. Once P'u-yi did us a special favor, allowing me to ask my mother to eat with me. When it came time to eat, a problem of seating arose. Who was to sit at the head of the table? Finally, both Mother and I sat together at the head of the table. The dishes of food were placed before both of us, and the others sat down in their successive positions. When P'u-yi heard that I had cried upon seeing my parents he said, "You shouldn't ever cry again. It makes it look as if you are very repressed here. Don't you want them to come?

You should be happy when they come. If you cry again I won't
let them come." From then on, when my parents came we just
had ordinary visits. I could not talk of anything personal, because
there was always someone standing nearby spying on us.

No Husband and Wife Relationship

After arriving at court, life was easy, and there were people to
wait on me. But I was invisibly bound by many rules and ceremonies. Fundamentally, we had no husband and wife relationship
to speak of at all. I was there simply to accompany him in his
leisure. I was not even free to sleep with him, and I dared not
even turn around when he was beside me. Later, when he was at
the Ch'i-hsi-lou and I at the T'ung-te-tien, I waited for him every
night until after midnight, and either he would come to my apartments or he would call me to him. If he did not send for me, I
dared not go on my own. He often did not come to my apartments for several days, and then, when he did come, he would
stay for just an hour or two before leaving again. Since at the
time I did not have a single relative with me, I of course really
looked forward to his coming to me. But he had a lot of people to
keep him company and often forgot about me. Several times I
looked down into the gardens and, seeing the lovely scenery and
beautiful flowers blooming, wrote him a note, which I sent by
one of the maids to ask him to come and enjoy them with me.
The first two times he did not reject me, but after that he did not
come again. Sometimes he would go with P'u-chieh and some of
the students into the garden, talking and laughing and having a
noisy good time, while I watched from my apartments wishing
that I could go down and join them!

I asked P'u-yi why he had not chosen a somewhat older
woman, instead of a child like myself. He replied, "Earlier, although T'an Yü-ling's illness had been fairly severe, it had not
reached the point of being incurable, and Yoshioka had insisted
on having a Japanese doctor look at her. Consequently, two doctors and several nurses came, and within less than two days she

died. I strongly suspected that those Japanese doctors were responsible for her death. Not long afterward, Yoshioka brought me the photographs of many Japanese girls, wanting me to select one. Their control over me was already suffocating enough. Could I stand having another spy sleeping in my bed, making it impossible for me even to breathe? But even a Chinese woman might possibly have been trained by the Japanese, so I thought I would choose a young girl, so that even if she had been trained by the Japanese, it would be easy for me to reeducate her." Being indeed young, I asked him, "Whatever Your Majesty commands I must obey and carry out always. For example, if two plus two equals four, but Your Majesty insists on saying they equal three, or five, I must go along and say that this is correct. But what should I do if in my heart I know clearly that it is not correct?" He could not give an answer to this question. He just said very sternly, "True, true. I can control your tongue, but I cannot control your mind!" Hearing this I hastened to bow to him and apologize. This ended the incident.

I had three maids waiting on me. They spied on every single movement I made. Every day at the end of their shifts they all had to go report to P'u-yi on all my activities that day. There were also several dependents of official students who came to keep me company, but they did not come of their own accord. Every day P'u-yi would designate their names, or I would designate someone through him, and a car would be sent to pick them up. They would arrive in the afternoon, we would eat dinner together, and then sometime after eight or nine o'clock they would be sent back home.

P'u-yi Has Frequent Hormone Injections

As for Wan-jung, who had fallen into disfavor, she was waited on by several maids and eunuchs, and probably her only means of passing the time was smoking opium. No one went to keep her company.

P'u-yi, the head of the household, had powers that were tightly circumscribed and limited to the puppet court itself. Around him were first of all those so-called students, all of whom were his brothers and cousins or nephews, including P'u-chien, P'u-ying, Yü-t'ang, Yü-yen, Yü-chien, Yü-lü, Yü-en, Yü-min, and so forth. They were called students because they studied every day. In addition to the teachers they invited, P'u-yi himself gave them ethics lessons and lectured on the edicts of the Yung-cheng emperor [r. 1723–36]. Yung-cheng was the emperor P'u-yi respected the most. P'u-yi instructed these several students so that he himself could nurture a group of confidantes loyal to the imperial line. But he never dared allow himself to trust them. They all spied on each other and periodically reported to P'u-yi.

Next were his attendants, such as Chao Yin-mao, Yen T'ung-chiang, Ts'ao Pei-yüan, Li Kuo-hsiung, and Tung Ching-pin, who were P'u-yi's high-ranking servants, and who waited on his personal needs, such as laying out his bed quilt, pouring tea, and serving meals. At the same time they were responsible for managing the imperial kitchens, dining rooms, the imperial chancellery and services, the storehouse, and so on. They could beat or fine the next level of servants. Among the attendants there should have been a relationship as among colleagues, but they never dared chat leisurely among themselves, much less visit or invite each other to their homes. If they had done so they would have been suspected of harboring treachery. Of course, they too spied on one another and made periodic reports. If the imperial countenance got angry they were all punished. When the students were at court they had to participate in the administering of punishments, or vigorously and loudly aid in the imperial indictments.

Next were those in the palace who performed various tasks solely within P'u-yi's living and study chambers. They were situated between the attendants and the male service staff.

The chancellery was composed of P'u-yi's accountants and bursars and was managed by Chao Yin-mao and Yen T'ung-chiang, who were also responsible for official communications.

The imperial kitchens and dining rooms were responsible for

boiling water, steeping tea, making various kinds of delicacies, and preparing dried and fresh fruit dishes. P'u-yi had three or four Chinese and Western-style cooks.

The most menial and lowest class was the janitorial service, made up entirely of orphans who had no homes to return to. They never had any time to rest. They were always on duty. They started working as soon as they got up in the morning, sweeping the T'ung-te-tien, doing laundry and other menial tasks, right up until P'u-yi went to bed, by which time it would be past midnight.

Toward those around him, P'u-yi was always on guard, suspicious, even feeling periodically that everyone was plotting against him. He had to inspect every communication I had with my family, and although there was a telephone in my rooms, it was not possible to make a telephone call in secret. Once, I happened to give a maid a few apples; P'u-yi received a report on it immediately and interrogated me in detail about it. If I wanted to send my family a little money, it had to go as an imperial favor from him. He did not allow me to have cash in my hands. He said, "My money is your money. Why should you have to touch it!"

P'u-yi was always worried about his health, anxious to live and afraid of dying. He was constantly taking medicine and having injections. He had frequent hormone injections, to prolong his life. He had two doctors who had to take his pulse every day, and had to make out a prescription. Even when he was not ill, they had to make out a prescription, called a tea-substitute drink.

"And What About Me?"

On August 8, 1945, the Soviet Union formally declared war on Japan and that evening dropped two bombs on Ch'ang-ch'un, one of which fell in front of the puppet palace, really frightening the emperor badly. As soon as the air-raid warning sounded, he came running over to the front of the T'ung-te-tien, shouting at the top of his lungs, "Yü-ch'in! Yü-ch'in!" When I came downstairs he dragged me by the hand down to the underground air-raid shelter to hide. After the planes had left he came out and offered incense to the Buddha for his protection. P'u-yi carried a revolver around with him all day long, and all those around him were armed.

On August 9, Yoshioka told P'u-yi that the puppet Manchurian government had to move to T'ung-hua, where it would be somewhat closer to Japan. In the evening Yoshioka came to say we would move on the 11th. On the 11th, most of those who did not want to leave with P'u-yi left to return to their various homes. All of those who were fleeing with P'u-yi gathered to leave for the train station. Of the puppet court there remained only P'u-chien and one or two male servants. Of the women, there were me, P'u-chien's wife, Yü-chien's mother, and P'u-yi's wet nurse! With Empress Wan-jung there were two eunuchs. Including both men and women we were just some ten persons. P'u-yi was very frightened and said to me, "In case of any unexpected event, we are totally defenseless. We could be seized without a fight." At nine o'clock in the evening, Yoshioka arrived to announce that we would go to Ta-li-tzu-kou in Lin-chiang County of T'ung-hua Province, leaving that night at midnight. At 12:30 A.M., we set out from the puppet palace. Four motorcycles accompanied the car containing P'u-yi and the empress. My car had none. At the train station where we boarded the train there were no ordinary passengers.

On August 12, we passed through Kirin and Mei-ho-k'ou, arriving at Ta-li-tzu-kou on the 13th. During the two days that we were on the train we had only two meals. We did not even have chopsticks.

At Ta-li-tzu-kou we stayed at an ordinary Japanese-style residence, of seven or eight rooms altogether. I stayed in the first room from the entrance on the left. The outside room on the right was used as P'u-yi's reception room. P'u-yi and the empress had separate rooms at the back of the house.

On the 16th, P'u-yi told me that he was going to Japan the next day. I asked him anxiously, "And what about me?" "You and the empress, and Second Sister, will follow by train." "But why don't we all go together?" I asked. "There are only three airplanes, and they won't hold that many people. Fortunately, we shall meet in two or three days." By the next day I was even more anxious and upset. Early in the morning I dashed into his dressing room and asked him whether we were leaving today. He replied that it had been decided that we would leave today. "Will the train be able to get here?" I asked. "What if by chance it doesn't come? Who will come to take care of me?" As I was saying this I involuntarily started to cry. He cried too. He comforted me, saying, "I have arranged everything carefully. Outside are P'u-chien and Yen T'ung-chiang, and inside are Second Sister and P'u-chien's wife. They will all look after you." "But what if by chance the train doesn't come? I have no relations here. Who will take care of me?" The more I talked, the more I cried, and the more sorrowful I became. He again held me and took me into the room, comforting me, saying, "We'll meet in a day or two." From that moment on, I endured ten years of pain and suffering, until the entire nation was finally liberated.

23

A Young Nurse in Manchuria

Ch'en Hsueh-chao

CH'EN HSUEH-CHAO (1906–1991), who recorded the following autobiography, is one of the better-known women writers in modern China. She was born in Hai-ning District, Chekiang Province. Her father, the principal of a local primary school, had been influenced by the new intellectual trends and was opposed to footbinding, so she escaped that painful experience. He died when she was six years old but left instructions that she should receive a modern education, which her brothers grudgingly obeyed. In 1921, she went to Shanghai to study, and by 1927 her success as a writer enabled her to travel to Paris on royalties. There she continued her studies, married a Chinese medical student, and was European correspondent for the well-known newspaper *Ta-kung pao*. In 1935 she and her husband returned to China, and in 1940, disillusioned with the Nationalist government and favorably impressed by the Communists, moved to Yenan, the Communist capital. Ch'en was attacked during the rectification campaign in 1942 and accused of being a "female chauvinist." After engaging in "productive labor" she was encouraged to join the Communist Party, which, after serious soul searching, she did in 1945.

   While in Yenan, Ch'en devoted most of her energies to being cultural and science editor of *Liberation Daily* and did little creative writing, but following the Japanese defeat she was sent to observe land reform, and after the establishment of the People's Republic she wrote two novels on the subject. In the antirightest campaign of 1957 she was expelled from the party, and she was attacked again during the Cultural Revolution. Ch'en fell into obscurity in these decades, but after Mao's death she reemerged and published two volumes of memoirs, both rich in ironic reflections on her life as a woman caught up in the turmoil of twentieth-century Chinese political life. One volume has been translated and published as *Surviving the Storm* (Armonk, NY: M. E. Sharpe, 1990).

The following selection is Ch'en's transcription of an interview with a twenty-two-year-old nurse, whom she met at a meeting making preparations to celebrate International Women's Day in 1946. For Ch'en, this young woman was an example of the kinds of changes that were occurring. She concludes her record of the interview, "If you ask me how many young men and women there are like this in the Northeast, I would answer: that's hard to calculate, but they are everywhere." This excerpt is from her *Man-tsou chieh-fang ch'ü* (Wandering in the liberated areas) (Ch'ang-ch'un, 1946), pp. 94–96.

HOW DID I come to join the Democratic Allied Army? Well, it's a long story. When we were under Japanese domination, we all believed that eventually the day of liberation would come, that such a day would finally arrive. In those days I was a student at the Japanese-run state nursing school of the puppet Manchukuo regime in Harbin. It was the one and only nursing school of the puppet Manchukuo regime. After we graduated, we had an obligation to serve them for three years. The vast majority of the students were Japanese women. They ate rice, while we ate sorghum, and we didn't even get enough of that to fill ourselves. But the leftover rice from the Japanese women was fed to the dogs, and when the Japanese women complained that their rice wasn't any good, it was just simply given to the draft animals. Every day we went hungry, but there was no way to buy something to eat or bring something from home because it was absolutely forbidden. When we got a day off, on our way back we would buy a steamed roll and hide it in a crevice in the wall around the lavatory. After we returned to the school, when we went to the lavatory we could eat the steamed roll on the sly. The Japanese women had apples after their meals, but not us; only if it happened to be some holiday of theirs did we ever get to eat apples. "These came from Japan. It's only because of us that you can have apples to eat." Those Japanese women were telling us all the time that this came from Japan and that came from Japan, that if it hadn't been for the Japanese we wouldn't have rice or apples, or this or that. One time I got into a quarrel with a Japanese woman over eating an apple. I said, "That apple was grown in China." They reported me to the head of the school for harboring dangerous thoughts. My punishment was to kneel on the ground for half a day. That's how they tormented us. We were constantly being insulted and despised. Besides all that, they fed us those Japanese feudal women's ethics, like when you eat, when you raise your rice bowl you're not allowed to look to either side but must look straight ahead at the rice bowl. When you're sitting, your knees have to be together, with your hands flat on your knees. . . . And they often made us sit in a kneeling position. Japanese women can sit kneeling all day long without getting tired, because it's their custom.

It just so happened that I returned home two months before the Red Army of the Soviet Union liberated Harbin. It was hard to get a leave of absence, but my mother was ill and my father came personally to Harbin to ask for a leave of absence for me and then took me back home. The school had reported the quarrel over the apple to my parents, saying my thoughts were tainted, and my father had been thinking of getting me back home because he was worried about me. I only regret one thing—I didn't get to see those Japanese women when they had to leave the school.

What about how I joined the Democratic Allied Army? For a long time my younger brother had been making a fuss that he wanted to go join the Democratic Allied Army. But Mother and Father wouldn't give their permission because they couldn't do without him. They only had the two of us. So one day my brother said he wanted to go over to a friend's home to have some fun, and he asked my mother for two hundred yuan. He put on a set of old clothes he had just washed himself the day before and left right after lunch. That night, the next day, and afterward, he didn't return. My mother cried and my father sat there gloomily the whole day long. After about half a month had gone by without a word from my brother, they decided to send me to hunt for him. I took a train to Pen-hsi, because my brother had said he was thinking of taking the entrance exam for Northeastern University. When I arrived in Pen-hsi, I went to the university and asked all around, in the offices, at the military unit, and so forth. There were a lot of young men my brother's age, but not my brother. When I got back to Hai-lung, I heard about a hospital for wounded soldiers there. I had looked everywhere along the way, but that was the one place I hadn't gone. I thought maybe he had been wounded and was in the hospital. The minute I entered the hospital I saw many wounded comrades; because the hospital was short on staff, they had just been set down anyplace, and the hospital couldn't even quickly wash and dress their wounds. But they just lay there quietly without complaining. When I saw the way they were, I almost started to cry. I visited all the wards but couldn't find my brother. Then I got an idea. I rushed to see the hospital director. I told him, "I came to find my younger brother, but I'd like to stay and help. I have gone to nursing school. Can you use me here?" "Wonderful," the director answered. So I stayed at the hospital for wounded soldiers, and every day I wash and dress the wounds of our injured comrades. They are all really nice, and they treat me like their little sister. They also agreed that everyone should help me find my brother. Sometimes they ask me in an innocent way, "Do you know who we were wounded for?" "I do know. It was for me, for us women."

Later, I helped them set up a second branch clinic. Everyone helped to look for my brother, and finally they located him. He was in X unit and doing very well in training. I wrote Father and Mother. "Please don't think about younger brother returning home, and even I won't be returning. I want to work. I belong to society, to the people of the Northeast, to the people of China."

My parents haven't gone hungry and the authorities say that they'll look after them while I'm working here. The hospital director and supervisors have urged me to suspend my work here for the time being, go visit my parents for a while, and then come back later, so that they won't worry about me too much.

Li Yu-ning received her Ph.D. in history from Columbia University. She has edited several volumes on Chinese women's history, including *Autobiographical Writings and Poems by Modern Chinese Women*, and co-edited *Documents on Women's Movement in Modern China* and *Collected Essays on the History of Chinese Women* (all in Chinese). She is the author of numerous articles in both English and Chinese on women in Chinese history. Professor Li has been the editor of *Chinese Studies in History* (published by M. E. Sharpe) since 1967, is a past president of the Historical Society for Twentieth Century China, and was awarded an Outstanding Faculty Medal by St. John's University, where she has been teaching Chinese history since 1973.